Capitalism

Geoffrey Ingham

polity

Contents

Introduction   1

Part I   Classical theories of capitalism   5

1   Smith, Marx and Weber   7

2   Schumpeter and Keynes   36

3   The basic elements of capitalism   52

Part II   The institutions   63

4   Money   65

5   Market exchange   92

6   The enterprise   119

7   Capital and financial markets   147

8   The state   175

9   Conclusions   204

Notes   227

References   247

Index   260

Introduction

Given the enormous accumulation of sociological literature on capitalism, it might well be thought that there is little need for another introductory text. Indeed, there have been a number of excellent recent additions to the genre, most notably Fulcher (2004) and Triglia (2002) and, at a more advanced level, Nee and Swedberg (2005). None the less, I believe that there is room for one more that attempts to do something a little different.

However, part of what I propose is, in the first place, rather old-fashioned. One of my aims has been to refocus attention on the classical sociological concern with the *systemic* nature of capitalism. By this is meant the fundamental elements, and their linkages, that characterize capitalism as a whole. Of course, this is precisely what Marx and Weber set out to do, but I believe that this aspect of their work has suffered some neglect in the recent past. For example, it has been surely a distortion of Weber's analysis of capitalism to devote so much attention to the *Protestant Ethic*. On the other hand, I have argued that the classic nineteenth-century sociological texts have very little to say about the monetary and financial side of capitalism, which has assumed a more obviously central role during the twentieth century. In this respect we get more guidance from the great economists such as Schumpeter and Keynes. But they and other economists concerned with the systemic structure of capitalism are, unfortunately, not likely to be encountered in an undergraduate sociology course.

The book is in two parts, the first of which deals with those theorists whose work I have found to be most valuable. It opens with a very brief outline of Adam Smith's analysis of 'commercial society' in *The Wealth of Nations* (1776). Apart from this book's intrinsic significance as one of the first systematic accounts of the modern market economy, the classical social theory of the next two thinkers on my list – Marx and Weber – is unintelligible without reference to Smith. Two other economists – Joseph Schumpeter and John Maynard Keynes – make up my list. They are included not only for their seminal heterodox contributions to the economic analysis of capitalism, but because this heterodoxy is implicitly 'sociological'. That is to say, they focus on the particular institutional structure of capitalism as a distinctive type of economy, rather than on the abstract mathematical models of decision-making and exchange to be found in mainstream economics. Schumpeter's economics provides a fascinating insight into the process by which the social science disciplines became separated in the early twentieth century – arguably to the detriment of both. But, unfortunately, this issue cannot be pursued here. However, it is my firm belief that students of sociology should have some basic understanding of Keynes as one of the towering figures in twentieth-century social and economic science. His economics might now be unfashionable, but his impact and influence on the modern world can scarcely be overestimated. However, this brief treatment of Keynes also aims to show that his critique of the orthodox economic analysis of the operation of capitalism, derived from Adam Smith, is unwittingly sociological in its understanding of the relationships between employment, money and capital.

The fact that my list of classical theorists of capitalism ends with Keynes, who died in 1946, might possibly be taken to reflect my outdated conception of the social sciences and rather old-fashioned concerns. In reflecting on this possible interpretation, I have reached the outrageous conclusion that no social scientist over the past half century has added anything that is *fundamentally* new to our understanding of the capitalist economic system. Indeed, some of those who might be thought to qualify for such a list have merely distorted and obscured much of the legacy of Smith, Marx, Weber, Schumpeter and Keynes.

After the somewhat crude extraction from their work of the basic elements that make up the capitalist system, part II looks at these more substantively – money, markets, the enterprise, capital and financial asset markets. However, the sociological literature on which to draw is very patchy in this respect. Reflecting classic sociological concerns, there is copious work on labour and the firm, but very little on money and finance. Consequently, I have relied on heterodox economic traditions and have made liberal use of material from the most valuable source on the operation of contemporary capitalism – the elite capitalist press. In the pages of the *Financial Times* and *The Economist* one finds the most expert reportage on what Schumpeter referred to as the inner workings of the capitalist engine, including the representation and disclosure of the capitalist elites' beliefs, their most pressing anxieties and the continuous evolution of capitalist ideology.

Finally, I should point out that this book lacks a thorough treatment of the very important question of the origins of capitalism. Given the constraints of an introductory text, I decided rather to concentrate on contemporary issues. For filling this gap I recommend two sociological histories of capitalism – one short and elementary (Fulcher 2004) and the other longer and more complex (Arrighi 1994).[1] Both make much use of Braudel's history of capitalism, which, in turn, was guided by one of the major influences on my own work – Joseph Schumpeter.

Part I

Classical theories of capitalism

1
Smith, Marx and Weber

Adam Smith (1723–1790): the market as a harmonizing 'invisible hand'

Published in 1776, Adam Smith's *The Wealth of Nations* was an attempt to explain western Europe's unprecedented acceleration in economic growth. Before this time, the wealth of a nation was relatively easy to explain – it was largely the result of the 'visible hand' of military power. Countries might differ in their endowments – such as climate, the fertility of the land and natural resources – but these advantages could always be obtained by conquest. Economic power was evidently a consequence of military power. By and large, rulers subscribed to the mercantilist doctrine which held that power should be founded on amassing and hoarding wealth within a territorial state. For some, even the export trade was interpreted as a loss of resources that, furthermore, might even strengthen an enemy.[1]

From the late seventeenth century onwards developments seemed to contradict this doctrine and to lend support to alternative explanations of the rise and fall of states. By the middle of the eighteenth century it was becoming apparent that the progression of society through a succession of increasingly wealthy stages of development could not be explained simply as the result of powerful rulers' conscious intent. Arguably the most mercantilist of all European states, Spain, was eventually brought down by a small country with negligible natural material resources of its own – Holland (Smith 1986 [1776]: 473). Here, the relationship between military and economic power was seemingly reversed. Whilst Spain had sought power by the conquest and seizure of south American silver, the Dutch East India Company's trading ventures produced the wealth that supported an expansion of military power. Successful wealthy European societies, Smith argued, were entering a new stage of economic development – based on 'commerce'.[2] Here, the creation of wealth was the result of myriad individuals pursuing their own interests, not the strategies of powerful rulers. Consequently, the two fundamental economic questions – the growth of wealth and its distribution – now required a quite different explanation.

Smith's answer to the questions is provided by his analysis of the interrelationship between three elements of 'commercial' society – *factors of production, the market* and *the state*. *The Wealth of Nations* was the first comprehensive examination of the emerging market capitalist system, and it remains enormously influential (Smith 1986 [1776]). It was written before the growth of industrial capitalism – that is to say, before factory production in large externally financed corporations. Rather, Smith was concerned with the first significant structural change in the evolution of the modern economy – the rapid development of market exchange. By the eighteenth century, the closed self-sufficient economic systems of the household and manor had given way to the market mechanism in which wages and prices were rapidly replacing traditional reciprocity and redistribution.[3] Moreover, Smith saw that there was a direct link between this expansion of the market and the division of labour. Extensive specialization of task and economic function eliminates the self-sufficiency of household and manor, making market exchange necessary, which in turn permits further specialized, divided labour and, consequently, greater efficiency and economic growth.

The factors of production

Commercial society comprises two sectors – agriculture and manufacture, in which capital (or stock), comprising mainly the instruments of production, employs labour (Smith 1986 [1776]: Book II). This gives commercial society its three factors of production – land, capital and labour. This fundamental division of function is the basis for 'three great constituent orders' of society – landlords, capitalists and labourers. Their mutual dependence can be traced through the exchange relations between rents, profits and wages in a 'circular flow' of production, income and expenditure. The capital stock provides the wages for the worker's expenditure and consumption of the production, which, in turn, creates profit, more capital and so on.

The division of labour and market exchange

The basic mechanism of the commercial system is the division of labour, the mutual dependence of the separate parts and their consequent need to exchange their products. Unlike feudal obligation or the compulsion of slavery, interdependency – that is, the connection between the parts – in commercial society is based upon the market price of the respective factors that are freely established in what Smith referred to as the 'perfect liberty' of exchanges.

Within each of the three divisions of society – land, capital and labour – there is further specialization of function or task. Smith illustrated the advantages of specialization in raising the productivity of labour with the example of the eighteen distinct operations performed by different workers in the manufacture of nails (Smith 1986 [1776]: 112–13).

Coordination of the complex functionally differentiated system is accomplished spontaneously by the 'invisible hand' of the market – that is, the interaction of supply and demand that represents the decisions of myriad otherwise unconnected individuals. The rise and fall of prices signal the existence of either scarcity or abundance to producers and consumers, whose self-interest ensures that any imbalances are corrected. For example, capital is attracted to sectors with rising prices and profits, causing them to fall as a result of the increase in competition. If left to operate unhindered, the invisible hand ensures that the 'circular flow' of production, income and expenditure, and the supply and demand for goods, will move to an equilibrium at which incomes and revenues from production cover costs, and all resources are fully employed.

However, the market was not merely a self-regulating economic mechanism; it was also a means of social integration. Exchange cemented society in networks of mutually advantageous interdependence, and it could also be seen as resolving the eternal ethical question of the relationship between individual conduct and the general collective welfare. If self-interest led to the wealth of nations, then, as Mandeville had expressed it earlier in his *Fable of the Bees* (1714), 'private vices' were the source not only of 'public benefits' but also of 'public virtue'.

This conclusion about the efficacy of the market depends on the important assumption that individuals do not wish to store wealth in the form of money. In his opposition to the mercantilist doctrine that the power of states is enhanced by the accumulation of precious metal money rather than the pursuit of commerce, Smith relegated money to a secondary, passive role in his analytical system. It was irrational, Smith contended, to hold money when it could either be used to obtain capital investment goods (fixed capital and stock) in order to make profits or spent to satisfy wants. Hoarded precious metal money was unproductive; for Smith, money should be nothing more than a medium to facilitate market exchange. This 'great wheel of circulation' was not to be confused with the real wealth of society that resided in the factors of production and goods that it circulated (Smith 1986 [1776]: 385).[4]

Commerce, politics and the state

In his polemic against the claims of absolutist monarchies and their false mercantilist policies, Smith relegated politics and the state to a minimal role in economic affairs. In the first place, the idea of the invisible hand's harmonization of individual and societal welfare was incompatible with politics understood as conflict between inherently opposed interests. Second, his insistence that economic coordination and wealth creation were the spontaneous, unintended consequences of self-regarding individuals in the marketplace was aimed at demonstrating that the state's direct involvement in economic activity was counterproductive. Governments must leave economic decision-making to individuals in the 'perfect liberty' of the competitive market.

This does not mean, as is all too commonly assumed, that the state is unimportant for Smith. On the contrary, he saw that it performed three indispensable roles in the commercial stage of society (Smith 1986 [1776]: Book V). First, the state should provide for the defence of the territory in which perfect liberty could be exercised. Second, and to the same end, the state must uphold the rule of law. Without secure property rights over the use and disposal of goods and capital the market cannot function. Third, the state should provide certain 'public goods' that it may never be profitable for individuals to produce 'privately' (see the discussion of 'public goods' in chapter 5). Smith's short list of 'public goods' refers mainly to infrastructure, such as roads, bridges, harbours and canals, where the level of capital investment and the difficulty of setting prices and of collecting revenue deter private provision. But he remained convinced that wherever possible general public services were better performed when supplied in the pursuit of profit by private entrepreneurs.

As we shall see, this partial qualification of the invisible hand's efficacy opens up the possibility that the state may be required under certain circumstances to play a more extensive economic role, or even replace the market mechanism. Smith was writing at a time when most goods and services could be more easily provided privately, as they required relatively less capital investment and coordination than today. Despite the recent privatization of public services in advanced capitalist economies, the modern state's role in financing public works, as we shall see, is far greater than it was in Smith's day. Rail transport, for example, is widely accepted in many, if not quite all, developed economies as being most effectively and efficiently run by the state. Furthermore, the deleterious environmental consequences of industrialism, financial crises and protracted economic depressions were less apparent in the middle of the eighteenth century.

Eventually, states were called upon to try to deal with what modern economists refer to as 'negative externalities' and 'market failure' (see the discussions in chapters 5 and 8). (But, eighty years or so after the publication of *The Wealth of Nations*, Karl Marx, as we shall see, had formed a clear view of the negative consequences of the 'perfect' economic liberty of commercial society.)

Value and distribution

The question of the source of value and its distribution remains the subject of an intense debate in economic theory that cannot be discussed here in any detail. Rather, the present aim is to focus on how Smith's answers disclose his conception of the structure of the emerging capitalist society – that is, his attempt to make the operation of the guiding 'hand' more visible to us.

Just as the power of states and their sovereigns no longer provided wholly satisfactory explanations of the growth of the wealth of nations, it could no longer account for its distribution among the three great constituent orders of society and labour's different occupations (Smith 1986 [1776]: 134). Commerce and industry had at least partially overturned traditional hierarchies based on religious sanction and political power. For example, the mediaeval scholastics' attempt prescriptively to regulate economic life with 'just prices' and the prohibition of unethical practices such as usury had long since been abandoned. But the question remained: why and how did the apparently free and equal exchange in the 'perfect liberty' of the market result in inequality? It remains, as we shall see, a central issue in the politics of modern capitalist democracies.

In a similar manner to the explanation of wealth creation as a spontaneous outcome of the market, Smith and the classical economists sought to locate the mechanism for the distribution of income among the factors of production (land, labour and capital) and the specialized occupations in the actual structure of the division of labour itself. Inequality was produced by the impersonal, and implicitly neutral, mechanism of the 'invisible hand', not by directly coercive exploitation as it had been in feudal society. The relative shares of rents, wages and profits were determined by their exchange value – that is, the price that had to be freely paid for the use of land, labour and capital for production.

Smith distinguished between the *natural* price – that is, that which exactly covers costs of production – and the *market* price, which is determined by scarcity and the balance of supply and demand at any point in time. The two prices frequently diverge in the short term, but in the long run the competitive market ensured their convergence. For example, if the market price were too low to cover costs, then the enterprise or sector would fail. On the other hand, if the market price met these with ease, then, as we have noted, more enterprise would be attracted to the sector in pursuit of easy profits, increasing both competition and supply and, consequently, reducing prices. In modern economic terminology, the economy would move towards equilibrium (Smith 1986 [1776]: chapter VII). At this point, the relative share of the distribution of income between the three factors and their respective occupations is that which brings about the full employment of society's resources. In this situation, produced by free exchange, the factors of production would receive precisely the return which rewarded their contribution to this perfect balance. Any other distribution would perturb the equilibrium. In the long run, rent, wages and profits were equivalent to the value of their contribution to the aggregate wealth. Not only was the 'invisible hand' efficient, it was also just and fair.[5]

Smith's legacy

In the third century after its publication *The Wealth of Nations* holds its place as the most cited work in economics. As we shall see, the economic and political crises of the early twentieth century led to a loss of faith in the effectiveness of the free market. John Maynard Keynes and others argued that the economy required greater levels of state involvement (see chapter 2), and for a short time communist economic systems appeared to be viable alternatives. However, as we shall see, the economic crises and inflation in the West during the 1970s and the disintegration of communism in the late 1980s led to the discrediting of Keynesian macro-economic management and the utter abandonment of socialist state planning. In the strong revival of the belief in the superiority of the free market as the means of organizing economic activity, Smith's analysis of the efficacy of the market experienced a strong revival. Together with the work of later theorists such as Friedrich Hayek (1899–1992) and Milton Friedman (1912–2006),[6] *The Wealth of Nations* forms the basis for the hegemony of today's economic 'neo-liberalism', which favours market deregulation, privatization and the reduction of the state's role in economic affairs.

Pro-globalization arguments for the extension of market capitalism are fundamentally Smithian in their advocacy of a world-wide division of labour and free trade, with states largely restricted to the provision of public goods and the facilitation of the market mechanism (Wolf 2005). Even his greatest critic, Karl Marx, agreed that the division of labour, competition and trade were responsible for the hitherto unprecedented expansion of human welfare; but he believed that Smith had misunderstood the nature of the 'invisible hand' and its eventual consequences. For Marx, the capitalist system was to be explained not simply by the technologically determined division of labour and market exchange, but, rather, by the inherent inequality of power of capitalist property relations. Furthermore, the market's efficiency was ultimately negated by contradictory and eventually destructive tendencies.

Karl Marx (1818–1883): exploitation and the fatal contradictions of the capitalist mode of production

As Lenin observed, Marx combined three strands of thought – German philosophy, French socialism and Scottish and English political economy (Kolakowski 1978). Our main focus will be on Marx's critical dissection of the last-mentioned, for which he used two related analytical tools taken from German philosophy: the distinction between appearance and essence, and the Hegelian idea of historical progress through the dialectical interaction of contradictory elements. First, Marx sought the 'laws of motion of modern society' at a deeper level than the superficial appearance of, on the one hand, equal exchange between freely contracting individuals and, on the other, the functional integration of the factors of production in the 'circular flow'. He also challenged the idea that capitalist society harmonized individual interests and collective social welfare in the way that Adam Smith had contended.

For Marx, capitalist production did not have the primary aim of creating 'use-values' for the satisfaction of genuine human needs; rather it was an economic system exclusively oriented to the realization of monetary profit by the production of commodities with an 'exchange value'. In Smith's scheme these two goals are reconciled by the invisible hand; but, for Marx, the capitalist mode of production places them in opposition. Use-values are subordinated to the pursuit of exchange-value and profits. Moreover, the seemingly free market of exchange between legal equals masks an underlying reality of increasing inequality and exploitation. Workers, unlike slaves, were free to choose which master to work for, but, without alternative means of subsistence, they were compelled to sell their labour to the bourgeois class. The fundamental market exchange in capitalism – that is, the buying and selling of labour power – was inherently unequal. Marx sought to tear away what he considered to be the 'masks' and 'veils' that bourgeois political economy had placed over the real 'laws of motion' – that is, to uncover the *essence* that lay beneath the superficial *appearance* described in what he referred to as Smith's 'bourgeois political economy'.

Second, the idea of a harmonious integration of the factors of production – land, capital and labour – was unable to explain obvious features of capitalist society. If capital, production, income and consumption were functionally linked in a 'circular flow' of equal exchange, in which the revenues from each were used by the others to the point where costs were covered, how were profits and economic crises to be explained? A 'circular flow' guided by an 'invisible hand' seriously misrepresented a type of society that was subject to ever more frequent economic booms and slumps and growing inequality. Marx contended that the pursuit of individual interest in the market not only failed to maximize collective welfare but also resulted in the anarchy of unco-ordinated economic decision-making that brought about unintended and uncontrolled fluctuations between over- and under-production.

In general, Marx argued that crises were expressions of the inherent contradictions between the elements that comprised the different modes of production in the development of human society – that is, the *forces and relations of production* (see below). Furthermore, these contradictions and crises were the driving force of history. Smith's circular flow was a static model of an equilibrium that could not explain how the historical stages in Smith's scheme developed one from the other. In Marx's theory, the inherent crises were resolved by the dialectical progression to a new mode of production which, in turn, developed its own contradictions. Society moved from primitive communism to the classical mode of production of the ancient world and thence to feudalism, followed by the intensification of contradictions in the capitalist mode of production which would lead to its collapse. Capitalism's basic institution of private property would be abolished and be replaced by a socialist system in which democratically controlled production would be devoted to the satisfaction of human needs rather than the pursuit of profit.

We can approach Marx's exposition of the 'laws of motion' of the capitalist mode of production in a little more detail, by looking at his fundamental distinctions between these basic concepts of his system of thought: *use-value* and *exchange-value*, *labour* and *labour power*, and *forces* and *relations* of production and their *contradictions*.

Use-value and exchange-value

At the beginning of volume I of *Capital*, Marx observes, as Smith and others had done, that all useful objects may be considered both qualitatively and quantitatively (Marx 1976 [1867]: part one, chapter 1). On the one hand, they possess qualities and properties that make them useful (*use-value*), and, on the other, the amount of labour that has gone into their production makes it possible to measure their value in relation to other commodities (*exchange-value*). In a departure from what he referred to as the bourgeois political economy of Adam Smith and others, Marx argues that a useful object becomes a *commodity* only in a social system that organizes production for exchange on the market with the primary aim of monetary gain. Of course, commodities are useful, but what is produced and in what quantity is not in the first instance driven, in the capitalist mode of production, by considerations of utility. Marx summarizes his argument by contrasting two forms of exchange – Commodity-Money-Commodity$_1$ (C-M-C$_1$) and Money-Commodity-Money$_1$ (M-C-M$_1$). In C-M-C$_1$, objects are produced and sold in order to obtain the money that will enable the producer to gain the satisfaction of other utilities. Bourgeois political economy assumes that this form of exchange is universal. But Marx argues that it masks the underlying reality of a particular capitalist M-C-M$_1$ form of exchange in which commodities are produced with the primary goal of realizing more money.

Marx argued that the distinctions between use and exchange value and the two different circuits of exchange uncover two distinctive and inherent features of the capitalist mode of production: first, that labour is transformed into the commodity 'labour power' and, second, that recurrent crises of over-production result from the production of commodities for their monetary exchange value rather than their utility.

Labour and labour power

Labour has use-value that is embodied in its products; for example, concrete labour is used to raise cabbages for sale in order to obtain money to purchase eggs (cabbages-money-eggs; that is, C-M-C$_1$). But in the capitalist mode of production this concrete labour becomes abstracted as labour *power* – that is, a general productive capability that can be sold for a fixed period of time (money buys commodified labour power in order to realize monetary profit; that is, M-C-M$_1$). In capitalism, a worker *appears* to sell a precisely fixed quantity of concrete labour, but actually sells the creative potential labour power that can be manipulated by the capitalist to extract surplus value (Marx 1976 [1867]: part one, chapter 2). This distinction is explicable only in terms of capitalism's social relations of production in which members of the social class of property-less wage-labour are objectively constrained in the absence of alternative means of subsistence to sell their productive potential to property-owning capitalists. Unlike the property-owing peasant who performs concrete labour in order to produce to engage in market exchange (C-M-C$_1$), the property-less wage-labourer can survive only by selling abstract labour power. This is the key to the deciphering of the mystery of the existence of profit in an apparently equal exchange between capital and labour that masks the underlying reality of exploitation.

According to Marx's labour theory of value, the value of labour power is determined like another commodity by the amount of concrete labour time needed for its reproduction. That is to say, the value of labour power is equal to the value of the other commodities – food, clothing and so on – needed to maintain the worker's family. But, in capitalism, the worker submits to the power of capital in a regime and a length of working day that uses the abstracted labour power to create exchange values greater than that necessary for the reproduction of the labourer and family. This *surplus value* represents the 'unpaid' labour power that is appropriated by the capitalist (Marx 1976 [1867]: part three, chapter 9). Smith saw this as the profit that represents the exchange-value of capital to the process of production; but Marx argued that this obscures the *exploitation* that is inherent in operation of the capital–labour relation.

The forces and relations of production and their contradictions

All historical modes of production – primitive communism, ancient slavery in Greece and Rome, feudalism and capitalism – comprise *material forces* and *social relations* (Marx and Engels 1968 [1859]: 180–4). The *material forces* are the means of production, such as machine technology, and also sources of energy, raw materials, land, skills and knowledge.

The *social relations* refer to the different historical patterns of ownership, control and organization of the material forces. In ancient slavery for example, all human and non-human material means and forces of production are owned by the ruling class. In feudalism, serfs are bound to the ruling class's land, but they are left in control of the process of agricultural production which is expropriated by the ruling class after the harvest. Capitalism is distinctive in so far as workers are legally free, but are none the less exploited.

Smith identified 'capital' with the material forces of production – tools and machinery, but Marx argued that these material means only become 'capital' in a system where they are appropriated by one class and operated by another. That is to say, *social relations* refer to the property relations which govern the organization of production. In Marx's view, Smith's focus on the material or technological 'factors of production' ideologically masks these relations of power between the classes by which labour power is transformed into surplus value. Bourgeois political economy presents the capitalist system as an objective, or natural, state of affairs which is determined by the characteristics of the material forces and means. However, capitalism, for Marx, is specified by its social relations rather than its technology. With the abolition of private property and the introduction of socialist social relations of production, these material forces could be put to work to provide for human needs, not simply to generate profits.

In Smith's scheme, landlords, capitalists and labour receive their respective revenues in rents, profits and wages as a consequence of the productivity of the material factors that they represent. Landlords with fertile land will receive higher rents; capitalists with more productive machinery will make more profits; and workers with scarce skills will receive higher wages. However, this did not explain why a consistently greater share went to rents and profits. Marx's explanation begins with the assertion that rent, profits and wages are not natural phenomena; rather, they are social categories that can only be understood in terms of the social relations of production, based on power and compulsion. Rents, profits and wages did not, in the first instance, express the relative functional contributions of the factors to the total social product.[7]

Rent, for example, did not simply express the productivity of the land, but was essentially a social category that was only intelligible in terms of the unequal property relation between landlord and tenant. Similarly, the profits of capital could only be realized if the means of production were appropriated by one class and operated by property-less wage earners. Capital did not comprise 'things'; rather, it was a social relation. The 'spinning jenny' of the early Lancashire cotton industry was a machine that only became capital by virtue of its ownership by one class and operation by another.

Moreover, if labour is the ultimate source of value, as Smith contended, then capital must comprise expended labour. Capital that *appears* in the form of the material means of production is, *in essence*, alienated and appropriated labour. Capital is not merely a material factor of production, but is actually constituted by the surplus value that is a result of the inequality of the social relations of production between owners and non-owners.

The capital–wage relation and the proletariat were the historical product of, among other things, the Enclosure Acts in England that dispossessed the peasants, who were consequently compelled to sell their only possession – labour power – and become the proletariat. For Marx, the state not only created, by design and default, the social relations of production, but was constantly required to maintain the inequality of power on which they were based. It was the 'executive committee of the whole bourgeoisie' whose competitive economic struggle often prevented them from seeing, and more frequently from acting in, their best general interest (Marx and Engels 1968 [1848]). For example, the British state intervened during the nineteenth century to shorten the working day, not simply as a result of workers' agitation but also to prevent the capitalists from weakening and demoralizing their most valuable asset – the actual creators of surplus value. In his early critique of Hegel's philosophy of the state, Marx formed the view that the extent of its role was in direct proportion to the severity of capitalism's contractions and crises. Far from playing the minimal role advocated by Smith, the state would become increasingly involved in the futile tasks of controlling class conflict and trying to resolve the economic crises (see the discussion of the capitalist state in chapter 8).

Marx's model of the evolution of modes of production was based on the Hegelian idea of dialectical progression. Applied to social and economic formations this meant that the basic elements of forces and social relations of production were bound together in a simultaneously positive and negative manner – that is to say, in a set of contradictions. For example, Marx agreed with Smith that competition between capitalists accounted for dynamic economic progress, in which the bourgeoisie had played their own revolutionary and necessary role in developing the forces of production. But, Marx contended, this competition resulted in an anarchical drive to produce commodities with exchange-value which led to periods of overproduction, followed by recessions, as capitalists tried to cut their losses by reducing output.

The most important expression of the contradiction between forces and relations was the falling rate of profit, which Marx believed gave his critique of capitalism an objective or scientific basis. That is to say, the bourgeoisie were powerless to prevent the normal functioning of capitalism from undermining the very thing that it was organized to achieve – profits. He divided capital into 'constant' capital (raw materials and machinery) and 'variable' capital (the amount spent on wages). 'Variable capital' is, in fact, 'labour power', which, in Marx's scheme, is the only source of surplus value and profits. In their intense competition the capitalists are pushed to increase the productivity of labour by constantly improving the technological means of production – that is to say, by substituting 'constant' capital for 'variable' capital. This is the bourgeoisie's progressive historic role – to make the means of production more efficient; but in performing it, they are compelled to substitute 'constant' for 'variable' capital and, consequently, become their own 'gravediggers' (Marx and Engels 1968 [1848]).

As 'variable' capital is the only source of surplus value, its replacement by the non-surplus producing constant capital causes a fall in the *rate* of profit (Marx 1976 [1867]: part three, chapter 9). This need not be a fall in *total* profits, as total output may grow; but the fall in the *rate* of profit has the effect of driving the capitalists to attempt to extract more surplus value by, according to this analysis, the only means possible – that is, lengthening the working day and increasing output. In turn, this not only further demoralizes, debilitates and antagonizes the workers, but also, as a consequence of the prior increase in constant capital (machinery) and subsequent increase in labour productivity, creates further overproduction. The cyclical crises continue to deepen as the bourgeoisie seek ever increasing levels of surplus value and, therefore, create further capital and production that the system cannot absorb. Although Marx's analysis of the falling rate of profit has been largely rejected, the assertions that capitalism inevitably produces class conflict and cycles of overproduction followed by recession commands greater acceptance (for an application of the falling rate of profit analysis to the economic crises of the 1970s, see Brenner 2002). As we shall see, for example, Keynes sought a remedy for capitalism's inability to maintain high levels of output and employment.

As we suggested above, for Marx the possibility of socialism rests on this distinction between the forces and relations of production and their contradictions. Capitalist social relations, not the means and forces of production, cause the crises. The forces were an expression of humanity's creative powers – that is, human labour in the most general sense. But these potentially limitless forces were stunted by the capitalist social relations of production. With their removal, and consequently the compulsion to realize surplus value, workers would no longer be compelled to sell their labour as the 'commodity' of 'labour power' with an 'exchange-value'. Labour would regain its true nature as a 'use-value', which could then be devoted to the production of other use-values and the satisfaction of wants freely and cooperatively established in the true democracy of socialism (on Marx's concept of 'true' democracy, see Avineri 1968). Socialism would make the 'machinofacture', developed by the bourgeoisie, more effective and able to free humanity from necessity by its unbounded productive capacity.

Is Marx's Capital relevant today?

Libraries are filled with over a century of compelling critiques of Marx's analysis of the capitalist mode of production and his confidence that the contradictions would lead to its collapse. And, despite the constant fear of global economic instability, there is no sign of the apocalypse that he envisaged. Indeed, as we shall see in part II, it is widely believed that modern capitalism is able to resolve its crises more quickly than before and that economies have not experienced such protracted periods of deep depression as they did before the Second World War. Moreover, since the collapse of almost all of the totalitarian communist regimes, which falsely claimed to have enacted his hopes for the future of humanity, Marx has fallen out of favour and capitalism endures and spreads across the world.

However, it would be a mistake to dismiss the general thrust of Marx's analysis (for example, see Wolff 2002; Callinicos 2003). In the first place, it is premature to think that the expert management of economies is able to eliminate serious dislocation, or even moderate the severity of the oscillations between boom and slump in the 'business cycle'. As we shall see in part II, such optimism was shaken twice in the late twentieth century – first, by the collapse in the 1970s of the post-Second World War so-called Keynesian 'golden age' and, second, at the turn of the twenty-first century, by the crash of the 'new economy'. Towards the end of the 1990s it was widely believed that the astonishing advances in information and communication technology would increase productivity to such an extent that economic fluctuations and recessions would be consigned to history. From a Marxian perspective, it would have been understood that in analysing capitalism attention should be paid not merely to such 'forces' of production, but also to the 'social' relations from which the dislocations and malfunctioning arise.

Overt class conflict might appear to have abated in the advanced economies during the very recent past, but this does not signify its elimination. During the post-Second World War period the 'withering away' of the strike was announced by those who did not hold to the Marxian idea of inherent capital–labour conflict (see chapters 4 and 8). However, an explosion of militant trade unionism followed. In Britain, for example, the Conservative government's project in the 1980s to reduce the power of trade unions is unintelligible without the notion of class conflict. And, of course, the conflict continues to be played out in the world's developing economies in ways more reminiscent of earlier days in western Europe and the USA. In short, the question is what has happened to the struggle between labour and capital? Has it been genuinely overcome by economic development and affluence, or is labour's opposition suppressed and stifled in advanced capitalism? These questions will be taken up in later discussions.

However, Marx's understanding of capitalism's instability is marked by an underestimation of the role played by money in the crises. Marx correctly identified the capitalist mode of production's distinctive Money-Commodity-Money$_1$ (M-C-M$_1$) circuit. But, in common with Adam Smith and most nineteenth-century economic thinkers, Marx was less clear about the way in which capitalism is uniquely characterized by a banking system that can create an unlimited amount of credit-money that fuels the crises either through the financing of overproduction and/or speculation.[8]

As we shall see in chapter 2, Joseph Schumpeter was one of the first to recognize that the *differentia specifica* of capitalism lay in its credit-money-producing banking system. Later John Maynard Keynes referred to capitalism as a 'monetary production economy' and focused on the role of credit-money creation. The nature of capitalist banking and finance is also an important, but neglected, theme in Max Weber's work (Ingham 2003). However, here I wish to focus on the synthesis, implicit in Weber's conception of capitalism, between the nineteenth-century economic theorists' emphasis on the market's efficacy and Marx's insistence that it was founded on inequalities of wealth and power.

Max Weber (1864–1920) and the historical specificity of capitalism: rationality, calculation and domination

Weber tried unsuccessfully to halt the academic specialization in the historical and social sciences that he believed had impaired the understanding of the development of modern capitalism. His original synthesis drew together, but at the same time transcended, economic theory, Marxism and histories of Europe's cultural uniqueness. Whilst he agreed with economic theory that the pursuit of self-interest was universal, he argued that this in itself was unable to explain the rise of the very distinctive kind of 'rational' enterprise capitalism that had first appeared in western Europe. The oriental trader's desire for profit was unsurpassed anywhere in the world (Weber 1981 [1927]: 355), but the economy of which he was a part remained traditional and backward. Here, production was organized domestically or communally and was undertaken, as Marx and others had explained, for direct use rather than exchange on the market. The market occupied a marginal position in pre-capitalist economies, and acquisitiveness was not the major economic motivation.

For Weber, the unique characteristic of modern European capitalism was not merely that acquisitive profit-seeking had permeated economic life. Rather, he focused on the distinctive way in which profit was pursued. Capitalism is defined as the satisfaction of human needs and wants by industrial production undertaken by bureaucratic enterprises in which net profit is rationally calculated (Weber 1981 [1927]: chapter XXII). Continuous calculation of the income-yielding activity by capital accounting is the essential element in this type of economy, and Weber's explanation of the structure and development of capitalism takes the form of an analysis of the conditions which make this possible.

In an immediate and direct way, this 'maximum formal rationality of capital accounting' was achieved by the invention of double-entry bookkeeping, in which a balance is struck between revenue and costs (Weber 1978: 164–6). But such techniques are only likely to develop in a society where they can be applied. And rational economic calculation is only possible where social reality exhibits a significant degree of predictability – that is, one in which the processes of economic production and distribution have become 'calculable'. In this respect, for example, the autonomy of the business enterprise is centrally important. The separation of work and production from the domestic household and community eradicated substantive and arbitrary considerations – grounded in emotional ties, family obligations and traditional social norms – that might interfere with strict economic rationality in the calculation and pursuit of profit.

How the world had come to be a range of options for the calculation of profitable opportunities required an explanation. Weber sought this in the history and social structure of early modern western Europe, which he contrasted with that of the Orient. This thesis, that the rise of modern rational capitalism was historically specific and unique to Western society, has been extensively criticized for being 'Eurocentric' (see Frank 1998). The question cannot be considered here, but the questions raised by Weber continue to have contemporary relevance – for example, in the debate about the compatibility of Islam with capitalism.

The ideal type of modern capitalism

In his *General Economic History* Weber lists those institutional features of Western society that enable rational capital accounting in the enterprise (Weber 1981 [1927]: 276–8; 1978: 161–4). To repeat: it is these changes in west European social structure that make it possible for the enterprise to calculate net profit. In other words, capitalist economic practice is not merely the consequence of *Homo economicus*'s capacity for rational calculation, as it is in economic theory.

1.   The appropriation of all physical means of production as the disposable property of private autonomous enterprises. This was a unique development in human history and permitted the flexible switching of production in the search for maximum net income. Physical capital can be disposed of for money which can be reinvested in alternative ventures. As I have indicated, arbitrary and non-rational intrusions into the conduct of the enterprise's affairs are minimized if the household or family budget is separated from the enterprise budget.

2.   The absence of customary limitations on market exchange in goods and labour, that is, free commodity and labour markets. For example, mediaeval European sumptuary laws restricted consumption according to status group, and certain

classes were prohibited from owning property and following specified occupations. The Indian caste system is one of the clearest examples of such restrictions on market exchange. With Marx, Weber viewed the market as the site of the 'battle of man against man' 'to attain control over opportunities and advantages' (Weber 1978: 93, 38). Market prices were the result of these struggles between the possessors of money, capital and other economic resources. Economic 'scarcity' could only be established by 'conflicts of interests in bargaining and competition and the resolution of these conflicts' (Weber 1978: 92).

And this kind of conflict, which was the basis for the rational economic calculation of money prices, was more easily accomplished when the struggle was freed from arbitrary constraints and regulation as occurred in traditional society (Weber 1978: 82–5).[9]

3. Rational capital accounting presupposes a level of technological mechanization that is capable of producing a calculable output. For example, steam-powered machines are not merely faster, but also more predictable than wind, water and, most importantly, recalcitrant human labour power.

4. With calculable – that is, predictable – law, enterprises are able to depend on calculable adjudication and administration and freedom from arbitrary interference by the state. This condition was not fulfilled until the Stuart dynasty's claim to absolute monarchy in England during the seventeenth century and its appropriation of business opportunities had been successfully challenged. Today, this point is very clearly illustrated by the disquiet shown by US and European capitalist interests at President Vladimir Putin's appropriation of Russia's energy industry for geopolitical ends and his imprisonment of the prominent capitalist Mikhail Khodorkovsky.

Weber would have identified this as 'political capitalism', in which the state attempts to monopolize profitable opportunities in order to increase its political power. But he considered this subordination of the continuous calculation of profit-making to the interests of the state to be 'irrational from an economic point of view' (Weber 1978: 166) (see the discussion of 'rent-seeking' in chapter 8). To this extent Weber is in agreement with Smith and the liberal economists' critique of states' 'mercantilist' economic policies.[10]

5. Without formally free labour, rational capitalistic calculation is impossible. But the determination of the wage-costs of production, by agreement in advance, is only possible when people are compelled, 'under the whip of hunger', to sell their labour. In a further departure from economic theory Weber argued that the rational calculation of opportunities for profit required a power inequality in the enterprise. Capitalists are able to calculate labour costs with precision because, unlike slave-owners, they can control costs by dispensing with workers if demand for their production falls. As we shall see, the right of capitalists to lay off workers has become one of the most contentious issues in modern capitalism. Thus Weber was in close accord with Marx that power and exploitation were necessary for the operation of capitalism, but he flatly rejected the latter's diagnosis of capitalism's demise and his prognosis for humanity's future.

6.   The commercialization of economic life means that all share rights in the enterprise and other forms of property and assets are represented by marketable paper instruments. This last condition is elaborated in two short consecutive chapters in *General Economic History* which place more emphasis on the financial character of capitalism (Weber 1981 [1927]: chapters XXIII and XXIV). The existence of extensive markets in which property and capital are represented by freely negotiable (marketable) paper is unique to the Western world and heralds the appearance of capitalism's great speculative crises. Prices of paper instruments representing property and capital are driven up by demand stimulated by expectations of further rises in price. A point is reached where a loss of confidence turns the market and mass selling brings about a precipitous fall in price. Financial crises were entirely new phenomena, as was the possibility of over-speculation in the supply of means of production beyond the economy's capacity for consumption, as Marx had explained. Both were made possible by the availability of finance in the form of bank credit; and

both types of crisis brought bankruptcy and the consequent disruption of production in a process which later became recognized as 'debt deflation' (see Minsky pp. 40–2; and chapter 7).

Weber devoted relatively little attention to money and banking, but he did see that the creation and circulation of bank credit in western Europe was an important and unique development (Weber 1981 [1927]: 255). He was aware that Western capitalist banks did not merely accumulate existing savings in deposits for lending on, but also that they had the power to create 'new' deposits of money in the form of bank loans. As we shall see, the process by which personal credit becomes money is a core institutional element of capitalism. Loans to individuals are private debts to banks and are transformed into public money by the banking system's linkage with the central bank and the state's debts (see Ingham 2004, chapter 7; see the discussion of Schumpeter and Keynes in chapter 2 below).

In addition to the explanation of *how* it was possible for the enterprise rationally to calculate and devise strategies for maximizing net income, Weber also posed the question of *why* they should do so (Weber 1981 [1927]: 354). The orientation to work and profit-seeking was quite different in Western capitalism from that in traditional societies. Economic maximizing behaviour of the kind described by the economists' model of *Homo economicus* was historically atypical. For example, in his early study of Silesian peasants, Weber observed what economists now refer to as a 'backward sloping supply curve' for labour. This describes the situation in which workers cease to respond to economic incentives once they have attained a level of income that provides for their traditionally limited pattern of consumption. Further inducements to elicit more work by linking pay to output are ineffective, as workers respond by producing no more than the level that achieves the income that satisfies their traditional wants (Weber 1982 [1927]: 355). Without the erosion of such traditional attitudes, the stimulation and satisfaction of new wants by industrial production would not have been possible.

Weber applied the same observation to his explanation of early entrepreneurs' motivation for the continuous calculation and pursuit of profits as an end itself rather than a means to other extrinsic goals. In a traditional society, making profits to reinvest in order merely to make further profits was an example of 'non-rational' action in which 'means' had become 'ends'. When competitive capitalist markets had become fully established, the relentless search for profits to be ploughed back into the enterprise was an externally imposed exigency. Failure to behave in this way could mean being forced out of business by more efficient competitors. But such pressures were very weak, if not entirely absent, in the early stages of capitalist development. In these circumstances, why did the first entrepreneurs appear to strive for profit as an end in itself?

Weber's answer is contained in his best-known work – *The Protestant Ethic and the Spirit of Capitalism* (2001 [1904]). Here, he attempted to show that there was an affinity between certain beliefs in Protestant theology and unremitting capitalistic profit-seeking. Unlike the hedonism of traditional elites, the Puritan's asceticism facilitated the reinvestment of profits and the expansion of enterprise which could be interpreted as the glorification of God on earth. The good husbandry of the gifts that God had bestowed might even be considered to be a 'calling'. In addition, Weber advanced the view that Protestant theology played an important part in expunging the superstition, magic and supernatural beliefs that he saw as inimical to the instrumentally rational manipulation of nature by means of industrial technology. In contrast, the oriental religious ethics contained in Hinduism and Buddhism reinforced the traditionalism and irrational beliefs that inhibited the development of a rational economic spirit.

However, in the mature capitalism of the early twentieth century, Weber observed that '[t]he religious root of modern economic humanity is dead; today the concept of calling is *caput mortem* in the world' (Weber 1981 [1927]: 368). By this stage he seems to agree with Marx that religion is more important as an ideology that pacifies workers by promising happiness in the next world in compensation for the rigours of life under the capitalist regime (Collins 1986).

In a further departure from economic theory, Weber argued that these essential elements of modern capitalism were not simply the spontaneous result of a natural predisposition to barter and exchange – as Smith had contended. On the contrary, it was the actions – intended and unintended – of the early modern European states that had brought about the conditions favourable to rational capitalism.

The development of capitalism in the West

The emergence of the social and political conditions that made possible industrial production on a large scale, conducted and organized by rational capital accounting, grew out of the destruction of traditional obstacles to domestic free trade in land, capital and labour, and by the creation of mass markets for industrial production on a large scale. Weber attributed these developments to the intended and unintended consequences of the development of the modern European state. Adam Smith acknowledged the state's role in the operation of markets; and Marx, of course, emphasized the coercive power of the state in creating and subsequently suppressing the class of wage-labour. But, characteristically, Weber went beyond these two views of the state as, respectively, facilitator and oppressor. His analysis remains of considerable importance for today's debates on the changing relationship between states and markets brought about by 'globalization' (see chapter 8).

In a direct way, the modern European state, based on rational-legal principles administered by professional lawyers, removed feudal and patrimonial relations, and thereby created the social and political space in which capitalist property relations and markets could develop. But Weber also considered the wider economic consequences of the political relations between modern states and their members and between the states themselves.

Most importantly, the members of modern European states became citizens with equal legal rights that provided a basis for formally equal contractual economic exchange and representative democracy. These institutional links between capitalism, liberalism and democracy will be considered in chapter 8; here I wish to draw attention to further economic implications of the state–citizen relation in modern Europe as noted by Weber. In superseding social relations based on kinship, tribe and status group, citizenship eroded ritualized communal exchange and the 'ethical dualism' in the exchange relations of traditional society (Weber 1981 [1927]: 313, 359). On the one hand, exchange within communities was normatively regulated by rules of fairness and an ethic of charity which minimized internal conflicts. For example, the prohibition on usury was aimed at avoiding the exploitation and the disruptive calculation of gain at the expense of other members of the community. Moneylending in traditional societies, Weber observed, was carried out by outsiders – Jews in Christian Europe, Christians in the Islamic world, and Parsees in India (Weber 1981 [1927]: 232). On the other hand, outsiders were cheated and exploited. Both sides of the dualism inhibited the formation of large markets – that is, of economic transactions based on impersonal trust between strangers.

Furthermore, in contrast to members of traditional, rigidly stratified societies, a mass citizenry of equal legal status can more readily become mass consumers of undifferentiated mass products. Perhaps it is by no means coincidental that the USA, in which status group consumption differences were relatively attenuated from its inception, was the first mass consumption society. Moreover, as Weber astutely observed, mass production technology is only cost-efficient if mass consumer demand exists. Of course, this can be created by marketing and advertising, but this would appear to have been more easily accomplished in some societies than others.

A strong bureaucratic state was a necessary, but not sufficient, condition for the development of rational capitalism. Only under certain historical conditions in which the state was faced with the countervailing power of an independent economic bourgeois class did rational capitalism develop. It was the largely unintended outcome of the resolution of the struggle between state and capitalist classes in a 'memorable alliance'. This mutual accommodation of state and bourgeoisie created the means to meet the fiscal needs of states when financing the wars by which the European state system was consolidated (Weber 1981 [1927]; 280). This was most clearly seen England, where the successful founding of the Bank of England in 1694 to finance the conduct of war by the king furthered the interests of both the state and the mercantile classes and had a pivotal effect on the development of capitalism (Weber 1981 [1927]: 264–6; Ingham 2004). As we shall see in chapter 4, fiscal systems based on 'public' banks and state borrowing, with interest payments on loans provided by taxation, were the means by which the credit-money and money markets financed capitalist development. Moreover, this financial relationship between the state and the bourgeoisie was not only a domestic affair; states had to compete on international markets for the mobile capital produced and controlled by the independent cosmopolitan merchant class and their new banks.

In capitalism, according to Weber, the dominant economic classes do not simply control the state, as cruder Marxist theories imply. They depend on the state's autonomous power, but they are not subordinated to it. The 'memorable alliance' is loose enough to allow capitalist classes to operate freely both within and between states. From the beginning, capitalism was an economic system which operated transnationally in a way that was beyond the control of any single state or alliance of states. By and large, capitalists are not in principle restricted in their freedom to seek profits, wherever this might take them. The state, Weber concluded, gave capitalism its opportunity for development; and he added the rather cryptic, but brilliant, insight that 'as long as the national state does not give place to a world empire capitalism will also endure' (Weber 1981 [1927]: 337). In other words, Weber believed that capitalism would flourish as a global economic system in which neither the state nor capital subordinates the other. Capitalism would not collapse under the weight of its economic contradictions, as Marx predicted. Rather, it involves a perpetual political conflict between states and an increasingly cosmopolitan bourgeoisie in which the balance of power swings from one to the other. The subordination of capitalists to the interests of the state would destroy the dynamism of the system; but the converse subordination of the state to the interests of capitalists would lead to excessive, debilitating exploitation and political turmoil. As we have noted, Weber's enduring relevance could not be more clearly seen than in today's struggle between President Putin and the Russian capitalist oligarchs. Their 'memorable alliance' has yet to be forged, but a Weberian perspective would suggest that without one Russia is unlikely to make a successful transition to capitalism. The case of China poses even more intriguing questions concerning the relationship between state and capitalist power (see Nolan 2004; Hutton 2007).

Weber's analysis remains the single most comprehensive account of the social structure of capitalism (see also Collins 1986). It replaced the timeless universals of economic theory's *Homo economicus* and the more narrowly materialist focus of Marx and his followers. Weber identified the specific historical elements of the unique form of economy that was based on the continuous calculation of opportunities for profit and was first developed in early modern western Europe. This had two basic foundations. On the one hand, the rational legal state and modern bureaucratic organization made possible, respectively, the removal of non-rational substantive prohibitions on market exchange and the reduction of arbitrariness in the conduct of human affairs. Both the modern state and the modern enterprise were bureaucratic, rule-governed and, in principle, calculable. Markets and bureaucracies are complementary and not opposed institutions, as cruder forms of economic analysis and ideology maintain.

On the other hand, in the absence of state or private monopolies, power struggles, conducted and regulated according to the 'rules of the game' enforced by the state, between opposed economic interests produce a level of predictability that makes it possible to express relative scarcity in money prices. Prices are the outcome of an economic power struggle; for example, rising price inflation expresses changes in the balance of power. The market is the means by which opportunities for profit can be calculated, as it is in economic theory, but, for Weber, it is the site of the 'struggle for economic existence' and the location of conflicts that are much more extensive than Marx's two-class model of capitalists and workers. To this Weber added lenders versus borrowers and sellers versus consumers and so on. He also emphasized that the various economic classes strove to monopolize any advantages of their market situation rather than overthrow the system. Thus capitalism involves the tension between the dynamism that the free market makes possible and the efforts of the participants to extend and preserve any advantage that they can carve out (Collins 1986: 126, 258).

Finally, as I have suggested, Weber's conception of capitalism contains the germs of an approach which recognizes the importance of distinctive forms of credit-money and public banking that appeared in early modern Europe – first in the Italian city states, followed by Holland and England (Weber 1981 [1927]: chapter XX; Ingham 2003). This was taken up by his one-time collaborator Joseph Schumpeter, as we shall see in the following chapter.

Conclusion

Marx and Weber cannot be fully understood without taking into account their opposition to economic theory's understanding of market capitalism and its origins in the work of Adam Smith and the other classical economists. The commonalities of their critiques are, arguably, more significant than the differences which have surely been overdrawn and exaggerated by generations of sociologists (see Collins 1986; Ingham 2003).

To be sure, Weber utterly rejected the implicit economic determinism in Marx's vision of capitalism's collapse. But he presciently argued that if socialism were to be brought about, by political revolution, in a large, complex, industrial society, then it would require a bureaucratic administration that might be more oppressive for the workers than capitalism. Moreover, such a regime would risk losing the dynamism that was produced by the general 'struggle for economic existence'.

However, in contrast to orthodox economic theory, both theorists understood capitalism as a distinctive historical social system that was based on institutionalized inequalities of power. Weber fully accepted Marx's emphasis on the central importance of the complete expropriation of the means of production as the property of the capitalist enterprise and, in the absence of alternative means of subsistence, the fact that workers were compelled to sell their labour power.

2
Schumpeter and Keynes

Money in Adam Smith's scheme was considered to be no more than a neutral medium that facilitated exchange on the 'great wheel of circulation'. Capital was understood primarily in physical terms as 'stocks' – the instruments of production and raw materials. These were the 'real' factors of production and they were not to be confused with the mere 'wheel' – that is, the money by which they were circulated (Smith 1986 [1776]: 385).[1] Similarly, Marx sharply distinguished money-capital and credit from the means of production, and frequently referred to the former as 'fictitious' capital. But as the capitalist system developed during the nineteenth century, its distinctive monetary and financial character became clearer and these elements began to assume a more prominent place in the analyses of the economy. The idea began to take shape that money was more than a mere medium of exchange and a measure of the value of actual existing physical capital; rather the creation of credit-money was an autonomous force in capitalist development.

Joseph Schumpeter (1883–1950): money markets as the 'headquarters of capitalism'

Schumpeter crossed disciplinary boundaries as they were developing during the first half of the twentieth century, but not to the same extent and with the same conviction as Weber (see Schumpeter's magisterial posthumous *History of Economic Analysis*, 1994 [1954]). On the one hand Schumpeter was attracted to the mathematical sophistication of the equilibrium models of academic economics, but he also saw the importance of the historical study of economies and admired Marx's project and method, if not its details and conclusions. The result was ambivalence about the best way to study capitalism, but Schumpeter's seminal contribution is precisely the result of this tension. His work sought to resolve two related problems in the theoretical understanding of capitalism. First, Schumpeter concluded that Smith's 'circular-flow' model, which was the foundation of the equilibrium theories he admired, could not explain the definitive characteristics of capitalism that Marx had correctly identified – that is, the realization of monetary profits and the continued dynamic expansion of the means of production. Schumpeter's second criticism of economic theory was that the function accorded to money in its circular-flow model meant that it was unable to grasp the particular financial character of capitalism.

In classical economic theory no factor should receive more in income than its input, as measured precisely by costs, to the process of production. We saw earlier that revenues accruing to each factor of production, in Smith's model, are consumed in the subsequent sequential phases of the productive process. Supply and demand in the competitive market eventually ensure that no factor can receive more revenue than that which covers its costs. Schumpeter agreed with Marx's critique that this does not account for profits and any accumulation of surplus for investment (Schumpeter 1961 [1911]: 30–2). In short, capitalism's capacity for dynamic growth and constant revolutionary transformation of the means of production could not be explained by the static 'circular-flow' model.

These distinctive characteristics of capitalism are frequently explained in economic theory as the result of 'exogenous' factors such as technological invention. But what called forth the new techniques and ensured their application? It was difficult to see how the 'invisible hand' could do this without the assumption that it would be profitable for individuals to do so. But the 'circular-flow' model did not contain profits.

Nor did it contain a further distinctive element in capitalism that Weber had touched on – the creation of bank credit-money. In short, Schumpeter set out to resolve these inconsistencies and anomalies in Smith's model and to explain what capitalists actually did.

Profits and the role of the capitalist entrepreneur

The implication of Smith's and other economists' models of the circular flows of production, distribution and consumption in which the entrepreneur merely plays a passive role, responding to price signals in the market, is clearly at odds with the reality of capitalism's dynamism. On the contrary, Schumpeter argued, the entrepreneur is a key figure whose role is constantly to revolutionize the system by restructuring the factors of production in new ways that yield a profit for the initiator either by an increase in their productivity or by the production of new goods. In other words, the entrepreneur doesn't simply compete, but, rather, changes the nature of the competition (Schumpeter 1961 [1911]). Old industries and methods are swept away in a process of 'creative destruction'. In capitalism, however, this is only a temporary advantage, as others are free to adopt the innovations and enter the new sector. The ensuing competition drives down prices, as Smith's 'circular-flow' model predicts, and the subsequent falling profits lead to a 'destructive' phase.

Unlike Marx's vision of a cataclysmic collapse of capitalism, falling profits in the 'destructive' phase are not terminal for the system, as entrepreneurs continue to search creatively for profitable innovation. Schumpeter adds that this dynamic process is accelerated by the existence of a certain degree of monopoly which gives some protection in the initial costly and risky stages of innovation. That is to say, monopoly plays a positive role and is not necessarily as inefficient as it is in the model of the perfectly competitive market (see the discussion in chapter 5).

In addressing the supplementary, but essential, question of how entrepreneurial innovation was made possible, Schumpeter observed that the entrepreneur was the only economic agent in capitalism who was a debtor by the nature of his economic function (Schumpeter 1961 [1911]: 70–4). His analysis of the process by which capitalism was carried on with borrowed money involved a further departure from a 'circular-flow' model.

Capitalism and credit-money

Schumpeter located the rise of capitalism in the development of the law and practice of transferable debt and 'created' deposits in an emerging banking system during the sixteenth and seventeenth centuries, not in the nineteenth century's industrialism (Schumpeter 1994 [1954]: 78). (These monetary innovations are considered further in chapter 4; here we may simply note that transferable debt refers to the practice whereby a creditor is able to use their debtor's acknowledgement of debt – an IOU – as a means of payment to a third party.) The 'capitalist engine' could not be understood at all, Schumpeter contended, without reference to its credit operations and distinctive monetary system (Schumpeter 1994 [1954]: 318). The money markets were the 'headquarters' of capitalism (Schumpeter 1961 [1911]: 126); it was access to credit-money that drove the capitalist system.

At this time, most economic theory, and common sense, understood savings, finance and investment in a similar way to Smith's 'circular-flow' model. Here, as Schumpeter observed, banks are merely intermediaries between savers and borrowers, creating financial reservoirs by collecting together little pools of savings for lending on. But, as we have already noted, Schumpeter and others saw that capitalist banks produced new money by the act of lending, in the sense that the deposits that were created when money was advanced to a borrower were not taken from existing savings or matched by incoming deposits (Schumpeter 1994 [1954]: 319–20, 1113). Money was produced simply by the debt contract between banks and borrowers.[2] Schumpeter clearly grasped that the essential capitalist practice was the actual 'production' of bank credit-money out of nothing more than the promise of repayment (Schumpeter 1961 [1911]: 70–4).

The idea that money was capital had been roundly criticized by Smith and the classical economists as an error perpetrated by false mercantilist doctrines. As we have noted, capital was rather to be seen as 'stock' – tools, materials and other physical means of production. This was 'real' wealth; money was simply the means for exchanging it in the form of goods, or for representing their value symbolically. Additionally, in the era of precious-metal money, credit instruments – such bills of exchange and promissory and bank notes – were to be distinguished from 'real' money. Thus, although credit was important in facilitating trade and production it was not an autonomous force or factor of production, which could only be physical capital 'stocks'. Schumpeter moved towards a different view which gave a clearer account of the workings of the capitalist system. As we shall see in chapter 4, he favoured a credit theory of money – that is to say, all money, regardless of form and substance, is a token claim or credit. Moreover, he also considered that we would have avoided these 'downright silly controversies' about whether credit was money or whether money was capital if economists had kept to the Roman jurists' conception of capital as 'essentially monetary' (1994 [1954]: 322–3).

Schumpeter's efforts to resolve what he saw as the anomalies and inconsistencies of the 'circular-flow' model of the economy had led him, not without equivocation and uncertainty, to view capitalism as comprising two relatively autonomous parts – on the one hand, the material productive factors and, on the other, the monetary and financial. Unlike earlier economic systems in which money was based on the natural scarcity of precious metal, capitalism's banks and money markets had the capacity to expand money-capital without limit. This expansion of money was an independent source of dynamism, but it was also simultaneously the source of capitalism's crises. This was taken further by Schumpeter's pupil, Hyman Minsky, in his 'financial instability hypothesis'.

Minsky believed that 'as long as an economy is capitalist, it will be financially unstable' (Minsky 1982: 36). Following Schumpeter's observation that modern capitalism consisted of enterprise carried out with borrowed money, and echoing Weber in the importance he attached to capital accounting, Minsky observed that in a firm's balance sheet, comprising cash receipts and liabilities, 'the present, past, and future coexist in time' (Minsky 1982: 19). He identified three possible sets of relationships between incoming revenue and debt liabilities which describe progressive fragility: *hedge finance*, *speculative finance*, and *Ponzi finance*. In the hedge finance enterprise, anticipated total revenue exceeds running costs, and debt and interest payments are met within conventionally accepted accounting time periods. A speculative finance enterprise can only meet its debt and interest payments by selling assets or by further borrowing from banks and capital markets. Ponzi finance, named after the Boston swindler's pyramid scheme (for further discussion see Kindleberger and Aliber 2005: chapter 5), describes a situation in which current and projected earnings cannot meet payment commitments 'except for some end points of the horizon' (Minsky 1982: 22). Large infrastructural construction projects, such as the Channel Tunnel, often fall into this category, and Ponzi finance is typical of firms in the financial sector which borrow to acquire speculative financial assets for resale. Under most circumstances, as the cost of debt increases with time, profitability is only possible if the financial assets continue to appreciate. Consequently, Ponzi finance is especially vulnerable to changes in market conditions and interest rates. As we shall see in chapter 7, modern firms in the productive sector increasingly acquire financial assets in this way and in some instances, such as the notorious Enron case, come to resemble purely financial enterprises (see pp. 170–2).

Contrary to the widely accepted view that financial instability is the result of individual irrationality or miscalculation, Minsky argues that as capitalist enterprise is debt-financed, crises are 'normal functioning events' (Minsky 1982: 37). The typical cycle begins with the successful expansion of production and revenues of the prudent hedge finance enterprises. The growing cash balances in their bank accounts enables the extension of further loans by banks. In search of profit, these 'merchants of debt' make the loans to enterprises which fall into the 'speculative' and 'Ponzi finance' categories. As the level of unserviceable debt mounts, there is the increasing likelihood that the inability of an enterprise to meet its payments will initiate a chain reaction of defaults. Or, the monetary authorities, concerned by the rising level of debt, might try to curb credit-money creation by raising interest rates, which will also cause defaults that might trigger a chain reaction.

As current income of 'speculative' and 'Ponzi-financed' firms is insufficient to meet payments, assets are sold to realize cash, causing a collapse of asset prices which exacerbates the situation. As firms attempt to cut their losses by reducing output and laying off workers, output and demand fall, triggering a debt-induced deflation and possible depression ('debt-deflation').

For Minsky, the capitalist system is inherently unstable because of the ease with which its banking system can create credit-money, but he does not, however, draw a Marxist conclusion that capitalism will collapse as a result of these internal financial contradictions. Rather, he implies a paradox which we will explore further in chapter 7. As capitalist finance becomes more efficient in creating credit-money it becomes more vulnerable, but at the same time governments and their central banks believe that they have become more effective at monitoring the system and preventing this 'fragility' from becoming a 'crisis'. For example, as we have noted, credit-money creation can be controlled by raising interest rates, but this increases the probability of defaults. As the risk of default mounts, banks become reluctant to lend ('risk averse') which further accelerates the defaults and movement towards a recession in the economy, and investment and consumption slows in the wake of this credit 'squeeze', or 'crunch'. It is at this juncture that central banks intervene as 'lenders of last resort' by advancing loans to the banking system in order to prevent bank failures and defaults and the unravelling of the credit network and payments system. This also enables banks to advance loans to otherwise sound firms which had been threatened by non-payment of debts and falling prices. However, this action creates what is known as 'moral hazard' in which the banks, in pursuit of profits, continue to make imprudent loans in the knowledge that the central banks will not permit a collapse of the banking system.

It was arguably the most threatening of capitalism's debt-deflations after the Wall Street Crash of 1929 that prompted Keynes's seminal analysis of the capitalist system. Like Marx, he wanted to know why it produced such paradoxical and unintended effects. If human society was capable of producing such vast increases in productive power and wealth, why was it prone to unwanted crises and depressions?

John Maynard Keynes (1883–1946): making capitalism work better

The First World War, the Wall Street Crash in 1929, the final collapse of the gold standard in 1931, global economic depression and mounting unemployment in the 1930s combined to present, arguably, the most serious threat that the capitalist democracies have ever faced. But whilst the democracies floundered, fascist and communist authoritarian regimes had embarked on programmes of state-funded development which had increased employment. Keynes's fundamental aim was to solve the problem of depression and unemployment without sacrificing the economic and political liberalism in the capitalist democracies.

Conventional economic doctrine in the early twentieth century followed Adam Smith in its belief that the 'invisible hand' would, in the long run, ensure the full utilization of all factors of production. Workers could be fully employed if wages eventually fell sufficiently to balance the supply and demand for labour. However, Keynes saw that even if such equilibrium were eventually to occur, it might come too late to avoid human misery and political unrest – in the long run we are all dead was his famous retort to orthodoxy.

This orthodox economic belief that the self-regulating market mechanism would eventually bring about full employment was firmly entrenched in the British Treasury and the Bank of England. Keynes set himself the intellectual tasks of persuasively demonstrating that the free market and the circular flow between the factors of production did not necessarily ensure full employment and, at the same time, of proposing remedial measures that were consistent with political and economic liberalism. Forced labour in road and railway construction, as practised by authoritarian regimes, was not an acceptable solution.

The General Theory of Employment, Interest and Money was published in 1936, but it was only during Keynes's guidance in securing the non-inflationary full employment of the British economy's resources during the Second World War that his analysis gained widespread acceptance in government. This conversion to his ideas was also reinforced by the political commitment to maintain full employment and to introduce comprehensive social welfare, should the war end in victory. The contention that this new social democratic settlement could be financed if Keynes's theory were put into practice became increasingly persuasive. Full employment, it was argued, would reduce the demand for welfare and social security and, simultaneously, increase tax receipts and contributions from employed workers which would help to finance the new measures. For almost a quarter of a century after 1945, Western democracies believed that Keynes's understanding of the capitalist system had enabled its economic problems to be solved and had ushered in a perpetual 'golden age'. The disintegration of this utopian vision during the 1970s will be examined later; here we need briefly to outline Keynes's basic arguments.

According to classical economic theory, as we have seen, money is a passive element in the economic process; it is considered analytically to be a 'neutral veil' behind which the factors of production of the 'real' economy operate. As money does not bring utility or yield interest, holding it is unproductive and, consequently, the rational maximizing individual will either spend it on consumption or invest it for income or profit. The price mechanism of the 'invisible hand' ensures that these activities bring about the full utilization of society's resources. Thus, as Smith had contended, the individual pursuit of self-interest ensured the maximization of collective societal welfare.

Keynes saw that this theory was appropriate for the barter exchange of what he termed the 'cooperative economy'; but, like Marx and Schumpeter, he argued that it ignored the essential historical fact that capitalism was a 'monetary production economy' with the goal of realizing profits. Here money played a pivotal, but paradoxical, role. On the one hand, money could be used to expand production and employment, but, on the other hand, assets could be sold and the money removed from the system as a store of wealth – in Keynes's terms, 'liquidity preference'. From the purely logical standpoint of classical theory, Keynes agreed that this would not be economically rational – it would be more profitable for the individual and society to invest and consume. However, a preference for holding money did occur from time to time and the hoarding inhibited the accomplishment of the full utilization of resources by society. This state of affairs required an explanation.

Although capitalist activity was based on calculation, which was made possible by money's role as a stable standard of value, uncertainty was an eradicable feature of human existence. Given certain facts, the probability of *risk* could be calculated; but Keynes distinguished this from *uncertainty* – that is, situations and circumstances in which we do not know and have no means of knowing how events will unfold. This becomes increasingly the case the further into the future we try to predict and project our endeavours. In the face of such uncertainty, holding money offered psychological security, but the withdrawal of purchasing power diminished production and consumption.

It was 'liquidity preference' that explained the 'outstanding characteristic' of modern capitalism of remaining in a chronic condition of less than optimum activity for long periods of time without either recovering or completely collapsing. In other words, Keynes was convinced by neither Smith nor Marx. All the evidence indicated that 'even approximately full employment is of rare and short-lived occurrence' (Keynes 1973 [1936]: 249–50). In a world of uncertainty, whether or not money was used as a hedge to lull 'our sense of disquietude' or was invested in production or expended in consumption depended on 'animal spirits' – that is, feelings of optimism and confidence. However, this is not simply a matter of individual psychology. As Keynes implies, it is the institutional structure of the capital market which makes this choice between liquidity (holding money) and investment in production and employment available to individuals.

Finance and the capital market

Keynes observed that stocks and shares have a dual character which, in an uncertain world, means that the mutually beneficial harmonization of individual self-interest (profit) and collective welfare (full employment) is not necessarily achieved. Stocks and shares are both a claim (in the form of dividends) on the long-term profits of business enterprise and, simultaneously, speculative assets whose current price varies in relation to expectations of the enterprise's prospective profitability. In a similar manner to classical theory, today's economic orthodoxy maintains that this dual character of financial assets ensures that the short- and long-term performance of the enterprise and individual and collective welfare are integrated. On the assumption that the share price accurately reflects prospective income based on the company's performance, it is held that enterprise managers will on the basis of self-interest endeavour to maximize profits in order to maintain a high stock-market valuation. High share prices act as a defence against take-over and, if pay is partly in the form of share options, they augment managers' remuneration. These issues will be explored further in part II; here we need simply to note Keynes's critique that the nature of the financial asset was not merely dual, but also potentially contradictory.

A central feature of the stock market is the precariousness of the knowledge on the basis of which estimates of the prospective long-term yield of stocks and share are made (Keynes 1974 [1936]: 149). The risk of uncertainty for shareholders is minimized by the liquidity of the shares on the market – that is, they are readily convertible into money. However, this short-term advantage for the individual creates potential long-term problems for business enterprise and, consequently, collective welfare. The stock market enables individuals rapidly to move in and out of investment. It is as though, Keynes whimsically explains, a farmer, having tapped his barometer after breakfast, decides to sell his farm and take his money out of farming during the morning, only to return it a few days later as the weather improves (Keynes 1974 [1936]: 151). There is, at the most fundamental level 'no such thing as liquidity of investment for the community as a whole' – the result is catastrophic depression (Keynes, 1974 [1936]: 160).

Furthermore, with the 1929 Wall Street Crash in mind, Keynes warned that capitalism would fail to provide for human welfare if investment were to become primarily speculative and its stock markets came to resemble casinos (Keynes 1974 [1936]: 159). Even in the absence of serious collapses, the routine uncertainty about the long-term prospects of an enterprise means that investors are constantly trying to anticipate, in the short term, the valuations of their shares. The resulting opportunity for speculative gains creates a short-term volatility in share prices and, consequently, instability for business. Moreover, speculation diverts money from long-term investment in productive enterprise.

Orthodox economic thinking, however, had a different explanation for the inability of society to achieve the full utilization of its resources – the failure of wages to adjust to market conditions.

The labour market and effective demand

This central tenet of classical economics, revived in the neo-liberal economics of the 1980s, held that workers would price themselves out of jobs if they failed to accept lower wages as dictated by the market competitiveness of their firm or industry. Thus all unemployment was 'voluntary' in the sense that it resulted from workers' decisions that a given level of wages was unacceptable as compensation for the 'disutility' of work. However, Keynes argued that unemployment was, in the main, 'involuntary' as, in effect, labour did not have the power to influence the overall level of employment because bargaining determined *nominal* money-wages but not *real* wages – that is, their actual purchasing power (Keynes 1974 [1936]: chapter 19).

Real wages were determined by the combined complex relationship between wages and profits and other prices in the economy, which labour could not directly control. An increase in employment was a possible consequence of a reduction of money-wages, but only if there was an expectation on the part of the entrepreneurs that more workers and increased output would result in greater profits. However, Keynes considered that other outcomes would be more likely. For example, given a competitive producers' market, a reduction of wages might lead firms merely to reduce prices but maintain the same level of output and, therefore, employment. Moreover, if wages were to be reduced this would mean lower effective demand in the economy and the possibility of a downward deflationary spiral as production is cut to adjust to lower consumption.

Keynes argued that private agents – labour or capital – could not easily break the impasse of inadequate effective demand – that is, insufficient purchasing power to maintain full employment. However, Keynes's remedy was not radically to alter the social structure of capitalism – despite his misgivings about the role of the capital market. Rather, he maintained that from time to time capitalist economies were in need of a deliberate stimulus from the 'visible hand' of governments. But they should not, as he put it, take over what was being done, rather, do what was *not* being done.

The management of aggregate demand

For all its virtues capitalism did not automatically produce the level of aggregate demand that was consistent with full employment. Only the government was in a position to do this, but Keynes insisted that, whatever it did, it should not limit individual freedom, which he wished to avoid out of sense of personal conviction. But he was all too aware that any form of public interference in the labour market would be opposed, on the grounds that it contravened the 'strict business principles' that were derived from classical economics. To illustrate his point, he suggested, again with typical whimsy, that it might be acceptable if the Treasury were to bury old bottles filled with bank notes and have private enterprise tender to dig them up, which would have the effect of creating employment and increasing the community's real income (Keynes 1974 [1936]: 129).

In effect, he advocated that governments should use their power to *enable* and *assist* private investment, production, consumption and employment to progress until all resources were fully utilized. It must be emphasized that Keynes never offered simple blueprints and that, after his death, 'Keynesian' was applied to a wide range of policies, some of which were not entirely consistent with his work. However, the basic Keynesian measure requires that governments abandon balanced budgets – that is, they should practice 'deficit finance'.

By their demand for goods and services from the private sector, all governments in capitalist societies create employment, income and further demand in the economy. But conventional 'sound money' and 'strict business principles' held that this expenditure should not exceed tax revenue for fear of introducing too much money into the economy and inducing inflation. However, in order to break an impasse where the level of aggregate demand was insufficient to secure full employment, Keynes advocated that government expenditure should be permitted to exceed revenues from taxation, at least in the short term. This could be achieved by borrowing from the private sector by issuing government bonds and/or by running up an overdraft at the central bank. Such unbalanced budgets would be self-correcting due to a 'multiplier effect' on employment and the consequent increase in tax revenue from the increase in production and employment.

Keynes exposed capitalism's fragile and precarious nature and its inherent tendency to produce unintended and unwelcome consequences. Its performance chronically fell short of its capacity to satisfy human welfare – there was 'dearth amidst plenty'. The 'invisible hand' could not be counted upon to maintain full employment. In the very simplest terms, this was a consequence of the connections between uncertainty, the contradictions between individual interests and collective welfare, and the nature of money in capitalism. In the first place, although money is the source of investment that leads to the employment of labour and the generation of income for consumption, it also provides individuals with the means for withdrawing from enterprise and storing their wealth. The short-term expedient for the individual to deal with uncertainty has unintended long-term negative effects for society as a whole. Second, the existence of speculative markets in financial assets creates price instability that exacerbates uncertainty and can affect employment and production.

As we shall see, speculation is particularly important in foreign exchange markets, where changing exchange rates affect an economy's price competitiveness and level of employment. Keynes was aware that attempts by a government to stimulate aggregate demand would be considered to be inflationary and that this would lead to the selling of its currency and a consequent falling exchange rate which, in turn, would affect domestic conditions (see chapter 4, note 13). Consequently, Keynes's design for the post-1945 international monetary system contained a somewhat contradictory proposal. Worldwide free trade was to be encouraged and supported in all commodities except money. As we shall see, the Bretton Woods international monetary system, which operated between 1945 and the early 1970s, attempted to control international speculative markets in currency and money-capital in order that the democracies could make good the wartime promises to maintain full employment (see pp. 84–6).

Keynes produced a penetrating analysis of the social structure of the capitalist system; but it contained two closely related blind spots. First, he tended to overestimate the efficacy of ideas and intellectual argument and to underestimate the nature of the struggle over the distribution of income. Having dissected the capitalist system, Keynes strongly implied, as did almost all professional economists, that the various groups in society – workers, entrepreneurs, rentiers et al. would all accept the judgements of the technical experts on the measures necessary to produce full employment. Economics, Keynes ventured, would become like dentistry, and, eventually, everyone would recognize the collective benefits of full employment. Second, it is surprising, given the importance he attached to expectations, that he did not consider more carefully the effect of full employment on labour's expectations and power to realize them. These defects were to become much more obvious during the 1970s, but as early as 1944 the Polish economist Michal Kalecki warned, from a left-wing perspective, of the political consequences of full employment (Kalecki 1943). Governments would be forced to discipline the workers' enhanced power and expectations for ever-rising and inflationary wage increases by the deliberate introduction of deflation – an ironic 'reverse Keynesianism'.

Conclusion

Schumpeter and Keynes moved beyond the classical nineteenth-century focus on the material components of the economy – technology and the capital–labour relations in production – to investigate the role played by money. In doing so they departed significantly from conventional nineteenth-century conceptions of money. In essence, both Schumpeter and Keynes held that all money was, in fact, 'credit' of one kind or another. They pointed to the fact that the pace and rhythm of capitalism's dynamic growth was largely dictated by the banking system's 'monetization' of debt, which financed both production and consumption. This pivotal element of the capitalist system, consisting of an entirely new set of banking institutions and practices for the production of credit-money, will be examined in chapter 4. It cannot be too strongly emphasized that these were, as Weber had also noted, unknown in previous types of economy. Their analysis further implies that the locus of power in capitalism lies in the money and credit markets, where Schumpeter's 'merchants of debt' assess creditworthiness and, consequently, determine when and where production takes place and how far credit-financed consumption can absorb it.

3
The basic elements of capitalism

It is possible to discern a gradual shift of emphasis in our classic theorists' analyses of the capitalist economy. Each gives special – but not exclusive – attention to a particular element. Although Smith devoted considerable attention to the way in which capital 'stock' was used to employ labour, he focused on the rapid extension of the division of labour and market exchange in eighteenth-century 'commercial' society. By Marx's time in the mid-nineteenth century, the enterprise factory system was more firmly established, the struggles between capital and labour had intensified, and cycles of economic expansion and contraction had increased in severity and frequency. By the end of the century, more attention was given to the expanding banking system and the increasing role of capital markets. For example, Hilferding augmented Marx's analysis to take the emergence of 'finance capital' into account (see the discussion in Scott 1997: 22–5). But Schumpeter realized that money, banking and finance had been capitalism's most distinctive characteristics from the very earliest stages of development and that these were the key to understanding the system's operation. Obviously, Smith and Marx were not unaware of the monetary and financial side of capitalism, but they looked elsewhere for its definitive features. With Keynes, as we have seen, money takes on even more significance.

Taking these accounts as a whole we can identify three fundamental elements, or institutional clusters, of the capitalist economy:

A. monetary system for producing bank-credit money;
B. market exchange; and
C. private enterprise production of commodities.

A. Monetary system and bank-credit money

Market exchange and enterprise production cannot exist without a viable monetary system. First, the impersonal coordination of sellers and buyers – that is, supply and demand – by price signals in large-scale markets presupposes the existence of a means of exchange and payment. Second, as Weber emphasized, the calculation of costs of production and net profits in the enterprise requires a monetary standard of value (money of account). Third, money-capital for both production and financial speculation is created with loans (debt), produced by a network of banking enterprises which realize a profit from interest. Following Schumpeter, it could be argued that the financing of production with money-capital in the form newly created bank money uniquely specifies capitalism as a form of economic system. Enterprises, wage labour and market exchange existed to some small degree, at least, in many previous economic systems, but, as we shall see, their expansion into the dominant mode of production was made possible by the entirely novel institution of a money-producing banking system. Capital is 'that sum of means of payment which is available at any moment for transference to entrepreneurs' (Schumpeter (1961 [1911])).[1]

B. Market exchange

The exchange of commodities in markets is based on competition between buyers (demand) and sellers (supply), which produces a price at which exchange is acceptable. This mechanism of bids (demand) and offers (supply) coordinates the three phases in the capitalist production of commodities:

(i) finance (money-capital) → (ii) production (capital + labour) → (iii) consumption.

Bank credit finances investment (in the form of loans, stocks and shares) in physical capital and the employment of labour for the production of both the means of production and of consumption goods in order to realize a profit – that is, Marx's M-C-M_1. As we shall see, capitalism also contains purely speculative markets in financial assets which involve purely M-M_1 exchanges.

All forms of property, goods and services, including the enterprise and its potential revenue, are marketable as financial assets – stocks and shares, bonds, securities and so on. The uncertainty of financial asset price changes over time gives rise to speculative markets involving purely financial exchange in which assets are bought and sold in the expectation of price changes – that is, M-M_1 deals.[2] In this way, capital is endowed with a dual character – as both productive resource and speculative financial asset.

Thus capitalism contains the following basic markets:

a. the money and money-capital markets by which the supply and demand for finance is coordinated and its price (interest) established;
b. the labour market which determines wages;
c. two markets involved in production: (i) the market for production goods (means of production); and (ii) the final consumption goods; and
d. financial asset markets, based on the fact that the title to the ownership of all forms of property in capitalism is represented as a marketable 'asset'.

As the discussion of our theorists has shown, there are two quite divergent analyses of these interrelations. On the one hand, theories deriving from Smith's account of the 'invisible hand' emphasize the effectiveness of the market's decentralized coordination and integration of complex economic systems. In this model of capitalism, competition produces the most efficient outcome in which all resources are fully utilized.

Moreover, economic agents – bankers, workers, managers and so on – are rewarded in accord with their functional contribution, which is, in turn, determined by a competitive process of supply and demand. For example, a shortage in the supply of highly productive labour will lead to the substitution of labour-saving physical capital. Furthermore, this approach strongly implies that the economic integration and efficiency creates social integration by binding economic agents together in webs of mutually beneficial exchange.

On the other hand, Marx, Weber and – to some extent – Keynes point to the power inequalities of the property rights between economic classes and agents and to the fact that the divided economic functions do not simply cooperate, but struggle over the surplus. For example, capital, but not wage-labour, has the right to control the operation of the enterprise and to calculate and distribute profits. Furthermore, this tradition places emphasis on the unintended negative or contradictory effects of market coordination.

By enabling capital to be withdrawn from unprofitable activity and reinvested elsewhere, financial asset markets are an essential source of capitalism's flexibility and dynamism. But, as Keynes warned, this capacity can quickly incapacitate the economy if there is a widespread withdrawal of capital from production and/or consumption and its storage of capital in the form of money. Furthermore, pure speculation under conditions of uncertainty can routinely create asset price bubbles and instability that can perturb the production of goods and services.

Despite these different views on the efficacy and stability of the market mechanism, there is widespread agreement that market competition accelerates economic growth by driving capitalist entrepreneurs constantly to revolutionize the means of production in a process described by Schumpeter as 'creative destruction'.

C. Private enterprise production of commodities

The production of goods and services for sale on the market takes place in private enterprises which are institutionally separated from the household and state, where consumption takes place. Money-capital and wage labour are brought together in the enterprise, which aims to calculate the net cost of producing marketable commodities with an exchange value in order to realize a monetary profit. All means of production are the private property of the enterprise and constitute its physical or material capital. Production is undertaken by legally free labour, employed for wages by the enterprise.

The physical means and money used in the process of production are 'capital' in that they are not owned or controlled by those who directly operate the enterprise – workers and managers. In other words, as Marx explains, capital is not defined by its functional role in the process of production, but by a power relation. 'Money' becomes money 'capital' only with the existence of property-less labour – that is to say, a class of economic agents that can only subsist by selling their only 'property' – their labour power.

With the development of the large-scale corporation, comprising shareholders and salaried managers, it was widely held that private ownership had been separated from control of the enterprise to such an extent that capitalism was no longer an accurate designation of modern economies. However, as we shall see in chapter 6, both ownership and control of capital remain highly concentrated and outside the control of almost all employees.

Private ownership is not necessary for the physical means of production to be capital. States also own means of production, but if workers do not exercise control over their deployment, use and disposal, then it is more appropriate to refer to this as a form of 'state capitalism', rather than socialism. From this standpoint, for example, Saudi Arabia's oil and gas enterprise Saudi Aramco and Mexico's Pemex, as well as communist China's enterprises, are state capitalist.[3]

Again, the enterprise – like the market – can be looked at from two perspectives – as the functionally efficient means for the coordination of economic activity, or as the source of exploitation and site of the most intense conflict between economic agents and classes. These different conceptions of the enterprise will be examined in chapter 6, but here we should note that coordination within the enterprise is not based on the 'invisible hand'. As Marx and Weber insisted, the wage contract does not merely specify the terms of the contractual exchange of effort for reward; it also entails the workers' subordination to the 'visible' authority of the owners and controllers of capital.

These elements A, B, and C comprise a structurally differentiated 'economy' which is, in Polanyi's terms, 'disembedded' from other non-economic institutions in society. Decisions about production and distribution of goods and services in the market capitalist economy are taken on the basis of an economic rationality – that is, costs of production and relative prices. In pre-market society the organization of production and distribution is 'embedded' in families, communities, manorial households or states. For example, the division of labour in simple hunter-gatherer societies was embedded in communal and familial relations. Men made tools and weapons and hunted; women made utensils, gathered vegetation and cooked. All labour was devoted to production for basic subsistence and use, not exchange; and distribution was governed by norms of in-group reciprocity. Traditional agrarian communities largely distributed production in accordance with an ethic or charity (Weber 1981 [1927]: 356). In empires – such as ancient Egypt – the surplus was collected and redistributed as rations by the central bureaucracy (Polanyi 1971 [1957]).

However, as we shall see, two crucially important related points must be borne in mind. First, the separation of the economy as a complex of distinct institutions does not mean that it is completely separate and autonomous from the other parts of society. Second, the market and other basic elements of the capitalist economy are not self-reproducing or self-regulating – that is to say, Smith's 'perfect liberty' of freely contracted exchange relations did not emerge spontaneously. Rather, the 'free' market and all other institutions of the capitalist system – the enterprise, the banking system and so on – are all produced and maintained by state law, norms and cultural beliefs. As Marx emphasized in his critique of Smith, the revenues (rent, profits/interest and wages) received by the factors of production (land, capital and labour) were the result of the social relations of production – that is, property relations. Property gives capital the legal right to organize production in the enterprise. These issues will be examined further in part II; here we need simply to outline the main points for consideration.

The state

In simple terms and notwithstanding considerable variations between different countries and across time, relationships between the state and the structurally distinct market capitalist economy are the outcome of the mutual accommodation between the emerging capitalist bourgeoisie and the early modern state, described by Weber as the 'memorable alliance' (see pp. 32–4). The struggle between monarchs and merchants for control of opportunities for profit-making was resolved by a tacit agreement in which the bourgeoisie ceded their claim to rule in exchange for the right to make money in conditions secured and protected by the state. In return, the state was financed by taxation and loans from the propertied classes. In short, as we shall see in more detail in part II, capitalism is characterized by two interdependent sources of power – the state's legitimate use of force and the private ownership and control of economic resources (capital).

Modern capitalist states provide:

(i)   a level of social order within which peaceful economic activity can take place;

(ii) an institutional and legal framework which specifies the rights of the various economic agents and the rules of competition and exchange – that is, the laws governing property rights and contracts between buyers and sellers;

(iii) a range of services and 'public goods' that would appear to be necessary for an effective capitalist economy, but which private enterprise is either reluctant or unable to undertake – for example, a sound currency, education and welfare to maintain the quality of the work force ('human capital'); and

(iv) attempts to correct the market's failure to achieve acceptable outcomes – for example, financial crises or persistent unemployment. In return, these activities are financed by taxation and loans with the consent of the economic interests of civil society.

Each of these 'functions' can be considered from the different perspectives on the operation of the capitalist system that we have encountered. Some would argue that the state's actions are based upon a disinterested search for the most effective and efficient means of running capitalism. Others contend that the regulation of the economy is the outcome of a conflict between irreconcilable interests that does not necessarily produce the most efficient outcome. In this regard, the Marxist perspective maintains that the state exists to ensure the dominance of capital and subordination of labour.

The scale and scope of the state's direct intervention and participation in the economy is continuously contested in a way that could almost be said to define the nature of politics in modern capitalist societies. On the one hand economic liberals, taking Smith as their guide, argue that the market has a capacity for self-regulation and, consequently, state involvement should be kept to a minimum. On the other hand, radical critiques, based in varying degrees on Marx, contend that market capitalism is crisis-prone and founded on economic inequality. State power should be used to curtail the depredations and destructive consequences of the capitalist class. Various 'middle' or 'third' ways have been sought, which seek to harness the productive efficiency of market capitalism to the attainment of politically determined goals and values – equality of opportunity, social justice, the eradication of poverty, health and even 'happiness' (for a critical survey of 'third way' discourse see Callinicos 2001).

The balance of power and interdependence between states and capital is characterized by a particular articulation of sovereign territorial space and market networks at the international level. Although capitalism is dependent on the social peace that states can bring about, it is by nature extraterritorial. In the most fundamental terms, what we now see as globalization may be understood as an acceleration of the process whereby capitalist networks and markets extend across the world. In this process, the complex relationship between the two 'logics' of political and economic power is revealed (see the discussion in chapters 8 and 9).

As we shall see, the idea that there exists a mutually rein-forcing connection, or 'elective affinity', between the liberal democratic state and capitalism is well established in the social and historical sciences. Most obviously, as we have noted, Smith's 'perfect liberty' of the market has its founda-tion in the politically liberal state. Weber agreed and drew further connections between citizenship and capitalism. Fur-thermore, it is argued that modern representative democracy is an almost inevitable consequence of economic and political liberty. As I have already suggested, these issues are of the utmost contemporary importance as capitalism continues to spread across the world and in doing so encounters hitherto unreceptive regimes and forms of state in Islamic countries and communist China.

Culture and capitalism

Like all social systems, capitalism is 'cultural' in the sense that its economic activities are guided, framed and rendered meaningful to the participants by shared symbols, norms, beliefs and values.[4] Attention has been given to two main issues: the 'spirit' of entrepreneurial capitalism, and acquisi-tive consumerism. Capitalism is historically distinctive in that both production and consumption are freed from the limits set by traditional cultural constraints. Some level of luxurious 'conspicuous consumption' is to be found in all except the simplest subsistence-level societies, but only in modern capi-talism does it become a major motive force in the economy. In short, if the culture of capitalism is unable to generate an ever increasing expansion and proliferation of consumers' wants, then the economy falters and enters a period of stagnation.

As Weber observed in late nineteenth-century Silesia, where traditionally limited patterns of consumption had not entirely disappeared, it was proving futile to increase the peasants' output by offering monetary incentives (Weber 1981 [1927]: 355). Raising the rates simply led the peasants to reduce their effort to the point that gave them the previous level to meet their customary level of consumption. Applying the same logic to enterprise production, Weber posed the question of why, in the absence of any economic compulsion, the early capitalist manufacturers persisted in their pursuit of profits far beyond the point at which their own consumption needs had been met. As is well known, he identified a distinctive 'spirit of capitalism' in which the pursuit of gain by the unceasing calculation of net profit had become an end in itself, rather than a means to affording a culturally prescribed style of life. But how did these entrepreneurs make sense of their historically atypical activity? Why, in early capitalism before competition in product markets, did they make profits only to plough them back into the enterprise? Protestantism's distinctive 'ethic', Weber famously concluded, had an 'elective affinity' with the 'capitalistic spirit'. The 'calling' to work and the glorification of God by the good stewardship of his gifts to humanity gave meaning to the relentless calculation and pursuit of profit for the improvement of enterprise, as opposed to mere avarice and greed.

In modern capitalism the compulsion to pursue profits now has a purely structural foundation; that is to say, it is driven by the quest for survival in competitive markets and by the demands of shareholders for dividends.[5] Nowhere is this more evident than in the absolute exigency that consumers' wants are stimulated without limit, lest falling demand triggers a recession and a downward spiral of factory closures, unemployment and ultimately social and political unrest. Marx's 'fetishism of commodities' is now institutionalized in the culture of modern capitalism, and personal identity in modern capitalism is largely achieved by the display of a distinctive pattern of 'lifestyle' of 'conspicuous consumption' (Slater 1997; Veblen 1994 [1899]).

However, it has recently been argued that purely materialist incentives fuelled by insatiable consumption demands can never provide sufficient basis for the continued willingness of individuals to participate in the capitalist system (Boltanski and Chiapello 2005). Unbridled hedonism, selfishness and greed can never provide an ethical legitimation for capitalism and, consequently, they will continue to attract critiques of the system. Paradoxically, this continually stimulates the formulation of new ideological justifications, that is to say, a 'new spirit of capitalism' which emphasises the 'collective benefits defined in terms of a common good' that it is claimed capitalism can produce (Boltanski and Chiapello 2005: 1–55). For example, discourse in management texts has appropriated values from the 1960s countercultural critique of capitalism and used them to characterize new non-hierarchical forms of work organization in which individuals can realize autonomy and self-expression.

With the exception of culture, these fundamental elements – the market mechanism in the capitalist economy, the monetary system and the production of bank-money, enterprise production and the struggle for its surplus, financial assets, and the state's roles in capitalism – will be examined separately and in more detail in the following chapters.

Part II
The institutions

4
Money

It might seem to be unnecessary to draw attention to the fact that money is an essential component of the capitalist system. As Marx complained, the 'cash nexus' comes to dominate all social relations, everything and everyone in society becomes a commodity, and the quest for profit gradually replaces all other motives in humanity's productive activity. Somewhat paradoxically, however, money's role in the development of capitalism is largely taken for granted in the social sciences. Economic development is seen to be triggered by other factors – the division of labour, technology, population growth, property rights and so on. There is a strong implication that money simply emerges in response to the functional needs of expanding economic activity. For example, it was naively assumed in the 'shock therapy' construction of a capitalist economy in Russia in the early 1990s that the creation of a monetary system would be unproblematic (Woodruff 1999). However, as this episode demonstrated, money does not appear spontaneously in this way; it is rather a fragile socially and politically constructed institution (Ingham 2004).

Money provides two essential conditions for capitalist economies. First, a stable measure of value makes it possible to coordinate supply and demand in large-scale impersonal markets by the price mechanism. Barter limits exchange to bilateral bargaining in which the exchange values of the goods vary by trade, thus limiting the size of the sphere of exchange. Second, stable money is necessary for the longer-term debt contracts which form the basic fabric of economic relations in capitalism. For the successful creation of the extensive debt that drives the capitalist system, lenders must be confident that their interest is not eroded by inflation.

Without a stable monetary system an economy will fail to become fully capitalist and a capitalist economy will fail, regardless of how well it is endowed with material and other resources – as Argentina has shown over the past century (see Ingham 2004: 165–74). The production of a trusted currency, including an integrated banking network, and the stability of money's purchasing power are the primary concerns of all capitalist states.

Money is, of course, much older than capitalism, but here it has distinctive characteristics. These consist in a particular set of social relations and institutions, involving the state and the banking system, for the production of what is, in principle, an unlimited supply of credit-money (money-capital) that finances dynamic growth. As I have stressed, it is a defining characteristic of capitalism that private debts can be readily transformed into money. However, this capability is simultaneously the source of capitalism's dynamism and its fragility. On the one hand, this elastic production of money can have inflationary consequences, as debt-financed investment and consumer demand are driven beyond the productive capacity of the economy. On the other hand, debt inevitably entails the threat of default and the subsequent 'disappearance' of money in a process of 'debt deflation' (see pp. 41–2). Financial and monetary crises are the most significant recurrent events in the history of capitalism – from the South Sea Bubble (1720) to the Wall Street Crash (1929) to the southeast Asian crisis (1997) to the 2007–8 'credit crunch' and countless others. Financial markets will be examined in chapter 7; here we need to understand a little more about what makes them possible – money.

Despite money's fundamental role in capitalism, considerable disagreement on the nature of money persists in the social sciences (Ingham 2004; 2005). The complexities of the disputes need not concern us here, but basic issues in the theory of money need to be examined in order to understand how money is produced in capitalism and how its two main 'disorders' – inflation and deflation – come about.

What is money?

Money is a pivotal social technology in the history of human society. With number and writing, it was a basis for the world's first large-scale complex societies in the ancient Near East during the third millennium BC.[1] Today, the electronic transfer of money across national boundaries and the rapid changes in the value of money wrought in the foreign-exchange markets are the major driving forces of globalization.

According to the familiar textbook list, money performs a number of crucially important functions: medium of exchange, means of payment (unilateral settlement), store of value and money of account (measure of value).[2] Media of exchange and means of payment make possible the operation of the division of labour and the subsequent exchange of production in large-scale markets. Second, money is a store of value – that is, abstract purchasing power. Third, money's most important attribute, upon which the others are based, is as a measure of value – or, money of account. The abstract notation of money in pounds and pence, dollars and cents, and so on, enables the calculation of prices, costs, benefits, debts and credits, profits and losses.

Money has a dual nature. As a social technology, it expands society's 'infrastructural power'; but this collective capacity can be appropriated by particular interests and used 'despotically' as a means of domination (for the distinction between infrastructural and despotic power see Mann 1986). More-over, the power of money is found not simply in the form of amassed wealth but also in the power to control the actual production of money in institutions such as mints and banks. Today, for example, the interplay between central banks' interest rate decisions and the money markets' reactions to them in their pricing of currencies and every kind of financial asset is arguably the most important institutional nexus of modern capitalism.

In the most elementary terms, there are two distinct and incompatible theories of the origins, development and nature of money (Ingham 2004; 2005). On the one hand, money is said to have first appeared spontaneously in the course of barter and is identified with money media or 'things'. According to this theory, one of the most highly valued and therefore tradable commodities against which all others could be readily exchanged – for example, precious metal, salt – becomes a medium of exchange.[3] It is assumed that other functions and attributes of money, most importantly measure of value (money of account) for the construction of price lists and debt contracts, simply follow from the existence of a widely accepted tradable commodity. However, although such a commodity could function, in Keynes's terms, as a 'convenient medium of exchange', its exchange ratio with other commodities would vary from trade to trade, according the different barterers' preferences. Only exceptionally would it be able to act as a money of account for price lists and long-term contracts. Money is the stable measure of value which makes it possible to establish the relative prices of all commodities. Simple barter exchange alone cannot produce a single stable price for a commodity that would enable it to act as a stable measure of value, or money of account (Ingham 2004).

In other words, a genuine market *presupposes* the existence of a single measure of value (money of account) in which demand and supply can be expressed in prices and debt contracts undertaken.[4] Moreover, the historical and anthropological evidence does not support the hypothesis that money originated in barter exchange (Ingham 2004; Aglietta and Orléan 1998).

The other school sees money as an *abstract* claim, or credit, measured by a money of account. Here money's nature is twofold: it measures and stores the abstract value of general purchasing power and transports or transmits it through space and time. In this conception, money has value not because it comprises a commodity with fixed intrinsic value (although an authority might declare it to have one, as in a gold standard). Rather, money is abstract purchasing power – 'the value of things *without* the things themselves' (Simmel 1978 [1907]: 121, emphasis added).[5] This abstract quality of money as a 'credit' or 'claim' on goods and for settling debts is much more obvious in today's monetary systems than it was in the era of precious metal coinage. In modern capitalism, most money consists of electronic impulses that record and transmit quantities of abstract value between bank accounts.[6] Thus, in this understanding, the unique specificity of money as abstract credit, rather than as an exchangeable commodity, lies in what Keynes referred to as the 'description' of money by a money of account – dollars, euros and so on (Keynes 1930: 4). Such a description, by which we understand some object or institution as being monetary, is assigned socially by 'collective intentionality' (Searle 1995). Commodity media of exchange (gold, beans) can become money, as opposed to readily exchangeable commodities, when they are further 'described' in the terms of the measure of abstract value – pound, dollar, euro and so on. Thus the commodity gold is transformed into money in a 'gold standard' when the monetary authority fixes its price in terms of the money of account – for example, 1 ounce of gold = \$10.[7] In such a gold standard, coins, paper notes and weights of gold would all become money when they were declared to represent a dollar.

In other words, money is a social and political construction, but this does not merely mean that money is produced socially. Rather, this theory argues that money is actually *constituted* by a social relation of credit–debt, denominated in an abstract money of account. First, issuers of money – banks and states – promise to accept, in payment of *any* debt owed to them, the form of money that they have issued and denominated in their declared money of account (Ingham 2004: 12, 178, 187). Second, money (with a known value, as opposed to tradable commodities with uncertain exchange rates) can exist as a credit, for the holder only if other debts exist, denominated in the same money of account, awaiting cancellation. In other words, money (as opposed to tradable commodities) cannot be created without the creation of debt (Innes 1914, in Ingham 2005).

The credits that constitute money can be issued privately or publicly. There is evidence of the use of private trade credit (acknowledgements of debt, or IOUs), recorded in a money of account on clay tablets, in ancient Babylon over 3,000 years ago – at least two millennia before the first known use of coins. But such credit instruments were generally restricted to commercial networks and their use was often strongly resisted by states, which wished to monopolize the advantages that resulted from the issue of money.[8]

Knapp's state, or 'chartalist', theory of money locates the historical origins of money in the debt relations between states and their members. In payment for goods and services, states issued credit tokens (*charta*), denominated in the declared money of account, which, in turn, they promised to accept in payment of tax debts. In this way, states create the sovereignty of a monetary space in which debts and prices are denominated with their single money of account (measure of value). This monopolization of monetary production overcomes the anarchy of variable exchange ratios of even the most tradable commodities and, consequently, forms the basis for large-scale markets.

As we shall see, the capitalist monetary system developed from the integration of private networks of mercantile trade credit-money with public currency – that is, state money. This was first effectively accomplished in Europe from the sixteenth century onwards. Capitalist credit-money was, arguably, the most important element in the 'memorable alliance' between the state and the bourgeoisie, which Weber considered to be so important in the rise of capitalism. The gradual detachment of money from scarce precious metal made possible a vast increase in its supply which financed the enormous expansion of production and consumption.

Capitalist credit-money

By the late fifteenth century increasingly stable feudal relations and more secure kingdoms had pacified large areas of Europe to a degree that permitted a significant growth of commerce. Using techniques borrowed from the Orient, merchants began to use credit instruments – such as the bill of exchange – to finance their trade. Bills of exchange require two networks – one of traders and another of bankers. Rather than risk the transportation of precious metal money, merchant A, for example, would remit a bill of exchange, drawn on his own bank, payable to the named merchant B. This was presented by merchant B to his own bank for payment. The bill of exchange would then become a credit for B's bank which would eventually be netted out in the bank giro network for the clearing of inter-bank debts, thus minimizing the use of coin.

At this stage of development the bills represented the value of specified goods and were payable only to the named trader. Eventually, bills unrelated to any particular transaction and pair of traders were issued as credit by reputable banks and began to circulate widely. In other words, these bills, representing bankers' liabilities, became depersonalized and transferrable (or 'negotiable') to third parties; in effect, they were private-sector commercial money.

By the seventeenth century bills and promissory notes circulated extensively across the major trading countries of Europe as transnational private money. Moreover, the banks were able to produce this money by lending, in the form of bills and notes, to individual merchants and producers. This lending created a deposit (the client's debt to the bank) against which further bills and notes could be drawn. This practice is quite different from pre-capitalist money-lending where the lender depletes their stock of coins. The 'new' money created by the bills and notes was based simply on two promises: on the one hand, the debtor's promise to the bank to repay the debt and, on the other, the bank's general promise to accept its notes in repayment of any debt owed by anyone.

For Schumpeter these monetary innovations were the hallmark of capitalism: 'the development of the law and practice of negotiable paper and of "created" deposits is the best indication we have for dating the rise of capitalism' (Schumpeter 1994 [1954]: 78). As a network, the banking *system* is able to generate an elastic production of credit-money by the creation of debt in a self-generating process, as 'banks can always grant further loans, since the larger amounts going out are then matched by larger amounts coming in' (quoted in Ingham 2005: 377). Further discussion of this credit-money 'multiplier' follows, but here it should be stressed that it was the means of expanding production and consumption, which inelastic precious-metal currency inhibited.[9]

However, early private credit networks were unstable; they were only as strong as the networks of commerce in which they were embedded. Defaults on repayments broke the chains in the banking system's expansion of credit by causing bankruptcies and triggering recessions, as they can also do in modern capitalism. Greater stability and, consequently, faster economic growth were gradually achieved when the private banking networks were integrated with the public currency and the sovereign debt of the most powerful and secure states. This occurred first in the Italian city states during the sixteenth century, spread to Holland, and was most successfully accomplished in England with the foundation of the Bank of England in 1694.

By the late seventeenth century England possessed both a strengthened metallic currency and a prosperous mercantile community, which proved to be ground for the integration of public currency and private credit, joining the power and security of the state with the ability of the commercial banks to produce credit-money. The process was accelerated by Charles II's default on his debt owed to the London merchants in 1672 (for a more detailed discussion see Ingham 2004, ch. 6). The subsequent conflict between the bourgeoisie and the monarchy culminated in the offer of the throne to the financially astute Dutch king, William of Orange, in the Glorious Revolution of 1688. Based on techniques first developed in the Italian city states, Dutch finances had been transformed by the founding of a 'public bank' to lend to the state by the creation of deposits based on the king's promise to repay the debt, in exactly the way that the private banks had begun to operate.

The offer of the English throne to William was accompanied by a political and fiscal constitutional settlement in which the new monarch was forced to accept financial dependence on Parliament in a binding agreement. Long-term borrowing to finance William's expenditure was arranged through the adoption of these new public banking techniques, and represented an alliance of bourgeoisie and state. The Bank of England, founded in 1694, was financed with £1.2 million of capital provided by the London merchants. This was then loaned to William and his government at 8 per cent interest which, in turn, was funded by taxes and customs duties. The loan and the king's promise of repayment were considered to be the Bank's *asset*, and consequently became the basis for a further loan issue of its banknotes to private borrowers, for the same amount of £1.2 million. In essence, the norms of new banking practice had doubled the money available to the economy.

Essentially the same process for manufacturing money was replicated over the next century in hundreds of local banks. Borrowers' *private* debts to banks created the deposits which became *public* money when spent. The Bank of England's notes and bills, which were based on the sovereign debt, were in greatest demand, and the Bank would exchange the notes and bills of local banks in exchange for its own at a discount and eventual profit. Consequently, Bank of England notes, denominated in the same money of account as the Royal Mint's currency, were spread widely across the country. It is important to understand that the notes were introduced into an existing sovereign monetary space that had been secured by the strengthening of the state and its precious-metal currency from the late sixteenth century onwards. Eventually the two forms of money – bank credit notes and precious-metal coinage – were linked by their convertibility, at a fixed rate, in a gold standard.[10]

The fusion of the two moneys – private bank credit and state currency – was made possible by the balance of power between the monarch and the bourgeoisie and their acceptance of mutual dependence. It represented a delicate balance between too much state power, which might readily have suppressed the private alternative credit-money, and too little state power, which would not have been able to impose an acceptable public currency denominated in a stable money of account.

These arrangements for producing capitalist credit-money were copied with varying degrees of success throughout the developing Western world. It is a mechanism that connects capitalist finance with the state in a relationship of mutual advantage in which each has an interest in the survival and prosperity of the other. The state has access to loan finance and money capitalists receive interest and repayment of capital from tax and import duty revenues collected by the state. As we have noted, many otherwise well-endowed modern capitalist economies – for example, Argentina – have fragile monetary systems largely because they have not been able to forge this kind of mutually advantageous alliance between state and bourgeoisie (Ingham 2004: 165–74). Capitalism is distinctive in that it contains a social mechanism by which privately contracted debtor–creditor relations – for example, bank loans or credit card contracts – are routinely monetized. The banking system converts private debt into the most sought-after means of payment – that is, the state's issue of money that is accepted in final settlement of tax liabilities. This conversion is achieved by complex linkages between the banking system and the state and, in turn, between the state and its own creditors (bondholders) and debtors (taxpayers). These relations are mediated by a central bank when it accommodates the private banks' debts by lending to them, at the base rate of interest it can impose, in order that they can balance their books. The central bank is able to do this because its loanable assets consist, in part, of the state's debt. This results from the central bank's acceptance of government treasury cheques presented by those who have received payment for the goods and services that the state has purchased. The state's sovereign debt – that is, its promise to pay – exists as its central bank's asset against which further loans can be made, in exactly the same way as William of Orange's debt in 1694.

The belief that governments could use this mechanism to control the supply of money and consequently the level of inflation influenced 'monetarist' policies during the 1970s and 1980s. However, it is now almost universally acknowledged that 'monetarism' failed because the supply of money is primarily determined by the demand for *private* loans and their monetization in the banking system, as noted above. It is now time to examine these definitive capitalist processes in little more detail.

The money market and the production of credit-money

The money market – Schumpeter's 'headquarters' of capitalism – links the demand for money with the supply, but the relationship between the two sides is quite different from that to be found in other markets. In the first place, the supply of money, unlike the supply of goods, cannot be permitted freely to respond to demand for the financing of production and consumption in both the private and public sectors. If money is not made relatively scarce in relation to the production of goods, *ceteris paribus*, inflation might result. Moreover, if money could be freely produced there would be little incentive to acquire it through work. Natural scarcity and costs of production set some limits to the production of precious-metal money, but modern capitalist money requires different methods for controlling its supply. Here, as we have seen, the creation of money is based exclusively on the creation of debt. States produce money by 'fiat' – that is, simply by writing cheques that their central banks promise to accept from the recipients. Similarly, private bank credit-money is produced by the creation of deposits for its borrowers. This non-precious metal 'fiat' money – existing only as entries in ledgers, paper notes, and electronic impulses and so on – can only be made scarce by the rules and norms that govern the contracting of debt by the state and the private sector.

Capitalist societies vary in the money-market institutional arrangements that link their states, central banks and banking systems, but they share certain fundamental features: (i) the private credit and the banking system 'money multiplier'; (ii) state debt as the ultimate foundation of credit-money; (iii) the pivotal role of the central bank; and (iv) the three-cornered struggle between state, money market and taxpayer.

(i) The demand for money to finance private production and consumption is met by the banking system. As we have noted, networks of capitalist banks produce money when they make loans, creating deposits which are drawn on, spent as money and, then, deposited back into the system by the recipients. Conventional banking practice specifies a 'fractional reserve' – usually around 10 per cent of deposits – that banks should keep in order that depositors can withdraw savings. Thus, for every £100 deposited (bank liabilities owed to depositors), a bank is able to advance loans (bank assets owed by borrowers) of £90. As the loan is spent, this monetized debt appears in other accounts elsewhere in the banking system. In turn, these allow the creation of further deposits against which these other banks may advance loans – in the first instance, a loan of £81 (£90 minus £9 fractional reserve = £81). Eventually, the initial £90 loan could produce £900 of new money in the form of loans.

In accordance with the conventions of double-entry bookkeeping, the totals of deposits (liabilities) and loans (assets) in the *entire system* cancel each other out. This gives the appearance of a one-to-one relationship between loans and deposits, as is suggested by common sense. However, accountancy conventions do not fully capture the dynamic money-creating role of capitalist banking, which consists in delaying payments and settlements in a way that makes possible the expansion of both sides of the balance sheet. The existence of outstanding debt constitutes the supply of money. The time frame for the repayment of loans is fixed by conventions and regulation and, of course, if these are not met the credit pyramid is threatened with collapse and the 'disappearance' of the newly created money. As we saw in part I, Minsky argued that the possibility of widespread contagious default was structurally endemic in the capitalist credit-money system and could induce debt-deflation. In order to prevent a serious unwinding of the credit system, central banks act as 'lenders of last resort' to the banking system.[11]

(ii)   If a state is viable and legitimate, and can tax effectively – that is, is an effective sovereign power – its promise to service its debts will be the fundamental basis for the creation of money, as outlined in the previous section. Being by far the single largest spender in modern society, a government's demand for money is the base for the money supply (this is often referred to as 'high-powered money' because of its ability to stimulate the money multiplier). In the same way as a private bank creates money by lending to a customer, the central bank creates a deposit for its customer – that is, the government – by accepting the state's promise to repay the debt. The government is then able to pay its suppliers with cheques drawn against its deposit account at the central bank. These will be first paid into the recipients' accounts held at their private bank which, in turn, presents them to the central bank for payment.

As the sovereign power a state can simply issue tokens in payment for the goods and services it buys from society, as outlined above, and, in turn, demand that these are used in payment of taxes. Tax receipts add credibility to the government's ability to finance its expenditure and repay debt, but central banks also typically accept the government's acknowledgements of debt (IOU) in the form of a government bond. Government debt in this form of a bond with a fixed rate of interest and term of maturity is also offered for sale, usually through the auspices of the central bank, to private 'rentiers' in the money market. As we shall see, taxation and bond sales are the means by which state expenditure and, therefore, the production of money is typically controlled in capitalist economies.

This institutional structure for the production of money is the result of an historical process that began with the mutually advantageous alliance in early modern Europe between the bourgeoisie and the monarchical state, as outlined above. However, this delicate balance of private and state interests could easily be disturbed. The state's creditors have to be satisfied, first, that state debt and the subsequent supply of money will not produce inflation and thereby erode the value of the fixed-interest investment in state bonds. Second, creditors have to be convinced that state revenue (taxation, customs duties, etc.) will be adequate for the service of interest payments. Consequently, governments attempt to establish their creditworthiness by conventions of 'sound finance' in order to secure the sale of their debt. These have varied over time. After the acceptance of Keynesian policy to stimulate demand and employment, the strict balance of expenditure and tax revenue in annual government budgets was largely abandoned. Balanced budgets were replaced during the twentieth century by norms of deficit financing that reflect a tacit consensus that the deficits and debts can be kept with conventionally acceptable limits. For example, member states of the European Union promised in the Maastricht Treaty (1997) to keep their budget deficits below 3 per cent of GDP (gross domestic product) and to maintain a debt-to-GDP ratio of no more than 60 per cent.

Capitalist states have to compete with each other on the international money markets and against other opportunities for investment such as corporate stocks and shares. However, a strong stable state – such as the USA or the UK – is *the* most secure form of investment available to the money market. The survival rate of such states is infinitely better than even the most powerful and enduring capitalist enterprises. On the other hand, weak states are ranked as riskier investments than the stocks and shares of many global corporations. Strong states are able to finance a far greater level of debt and, therefore, expenditure and in doing so they create money – as Keynes explained. It is significant that the two most successful states of the capitalist era – Britain and the USA – have also been the most indebted (Ferguson 2001: 133–41).

(iii)   In essence, states and their central banks must try to establish the 'working fiction of an invariant standard' (Mirowoski 1991: 579). That is to say, they must establish credible inflation credentials in order to sustain the creditworthiness that enables them to raise finance for spending by selling government bonds to the money markets (see Ingham 2004: 144–50, 152–8). In other words, the government must convince holders of this government debt that the value of their investments will not be eroded by inflation.

In the 1980s, as we have already noted, 'monetarist' theory contended that the *supply* of money to the economy was mainly determined 'exogenously' by the level of government debt and expenditure – the 'high-powered money' which found its way into the banking system. Consequently, it was believed that controlling government spending would control inflation. However, monetarism failed significantly to restrict the *supply* of money because this is also determined to a considerable extent from inside the economy ('endogenously') when banks extend loans to borrowers, creating deposits, as we saw in (i) above. Banks make the loans, creating deposits of money, and then look for loans from other banks and, ultimately, the central bank to maintain their reserves. In short, central banks cannot refuse to extend loans to the banking system for fear of the collapse of the payments system.

Consequently, since the failure of monetarism, governments now ask their central banks to control inflation by controlling the *demand* for money by its price – that is, by interest rates. First, central banks and monetary authorities now promise to maintain the purchasing power of money as an invariant standard by manipulating, through changes in interest rates, the willingness to borrow for private production and consumption. In other words, central banks make bank debt more expensive and, consequently, money more 'scarce' in relation to available goods.[12] Second, as outlined above, governments agree to limit their own *demand* for money by restricting expenditure, which is the major source of its supply, by adhering to conventional fiscal norms, implicitly negotiated and agreed with creditors in the money market for government debt.

The rate of interest that a government must pay for its long-term debt is determined, to a large degree, by demand for government bonds which expresses the money market's judgement on a government's credibility in maintaining the 'working fiction' of an invariant monetary standard – that is, low inflation. Adherence to what are considered to be the most prudent policies for managing state expenditure and, consequently, the injection of money into the economy is viewed favourably. With state expenditure – a major influence on inflation – under control, governments are able to sell their bonds at a low rate of interest and to finance their spending on favourable terms.

In the case of a creditworthy state, the interest rate on its bonds is the benchmark against which all other investment risks in the wider complex of the overall money market are calculated. Credit-rating agencies such as Moody's and Standard and Poor now play an important role in ranking the states and corporations across the globe according to acknowledged criteria (Sinclair 2005). The provision of what is deemed to be sound low-inflation money by states is a basic source of stability for the capitalist system. Without it, capitalist money markets would become anarchic and intolerably volatile, as financiers and money-capitalists scrambled to find secure assets in an uncertain world. Notwithstanding their sophisticated mathematical financial tools, the money markets hang on every carefully chosen word uttered by the finance ministers and central bankers of the major economies. Stability, steadiness and prudence according to accepted principles are their watchwords. If governments deviate from the tacitly agreed consensus on best practice, the money markets are swift in their judgement and punishment. Increased uncertainty triggers the selling of government bonds, and even in the twenty-first century investors still turn to gold from time to time. Money-capital can only be lured back with higher interest rates that, in turn, might have a deflationary effect on production and employment and, consequently, a government's political fate. Consequently, in attracting loans to finance their expenditure, today's democracies are constrained by the demands of money markets to maintain a low inflation regime and an acceptable *real* rate of interest (nominal rate minus inflation rate). On the other hand, expectations for public services, education and health care place demands on government expenditure which taxation cannot finance without incurring electoral disaffection.

(iv)   The struggle between debtor (producers and consumers of goods) and creditor (producers and controllers of money) classes in capitalism centres on the 'real' rate of interest. The ideal situation is one in which there is a positive real interest rate that is high enough to motivate money-capitalists to lend, but not so high as to deter borrowing to invest in production and to consume. The fundamental threat posed by inflation is that even relatively short periods of very high negative real rates of interest threaten capitalism's dynamic engine – the creation of credit-money in the money market. Inflation might accelerate to a point where it becomes impossible to maintain an acceptable positive real rate of interest by raising the nominal rate without causing widespread defaults. As debtors find themselves unable to service their loans out of current income they may press for higher wages, which merely accelerates the inflationary spiral. In short, if the creation of credit-money becomes unprofitable, capitalism can be in danger of grinding to a halt. Inflation and deflation are ever present threats to capitalism due to the interplay between its two relatively autonomous sectors – money and production.

Monetary disorder in capitalism

The two basic monetary disorders in capitalism – inflation and deflation – are not simply 'economic' phenomena. They can also have political causes and consequences, and both are very closely tied to the strength and viability of the state. On the one hand, both inflation and deflation can develop within the economy to a point where they perturb the existing social and political order and threaten the state's legitimacy and stability – for example, in Britain during the mid-1970s. On the other hand, causation often runs in the opposite direction. Severe political crises undermine confidence in the state and, consequently, its currency. Rapid inflation follows as people try to transform their money into valuable commodities and spend in anticipation of further price rises. As we have noted, it is striking that the monetary difficulties – including bouts of inflation – experienced by Russia and some other transition economies are in large part a consequence of the inability of the state to forge a stable and trusted monetary system (on Russia see Woodruff 1999). In short, stable money is an essential prerequisite for successful capitalist development, and this can only be produced by strong stable states.

Despite the fundamental importance of these interrelations between the economic and political spheres in capitalist societies, here I wish to focus most attention on the way in which inflation and deflation can be seen as an ever present possibility that accompanies what Minsky saw as the 'normal functioning' of the capitalist economy (see pp. 41–2). As the proponents of 'sound money' have always insisted, the disorders of rapid inflation and severe deflation are very often consequences of the relative ease with which money can be produced in capitalism. Although not unknown, inflation was infrequent and less severe in pre-capitalist economies, due to the much lower levels of monetized market exchange and the absence of money-producing banking systems.

Inflation

There is considerable disagreement amongst economists on the effects of inflation and on the level at which it begins seriously to disturb economic relations and activity. Indeed, moderate and steady increases in prices are taken to be a sign of a growing healthy economy. Many argue that deflation is the more serious condition. A price index that fails to increase a little each year is taken as a signal of the onset of stagnation, and this can create self-fulfilling expectations of a recession. Rather, it is rapidly increasing annual changes of, say, over 10 per cent that begin to perturb economic activity. Large and potentially rising increases in prices make rational capital accounting difficult, creating an atmosphere of uncertainty that inhibits capitalist enterprise.

However, high levels of inflation pose a far more serious threat to capitalism than difficulties with accountancy. Inflation can have a redistributive impact to the advantage of debtors and the disadvantage of creditors. On the one hand, the real value of debtors' liabilities can be eroded by inflation. For example, inflation increases the market price of houses, but interest is payable only on the original nominal value of the mortgage loan. On the other hand, however, a serious problem can arise if inflation continues to a point where it is no longer possible for nominal interest rates to be increased to maintain them at a positive real level (real interest rate = nominal interest rate minus inflation) without causing widespread defaults. In short, there is the danger that either the fundamental capitalist process of credit-money creation to finance production and consumption will cease to yield an acceptable level of profits, or that increased rates of interest will trigger the process of debt-deflation.

Stable prices express a stable, but not necessarily equal, balance of power in which the economic interests that comprise supply and demand in both production and consumption have reached acceptable positions in the market (Weber 1978: 107–8). This balance may be perturbed from the outside by what economists refer to as 'supply shocks', usually in raw materials and sources of energy, that send a chain reaction of price increases throughout the economy – for example, the oil price rises imposed by the Organization of the Petroleum Exporting Countries (OPEC) in the early 1970s, and today's threat of rising global food prices. But it should be noted that such 'shocks' are produced not merely by a natural scarcity but by the control of supply and the power to raise prices. In the 1970s, the highest levels of inflation occurred in those countries where strong trade unions were able to increase the price of labour.

Inflation might also be triggered by what could be seen as the 'demand shock' of large increases of state expenditure, especially in wartime. Such sudden increases in demand financed by government debt may create a similar chain reaction as the various economic interests struggle to maximize their advantage. Furthermore, production for war pushes the economy to the limits of its capacity and creates shortages that can be exploited by monopoly producers and suppliers.

However, the most spectacular cases of rapid hyperinflation usually follow a serious crisis of the state. As we have noted, a loss of legitimacy may trigger a loss of confidence in the sovereign currency as a store of value which, in vain attempts to avoid further loss of wealth, is spent as quickly as possible, thus intensifying the inflationary process. Inflation may reach a rate of over 1,000 per cent per annum before a new political regime comes to power and abandons the old monetary unit of account in an attempt to create a new monetary system. This is essentially a problem of political reconstruction and a new settlement between the classes and economic groups, as all old debts and contracts between individuals and between individuals and the state are wiped clean before renegotiation. Germany in the 1920s, Russia in 1991 and Latin American countries frequently during the second half of the twentieth century experienced this kind of inflation (Orléan 2006; Woodruff 1999; Maier 1978).

Crises of the state aside, high levels of inflation generated by the struggle between economic interests have been surprisingly infrequent in capitalist economies. Even the rapid industrial expansion of the nineteenth century was accompanied by price stability in the leading economies (see Fischer 1996: 156–78). However, as the twentieth century progressed there occurred a fundamental shift in the balance of power between the major groups and classes in the advanced capitalist states which eventually led to levels of inflation that were deemed to be problematic. There were no proletarian revolutions, but conflict between capital and labour was a driving force in the extension of representative democracy and the forging of social democratic settlements entailing a commitment to securing full employment and social welfare (see the discussion in chapter 8). Full employment empowered labour to demand ever increasing wage rises. These were readily granted by large-scale monopoly producers who were able to absorb the increased costs by passing them on in higher prices and by borrowing more working capital from the banks, exacerbating the wage–price spiral.

Although it was not the only factor, welfare and social security provision contributed to the growth of government expenditure and debt which provided a basis for credit-money creation in the banking system and, consequently, a potential for inflation. It is, perhaps, difficult today to appreciate the impact of fascism's and communism's apparent ability to eliminate mass unemployment and economic depression in the early twentieth century. The inter-war period saw the first systemic failure of capitalism on a global scale and with it a wavering of faith in economic liberalism. Finance and money markets were demonized and the free market was viewed with suspicion. It was in attempting to devise a liberal solution to the problem that Keynes and others realized that the recently discovered 'money multiplier' could stimulate an 'employment multiplier'. Keynes, Myrdal, Kalecki and others began to develop the economics of social democracy and instigate the corrective action that Polanyi saw as part of the 'double movement' in capitalism (see pp. 113–14).

However, until the outbreak of the Second World War, the orthodox economic policies of 'sound money' and balanced budgets prevailed, and the expansionary measures proposed by Keynes and others were resisted. By 1945 the situation had changed. First, banking and finance capital, whose interest lay in maintaining the value of money above all else, had been temporarily subordinated during the war to the needs of ensuring that the productive economy operated at full capacity. Moreover, global banking networks cannot operate during a global war and the control of capital flows was ceded to the states. Second, the war had altered the balance of power in society as the elites sought full cooperation from the masses in the war effort with promises not to return to the discipline of market forces and austerity of the inter-war years. Managed money, full employment and social welfare were introduced in various forms across the capitalist world.

By 1945 it was widely believed that the inter-war world depression was, to some significant degree, due to the collapse of the gold standard and the absence of a viable means of international exchange and payment. Thus at the negotiations at Bretton Woods in the USA priority was given to the construction of an international monetary system that would enable world economic growth based on international specialization and free trade (Helleiner 1994; Gilpin 2001: ch. 9). However, Keynes was fully aware that unregulated global money and capital markets could endanger the domestic commitments to full employment. Any political pledge to maintain full employment could not be credibly made unless governments had some control of their domestic interest rates. Private owners and controllers of money-capital could not be allowed freely to move it from one state to another in search of higher interest rates or in fear of what was believed would be the inflationary consequences of high levels of government spending by left-wing and social democratic governments. As Keynes explained,

> [T]here will continually be a number of people constantly taking fright because they think that the degree of leftism in one country looks for the time being to be greater than somewhere else ... [T]he whole management of the domestic economy depends upon being free to have the appropriate rate of interest without reference to rates prevailing elsewhere in the world. Capital control is a corollary of this. (Keynes 1980: 149)[13]

In other words, from the perspective of orthodox economic theory, the plan for the reconstruction of the capitalist world order after 1945 was contradictory, in that it sought to establish free markets in everything except money and capital. Controls were placed on speculation on foreign-exchange markets; foreign currency could only be acquired for legitimate import and export trade. In this way, it was hoped to avoid fluctuations in exchange rates that might have an impact on the level of employment through changes in the relative prices of imports and exports and/or changes in interest rates. It was the result of a change in the balance of power between money-capital, productive capital and labour, in which the first temporarily lost its position as the 'headquarters' of capitalism. Governments sought to maintain full employment and encouraged the formation of large monopolistic corporations where workers and management were able bid up their wages and salaries. In the increasingly prosperous quarter of a century after 1945, these three classes – money-capital, productive capital and labour – coexisted in a fragile compromise. Labour and productive capital expanded their shares of national income in relation to money-capital and banking, which did, however, have the consolation of positive, if low, real rates of interest (Smithin 1996: 5).

However, with the gradual post-war return to normal peacetime capitalism, two shifts occurred in this balance of power. On the one hand, all three groups gained power vis-à-vis the state. The commitment to full employment meant that large monopoly producers in key industries could not be allowed to fail for fear of both political and economic consequences. The corporations and their labour forces, empowered by the absence of the 'reserve army of the unemployed', used their leverage continuously to mark up prices and wages, which eventually set in train an inflationary spiral (Phelps Brown 1975; Hirsch and Goldthorpe 1978). On the other hand, as capitalist activity restarted after the war, banking and money-capital gradually resumed its dominance. This was particularly evident internationally, as private bankers began to evade the capital exchange controls of the Bretton Woods system. The City of London became a centre for organizing so-called 'eurodollar' markets using the foreign-held dollar surpluses that the US balance-of-payments deficits had created (Helleiner 1994; Ingham 1994; Germain 1997; Burn 2006).

In the early 1970s, inflation began to accelerate rapidly in the Western democracies. Large increases in commodity prices, especially oil, added impetus to the underlying structural causes of increased government expenditure and the power of monopoly capital and their labour forces to mark up their respective prices (Fischer 1996: 200–5). By mid-decade, inflation was at 15 per cent in the USA and over 25 per cent in Britain. The time had arrived when it was no longer possible, without causing widespread defaults and bankruptcies, to raise nominal interest rates high enough to compensate for the depreciation of money and produce a positive real rate of interest for creditor and financier interests. This crisis point marked an intensification of the political struggle to rebalance the market positions of the classes and interest groups – in the 'revenge of the rentier' (Smithin 1996).

Fundamentally, the demands and expectations of the postwar era were to be reined in a return to liberal economics – by 'Reaganomics' in the USA and 'Thatcherism' in the UK. Inflation was to be curbed by a return to 'sound money' principles in the guise of 'monetarism' and by measures to weaken the power of organized labour. The USA's New Deal legislation of the 1930s, which had introduced interest rate limits to encourage borrowing to finance production and consumption, was repealed. The action of President Reagan in breaking the 1981 air traffic controllers' strike sent a clear message to the labour movement, but this show of strength was surpassed in the UK by Thatcher's long struggle with and eventual defeat of the coalminers in 1984–5. The Thatcher government's confrontation with the miners, steelworkers, newspaper printers and others was supported by legislation designed to weaken the labour unions.

Redistribution in favour of creditor-financier interest slowly began to occur. By the 1990s, the US economy had rising real interest rates and falling real wages and profits in the productive sector (Henwood 1997; Lévy and Duménil 2004). Even when inflation had fallen and economic growth had resumed, high real rates of interest persisted, signifying the new balance of economic forces. Within the corporation, financial and creditor interests regained their dominance after a period of subordination to the tacit alliance between workers and corporation managers (see also the discussion in chapter 6). In the USA, for example, the financier/rentier share of corporate surplus rose from between 20 and 30 per cent in the 1950s to between 60 and 70 per cent in the late 1980s (Henwood 1997: ch. 2). Higher returns to shareholders were often achieved by reducing wage costs by 'downsizing' the workforce and 'de-layering' management.

With one or two short-lived exceptions, inflation diminished after the 1980s throughout the advanced capitalist world, and the competitive pressures unleashed by an expansion of global product and labour markets have maintained the relative stabilization of prices.[14] Many governments attribute this to improved monetary policy, including the formation of self-fulfilling expectations of low inflation through the announcement of inflation targets and the publication of the deliberations of newly independent central bank expert committees on the most appropriate rate of interest to achieve them (see Ingham 2004). To be sure, maintaining confidence that monetary policy can control inflation, and dampening demand with immediate incremental increases in the rate of interest, may have some effect in maintaining the 'working fiction of a monetary invariant' (Mirowski 1991: 579) However, in the absence of inflationary shocks and/or the unlikely shift back to labour in the balance of market power, the claims for the efficacy of monetary policy have yet to be rigorously tested.

None the less, it is true to say that measures to control inflation, whatever they may be, are invariably more successful than those aimed at reversing deflation. As we shall see, it would appear to be easier to prevent people from creating money by borrowing for production and consumption than it is to induce them to do so.

Deflation

Deflation is the arguably the greater danger to the capitalist economy because it is even less amenable to a purely monetary solution. Despite the difficulties, it is easier effectively to deflate an economy – through large reductions in government spending and very high interest rates – than it is to stimulate it out of a depression. For example, Japan's central bank base rate of interest has been close to zero per cent since the early 1990s, and its governments have pumped money into public works. Money has been cheap and in ready supply, but prices have continued to fall. Injecting money into an economy to encourage private investment and consumption has been likened to 'pushing on string'.

The capitalist system's inherent potential for debt-induced deflation following a speculative boom first became apparent in the aftermath of the Wall Street Crash in the USA, where interest rates were raised in the mistaken belief that this would increase savings and preserve the value of money. As

Keynes and others were soon to realize, it would be better to make money more freely and cheaply available in order to stimulate production and consumption. However, if economic expectations – Keynes's 'animal spirits' – remain dampened, the mere availability of cheap credit-money is not enough. State spending and investment might be more effective, but, as Japan's long period of stagnation shows, it is not a fool-proof remedy.

Towards the end of the 1980s it became increasingly difficult for the Japanese economy to absorb and utilize the wealth generated by its success in any further expansion of domestic production. Profits and the international trading surplus poured into investment in land, commercial and residential property, and stocks and shares, causing rapid price inflation in these assets. In turn, the rising prices encouraged a surge of demand for bank loans to finance further speculation that these asset prices and, therefore, profits would continue to rise. Between 1985 and 1989 the Nikkei stock-market index rose from 13,000 to 38,915, property prices increased by an annual average of 22 per cent, and it was estimated that the property value of metropolitan Tokyo exceeded that of the whole USA (Van Rixtel 2002: 171). During the period, Japan's domestic bank lending was far greater than anywhere else in the world – doubling to 300 per cent of GDP (Warburton 2000: 11). The close institutionalized informal links (*amakudari*) between the private sector and the monetary authorities in Japan had supported a forbearance that allowed the bank-financed expansion of the speculative bubble to continue way beyond the early warning signs (Van Rixtel 2002: 177).

When, in 1989, the indulgent monetary authorities acted to curb the speculative boom by raising interest rates, it was too late and their actions triggered a crisis. Speculative financial assets had to be sold to meet the increased interest payments, causing an accelerating downward spiral of asset prices. The Nikkei index fell from its peak of 39,000 in 1989 to 14,000 by 1992, and land and real-estate prices halved during the same period (Van Rixtel 2002: 174). The effects of the crash of the financial assets and property markets soon spread to the rest of the economy. Investment and consumption were cut to service the 'debt overhang'. Stagnation resulted. The deflationary shock has persisted since the 1990s, and after many false hopes Japanese consumers and investors have still not responded as positively as expected to almost two decades of near-zero interest rates.

There is considerable disagreement about the reasons for the unusually long period of falling prices and stagnation of demand in Japan, but the particular social structure of its economy and society offers some clues. Fundamentally, capitalist economies move out of stagnation and depression when entrepreneurs and consumers are willing to take on new debt to finance production and consumption. As long as the 'debt overhang' persists this is inhibited. Debtors must use income and profits to service their debts rather than investing and spending on consumption. Moreover, until debts are settled they remain a 'credit risk' and cannot easily acquire new loans. The impasse in the economy at large can be broken if debts are written off. Resulting bankruptcies remove failed firms from the economy, and the removal of the non-performing loans from the banks' balance sheets enables them to advance new loans. Economic power in Japan is located in the highly concentrated monopoly sector of six or so conglomerate company groupings – the *keiretsu*.[15] The member companies are linked through cross-holdings of shares and by their indebtedness to the 'main bank' of each particular *keiretsu*. Writing off debts would increase bankruptcies if banks foreclosed on companies with bad debts, which would have the effect of weakening a particular *keiretsu* vis-à-vis the others. A stalemate ensued; despite the occasional collapse of a bank or company the level of bad debts ('non-performing' loans) remained high enough to constitute an important factor in prolonging the disability of the Japanese economy.

Monetary policy in modern capitalist economies uses changes in interest rates either to inhibit or to encourage borrowing to finance economic activity – production, consumption and speculation – with the aim of avoiding inflation and deflation. In order to avoid large abrupt changes that might trigger either an inflationary surge or a deflationary contraction if debts become too difficult to service, central banks attempt to anticipate the level of economic activity and to make small pre-emptive changes. With the exception of Japan, serious inflation and deflation have been absent from the major advanced economies since the early 1980s. But, as we have noted, it is not entirely clear whether this state of affairs has been due primarily to the conduct of monetary policy or rather to the effects of economic globalization. The expansion of production of competitively priced exports by low-wage economies such as India and China has tempered both global deflationary and inflationary tendencies in the advanced economies. However, by 2008 there were signs that both inflation and deflation might become widespread in a reoccurrence of the 'stagflation' that was experienced in the 1970s. Economic growth in China and India has greatly increased global demand and has led to rapidly rising prices for raw materials, food and energy. Furthermore, inflation is being stoked by shortages in the supply of skilled labour in these countries, which has led to rising wages and consequently the prices of goods exported to the advanced economies. In addition, by 2008 fears were growing that the contraction of credit – that is, the 'crunch' or 'squeeze' – on the international money markets, triggered by defaults on US subprime mortgages, might set in train a debt-deflation global recession (see pp. 168–9).

Conclusion

Money provides two indispensable foundations for capitalism. First, without a trusted standard of value economic calculation becomes increasingly difficult and causes capitalism to falter. Second, capitalism is virtually synonymous with the existence of money-capital in the form of bank debt which finances production, consumption and speculation. There are two relatively autonomous parts to a capitalist economy – the monetary and the material – which are entwined in a delicate interdependency. Technological innovation can be dynamic only if the risk is taken to finance it into an unknowable future. It is this risky temporal projection, based on the premise that debts will be repaid, that endows capitalism with its inextricably linked dynamism and fragility.

5
Market exchange

The exchange and distribution of goods and services in terms
of money prices, determined by competitive bargaining
between buyers and sellers, has existed for many millennia,
but until the advent of capitalism such market exchange
played only a marginal role in the coordination of economic
activity. Rather, subsistence needs and other wants were produced and distributed, as we have noted, either in accordance
with traditional customary norms and/or directed by the
ruling elites in early 'command' economies such as ancient
Egypt and Babylon (Polanyi 1944: 1971). But, as Adam
Smith explained, with labour's increasing specialization of
economic function in large-scale economic systems, self-
sufficiency is impossible and, consequently, the market mechanism assumes a greater role in coordinating production,
exchange and distribution. However, it is important not to
overlook the fact that norms of reciprocity, the power of
command and administered redistribution continue to play a
significant role in capitalist societies. The circulation and
exchange of goods and services between family members in
domestic households, for example, is not typically governed
by the price mechanism; and redistributive transfers by state
welfare systems account for over 20 per cent of GDP in many
capitalist societies. Moreover, even within what is generally
understood as the capitalist economy, most economic
exchanges between divided labour in the production process
are, in fact, determined by command in bureaucratically

organized enterprises (see chapter 6). These significant qualifications aside, modern capitalism is, nevertheless, the first
economic system in history in which market exchange is the
basic means of coordination. The main markets which comprise the capitalist economy
were listed in chapter 3:

a. money and money-capital markets
b. labour market
c. producer markets for:
   (i)   production goods (means of production)
   (ii) consumption goods
d. financial asset markets

Money, capital and financial markets are the subjects of
chapters 4 and 7. Producer and labour markets are not dealt
with separately, but will be considered in the following explo-
ration of the divergent conceptions of the general nature of
the market.

The fall of the alternative state-socialist planned economies
and the absence of the kind of severe and protracted economic stagnation that occurred in the 1930s have reinforced
the view that the competitive market brings about an efficient
and, ultimately, harmonious integration of the specialized
sectors of the economy. Indeed, many recently influential
works tend to identify capitalism exclusively as the 'free'
market system – for example, Fukuyama, *The End of History*
(1992); Rajan and Zingales, *Saving Capitalism from the
Capitalists* (2003); Lal, *Reviving the Invisible Hand: The
Case for Classic Economic Liberalism* (2006); and Wolf, *Why
Globalization Works* (2005).

On the other hand, the tradition drawn from classical
sociology and heterodox economics offers a different understanding of markets in the capitalist economy. First, the
market is only a part of the capitalist system, which, as we
have seen, also contains non-market elements based on relations of power and authority – most notably the enterprise.
Second, the market is seen as the site of conflict and struggle
between inherently unequal economic classes and interests.
Here, prices do not merely express an efficient balance of
supply and demand that is determined spontaneously by

myriad unrelated individuals aiming to maximize their utilities. Rather, prices represent the outcome of a struggle for economic power between distinct group interests constituted by their position in the capitalist system. Furthermore, this tradition maintains that the great and ever increasing concentrations of economic power significantly limit, but do not entirely eliminate, competition. It is in the very nature of competitive markets to produce winners and losers, and the former are able progressively to monopolize their advantageous position and to manipulate the market. The domination of the upper levels of both the productive and financial sectors of the advanced economies by powerful monopolies and oligopolies is seen as a normal state of affairs which requires the constant intervention of the state to maintain an acceptable level of competition. Third, it is held that the market inevitably and continuously produces unintended contradictory effects that undermine economic, social and political stability – periodic unemployment, financial crises, resource depletion and so on.

The competitive market

It is a universally held tenet in today's hegemonic economic 'neo-liberalism' that an economy will operate more effectively as a generator and distributor of wealth and material welfare the more closely it approximates the textbook model of the perfectly competitive market. These theories are 'performative' – that is to say, they are used as blueprints to construct and shape the economy (Callon 1998; MacKenzie 2006).[1] The introduction of 'shock therapy' rapidly to create capitalism in post-communist states during the 1990s was based upon a belief in the superior efficiency of the market – and, it should be noted, the belief that capitalism was synonymous with the market. Similarly, privatization and deregulation policies in Western economies since the 1980s and pro-globalization arguments for free trade also assume that there is a direct linear relationship between what might be called 'marketness' and economic growth. It is, therefore, necessary to examine these influential theories.

As we have seen, Adam Smith held that the free interplay of supply and demand eventually produces a price which 'clears' the market for a good, that is to say, the price at which there is no supply of unsold goods and no unsatisfied demand. At this point, the impersonal market mechanism, produced as the unintended beneficial outcome of individual strategies to maximize self-interest, ensures that all resources are fully employed and that all agents are rewarded in accordance with their functional contribution to the economic process. In other words, the market is efficient and fair, and, by its demonstration of the manifest collective material benefits of economic interdependence, has the potential able to harmonize divergent interests in society.

This optimum outcome is based on a highly abstract model of the market economy, comprising myriad utility-maximizing agents, each making rational individual decisions on the basis of perfect information. The large number of players ensures that no participant can influence prices to their advantage at the expense of others. Market power is equally distributed; or, one might more accurately say, power is absent from the perfectly competitive market. All participants are 'price-takers' and there are no 'price-makers'. The model is widely criticized for the unrealistic nature of these assumptions and the fact that they do not adequately capture the operation of actually existing capitalism. However, it is also important to understand that the internal, or logical, coherence of the model is also open to question.

In the first place, and somewhat paradoxically, there is actually no competition in the perfect competition model. If all agents were to have equal resources and perfect information about the quality of goods and their competitors' strategies, then the result would be stasis – similar to a stalemate between chess grandmasters or equally matched soccer teams which were also able perfectly to anticipate each other's moves. We shall return to the question of how capitalist competition is actually structured, but here we might note that genuine competition can only exist in relation to differences – that is, *inequalities* – that are turned to advantage by some participants and challenged by others. That is to say, dynamism is the result of a struggle between unequal players. The perfect competition model merely describes the hypothetical end state of 'perfection' *after* the interplay of supply and demand, when the competing forces have reached an equilibrium price that has cleared the market. But beyond the assumptions of perfect information and myriad participants, the model does not explain how the forces of supply and demand come into existence and how they actually interact to produce the price.[2]

Few would argue that the real world could be made closely to resemble the perfect competition model. None the less, it is taken for granted that there is a direct linear relationship between efficiency and the degree to which the model is approximated in reality – that is, 'marketness'. For example, global perfect competition might be impossible to achieve, but it is almost universally accepted that *any* reduction of barriers to free trade, however small they might be, will increase efficiency and global welfare. Aside from the empirical objection that globalization and freer trade appear to be associated with increasing inequality, there are no logical grounds to support this deduction. As we have noted, the perfect competition model describes what the end state of perfect efficiency and welfare maximization would look like. But, without the assumptions of perfect information and myriad players who are individually unable to influence the outcome, it is not possible to demonstrate that any incremental step on the road to 'perfection' will bring precisely commensurate benefits (Etzioni 1988: 200–2). Short of 'perfection' in which all participating economies start from positions of equality, imbalances of trade and inequalities between rich and poor are just as likely, from a theoretical standpoint, to be exacerbated as they to be corrected by the reduction of barriers to free trade. The perfect competition model only yields the welfare-maximizing outcome if all the model's conditions are met in full – perfect information, foresight and so on.

A quite different, and more persuasive, argument for the efficacy of the market, based on the contrary and more realistic assumption of the inevitability of *imperfect* information, is offered by Austrian economic theory, developed in the late nineteenth and early twentieth centuries. In what became known as the 'socialist calculation debate', von Mises and his student von Hayek contended that free markets are more efficient than socialism could ever be because we could never have all the necessary information to plan production and consumption and balance supply and demand (for an accessible discussion see Bottomore 1990: ch. 4). As the scale and complexity of economic life increases, this cognitive problem becomes more acute, and coordination can only be made manageable by reflexive and adaptive adjustments that result from continuous bargaining in the market. In this theory there is no presumption that bargaining between buyers and sellers will eventually produce an equilibrium price that clears the market. Rather, it is argued that the 'spontaneous' interaction between free economic agents produces the best possible solution to the coordination of economic life in an irremediably imperfect world. Furthermore, the flexibility of decentralized market competition encourages innovation, leading to economic dynamism.[3]

Both advocacies of the market do, however, concede that there are certain circumstances that produce 'market failure'. First, there are exceptional 'public goods', as Adam Smith observed, for which the free interplay of supply and demand fails to produce the price that signifies an equilibrium between supply and demand. In modern economics' version of this theory, a 'public good' is a good that is 'non-rival' and/or 'non-excludable'. On the one hand, a good is 'non-rival' if consumption by one individual does not reduce the amount available for others; and, on the other, it is 'non-excludable' if it is difficult to exclude others from consuming it. For example, street-lighting is both 'non-rival' and 'non-excludable'. In order that bargaining produces a market-clearing price, there must be secure and enforceable property rights that create the necessary 'scarcity' of supply.[4]

Second, private market exchanges can have costly consequences, unintended by the transacting parties, which are not fully accounted for in the price paid by the buyer in the exchange. In the terms of economic theory, such 'social costs' are known as 'externalities' – that is to say, they are 'external' to private transactions. For example, the social costs of pollution and 'greenhouse' gases produced by air travel are not accounted for in the ticket price.

Third, the free interplay of supply and demand can produce perverse outcomes. Many examples are found in insurance markets. Here the supply of insurance brings forth 'adverse selection' – that is to say, demand from high-risk purchasers that makes it impossible for insurers to charge a single price for a uniform good to clear the market. For example, premiums high enough for the profitable provision of insurance to the old and unhealthy would deter the healthy low-risk individuals which the insurance companies want to attract. Consequently, different prices are determined for different categories of insured by the calculation of actuarial risk – for example, smokers pay higher premiums. The market for bank credit is, perhaps, the most significant instance in capitalism of this kind of 'market failure' through 'adverse selection'. A single rate of interest on loans that is low enough to stimulate maximum demand will attract both high- and low-risk borrowers. However, raising the rate to compensate for defaults by the high-risk individuals also deters the low-risk borrowers which the banks wish to attract. Consequently, the supply of credit is 'rationed' by the use of differential interest rates (prices) determined by the calculation of risk of default (on the economic theory of 'credit-rationing', see Stiglitz and Weiss 1981). In this process banks and credit-rating agencies, such as Moody's and Standard and Poor's, wield great power; it is their decisions on creditworthiness that determine the allocation of the money-capital that fuels the economy (see Sinclair 2005).

However, supporters of the market do not consider these 'market failures' to be insurmountable problems. Unlike Marx's 'contradictions' they are, in principle, remediable. 'Public goods' can be made private and thereby 'scarce'. For example, the consumption of street lighting could be measured by scanning bar-coded microchips which, if not implanted in individuals at birth, could be embedded in identity cards and car registration plates. Negative 'externalities' are also considered to be manageable. Currently attempts are being made to cut the costs of atmospheric pollution which are not borne by the price of fuel, for example by using the market mechanism of 'emissions trading'.[5]

The inability of the inherently 'imperfect' world to meet the strict conditions of the perfect competition model is an obvious source of the market's failure to 'self-regulate' – that is, to bring about equilibrium between supply and demand.

Two 'imperfections' have received considerable attention from economists: the monopolistic control of supply and 'asymmetric' information – that is, where one party's superior information can be used to exploit the other in a transaction.[6] Monopoly control over the supply of goods and resources, which can be used to exploit both consumers and other producers, is, in principle, controllable by determined government regulation. But nowhere has state intervention successfully eliminated monopoly and oligopoly in the mature capitalist economies. This is part of the struggle for power in capitalism and not merely a technical economic question. Populist democracy in the USA in the early twentieth century led to strenuous efforts to rein in capitalist power, but it had a negligible effect on the large US corporations that came to dominate the capitalist world. As we shall see, the competitive market plays a more limited role than is generally thought to be the case, and highly concentrated economic power is a permanent and normal state of affairs in capitalism.

The existence of the market imperfection of 'asymmetric' information has recently been used to try to explain the failure of wages to fall during periods when the supply of labour willing to accept lower rates is increased by unemployment. In this case, it is argued that employers are reluctant to take advantage of labour market conditions to hire new workers at lower wages because of the difficulty of establishing their quality with any reasonable degree of certainty. Better to retain the 'devils they know', despite their higher wages. However, in his earlier departure from orthodox economic analysis, Keynes did not see this 'wage stickiness' as a mere 'imperfection' that was, in principle, remediable with better information. Rather, as we saw in chapter 2, he argued that persistent unemployment was the result of a structural impasse from which the participants themselves were unable to escape – however 'perfect' their information. This scepticism about the labour market's capacity for self-regulation has more in common with the Marxist idea of contradiction and will be considered shortly. Here I wish to pursue the question of the common misidentification, in neo-liberal economic thought, of capitalism exclusively with the competitive market.

Large-scale impersonal markets, where the invisible hand is an apt metaphor, are typical of modern capitalism, especially as it extends its global reach. For almost two centuries successive waves of mass production by myriad enterprises in highly competitive markets have led to lower real prices for an ever increasing range of consumption goods, for example, from the large-scale production of household cutlery in Sheffield, England, in the mid-nineteenth century to the t-shirts and jeans in the discount store today and the falling price of personal computers. However, capitalism has another level – arguably its most characteristic – where great concentrations of monopoly economic power bear little resemblance, in any meaningful sense, to the competitive market model. Indeed, as the great French historian Fernand Braudel observed, the market sector 'where a degree of automatic communication usually links supply, demand and price' is not to be confused with capitalism. Rather, 'the real home of capitalism' is in the 'zone of the anti-market, where the great predators roam and the law of the jungle operates' (Braudel 1984: 229–30). The following discussion focuses on the monopoly power that is found at the upper levels of the productive sectors of typical advanced capitalist economies. (The arguably greater 'predatory' monopoly capitalist power of the even more highly concentrated financial sector is examined in chapter 7.)

Monopolistic competition and mass consumption

With the appearance of the large corporation in the twentieth century, the level of concentration in many industries increased dramatically in many economies. In the USA, by 1935, the average four-firm concentration ratio was over 40 per cent – that is to say, on average four firms accounted for 40 per cent of production or sales in manufacturing and retail. In some industries the level was much higher – over 80 per cent in tobacco products, breakfast cereals, automobiles and so on (see Chandler 1962; 1990). Such concentration enables collaboration between firms to avoid what they see as destabilizing and counterproductive 'cut-throat' competition, and also to make higher profits. Eventually, explicit price fixing by cartels to exploit consumers was outlawed. But this has had no effect on the levels of concentration, and the large corporations have been able to devise strategies that limit competition without recourse to illegal collusion. In these highly concentrated industries the coordination of supply and demand typically takes the form of 'monopolistic competition' on the supply side and mass consumption on the demand side. 'Monopolistic competition' describes the way in which large, modern corporations use their market power to transform a basic good into a 'branded' product that is differentiated by advertising and marketing from others within a given sector (Chamberlain 1933). In this way corporations seek to reduce the level of competition and to control the profitable opportunities that follow from their relentless stimulation of new wants for the mass of the population.[7] In the modern world, mass production and mass consumption, together with consumption by states, comprise capitalism's main dynamic driving force.

With the exception of existence on the edge of mere subsistence, consumption beyond needs that are largely shaped by biological necessity is present to some degree in all societies. Surplus production can be appropriated and used by dominant groups for the monopolization of the means of coercion and to express their power through the consumption of symbolic goods. In pre-capitalist society, luxury products and weapons were restricted to the ruling classes, whilst the masses toiled to provide for their own basic physical needs for food, clothing and shelter.

However, modern capitalist production is based on the expansion of private consumption for the satisfaction of ever expanding culturally defined wants that have become increasingly divorced from basic needs. Indeed, if all strata in society during the eighteenth century had behaved like the ascetic entrepreneurs depicted in Weber's *Protestant Ethic and Spirit of Capitalism*, demand would not have expanded and the emergence of capitalism might well have been retarded. However, cultural changes during this period acted as a stimulus to new kinds of consumption. Whilst some of the bourgeoisie saved their profits for reinvestment in enterprise, others took the first steps towards modern consumerism. Campbell's *Romantic Ethic and Spirit of Consumerism* argues that the rise of the novel and romantic love, for example, were expressions of a new form of pleasure-seeking in the upper classes in which individuals imaginatively constructed objects of desire by the 'widespread adoption of the habit of covert daydreaming' (Campbell 1987: 88–9).

With the expansion of wage labour and rapid urbanization, this kind of consumption was very gradually spread across society by the creation and manipulation of demand by producers and retailers. Consumption has become a 'mentalistic' process in which individuals are invited to identify with the scenarios in which products are placed by the media and advertising industry (Baudrillard 1988). By the mid-nineteenth century American department stores had introduced advertising and marketing to encourage the purchase of their suppliers' goods (Leach 1993). The USA's egalitarian culture, as we have noted, facilitated consumption by the 'masses' of standardized goods. Henry Ford could quip that his assembly-line-produced Model T was available in any colour as long as it was black, but in Britain the mass production of motor cars was, to some extent, held back by the belief that they would remain luxuries for the upper classes.

As the twentieth century advanced, mass consumer markets became more differentiated in terms of quality and symbolic prestige in order to stimulate demand further. Even basic products are made increasingly heterogeneous by being differentiated into a range that is ordered by degrees of symbolically attributed luxury that departs from the standard model. Again, this is most obvious in the automobile industry. Hand-built Ferraris continue to be produced for the wealthy, but there also exists, for example, a complex range of Fords in which the driver of the 'luxury' version Mondeo model can claim some superiority within the reference group of middle-income car owners. Thus the process of status competition, referred to by Veblen in the late nineteenth century as 'conspicuous consumption', has become transformed into a more widespread 'democratization of luxury' in which an ever-increasing proportion of private household expenditure is devoted to 'non-essential' goods (Veblen 1899).

By the end of the nineteenth century women's magazines, for example, were aimed at particular income groups and sought to foster a sense of the appropriate lifestyle that could be attained through consumption (Leach 1993). Today, mass media transmit brands and logos that proclaim the wearers' and users' claim for status. Moreover, desire in this form of consumption is inherently insatiable in that new limitless wants can be created by the constant and continuous cultural repackaging of human needs (Baudrillard 1988: 22). Basic needs for sex, food and drink are given myriad diverse cultural expressions in products whose increasing fragmentation and rapidity of change comprise the 'cultural logic' that drives production in 'late capitalism' (Jameson 1991). The process has a built-in dynamic in which competitive status struggles and efforts to create and maintain identity are eroded as the consumption of commodities by which they are signified spreads to other groups. Luxury goods are marketed, as ever, to specific class and status groups, but many of these eventually trickle down the income strata – for example, automobiles, television and so on.

Mass luxury consumption is financed by the banking system's advances of an increasing amount of credit-money to private individuals. Legal restrictions on consumer credit were eased to finance the post-1945 boom in most societies, culminating in the issue of credit cards to all but the most high-risk individuals in society – as Schumpeter's 'merchants of debt' push further down the income hierarchy in search of profits from interest on loans. In a development not envisaged by Keynes in the 1930s, personal 'deficit finance' is now an important adjunct to government expenditure and debt in maintaining aggregate demand, and consumer debt continues to grow to unprecedented levels. In the UK the ratio of household debt to income rose from around 100 per cent in the early 1990s to 150 per cent in 2006 (*Financial Times*, 31 August 2006: 3). Competition drives the banks to make increasingly risky loans, and by the early twenty-first century personal insolvencies and bankruptcies were rising rapidly year by year, for example in the UK from around 5,000 a year in 1998 to over 25,000 in 2006 (*Financial Times*, 5 August 2006, 31 August 2006: 3). As we shall see, this has become the major source of general economic instability in modern capitalism.

In 'monopolistic competition' each producer tries to create and defend a monopoly of their own brand niche – that is, a uniquely defined segment that is relatively secure from encroachment by competitors (White 1981). Typically, they try to maintain the stability of this segmented market structure by tacitly agreeing not to threaten one another in a price war. For example, business plans are publicly announced in order that the other producers in the industry can formulate theirs in a way that does not disrupt their relative positions in the overall market.

Furthermore, a self-stabilizing market mechanism is created by the status hierarchies – based on consumers' 'brand loyalty' to symbolically meaningful goods – that crystallize around consumer/producer niches in segmented markets. The expansionary invasion of product niches that lie either above or below the predatory producer's own segment is inhibited by the relative symbolic values of the niches. Occupancy of a high-status niche brings considerable cost advantages which from a strictly economic standpoint would enable expansion into other, lower-level segments of the market (Podolny 1993). In the first place, a high-status niche permits the producer to signal the symbolic prestige of the good with a high price; indeed, this is almost an essential signifier of quality. Advertising costs will be lower as once the brand is established there is less need to persuade potential buyers – the brand and logo are often sufficient. Bank credit might also be cheaper. In the standard view of the competitive market such a favourable cost/revenue profile should enable the producer to gain near-total domination of the market. However, the invasion of a lower status niche could devalue the symbolic value of the original product and, consequently, erode the cost/revenue advantage. (Conversely, the lower symbolic status of a mid-market producer will make it difficult to invade a luxury niche.)

In some industries, such as women's clothing, these barriers to entering different niches can be overcome by marketing goods of similar objective quality and cost of production under different brands or logos for sale in retail outlets that occupy different places in the status hierarchy.

However, in the automobile industry, for example, this is not easily accomplished. Here, there are numerous instances of producers, such as Mercedes-Benz, who have damaged their original high-status niche by invading a lower, small-car market.[8]

Aside from the tendency of successful enterprises to remain dominant, there are other reasons to think that monopolistic competition might be the typical product market structure throughout capitalist economies. Producers are unable to aim at profit maximization based entirely on costs of production in the manner suggested by the textbook model of the competitive market, because the information needed to do so is not readily available (White 1981). As the number of market participants increases arithmetically, the number of comparisons to be made by the participants grows geometrically to the point where the information cannot be processed and the market becomes unstable – Marx's 'anarchy of production'. Markets with large numbers of small producers exhibit price volatility – including special offers, discounts, promotions and so on – and also high levels of failure and bankruptcy. Consequently in some industries, as we have noted, producers devise a survival strategies which they explicitly signal to each other. New entrants to a market examine these signals, choose a particular price or quality niche and attempt to compete within it. This form of competition by signalling favours the formation of oligopoly. In some industries the anarchy of competition gradually evolves into monopolistic competition, as in car production during the twentieth century. In other industries, such as catering and restaurants, where, among other things, entry costs are low, the volatility and attrition persists.

However, producers' efforts to create a stable oligopoly are constantly threatened by the dynamic process of entrepreneurial 'creative destruction' that drives the capitalist system (Schumpeter 1942: 84). The relative stability of monopolistic competition is typically overturned when one of the existing firms or, exceptionally, a new entrant achieves a competitive advantage by the application of an innovation that effectively supersedes the existing products or creates an entirely new market. For example, motor cars destroyed the market for hansom cabs, compact discs rendered record turntables obsolete and so on. Moreover, as Schumpeter contended, monopoly profits give the security and stability to enable taking the risk of introducing innovations that revolutionize the market. Such secure large firms have the resources to devote to research and development of new products and, furthermore, are able to attract finance on favourable terms.[9] At this upper level of modern capitalism, the struggle to control the opportunities for profit is also conducted through mergers, acquisitions and hostile takeovers orchestrated by banks and other financial enterprises. This means of eliminating competition is also highly profitable for the investment banks, where we also find a similar kind of monopolistic competition (see chapter 7).

Although it is a question of enormous complexity, there is evidence to suggest that economies characterized by monopolistic competition between large firms do experience the fastest economic growth (Chandler, Amatori and Hikino 1997). Dynamic capitalism, it would appear, is the result of a delicate balance between too much and too little competition, that is to say a state of affairs between market anarchy and the stagnation that results from absolute monopoly. For example, it could be argued that the high level of monopoly control exercised by the all-powerful *keiretsu* conglomerates that sit at the top of the Japanese economy has inhibited the kind of 'creative destruction' that could break the cycle of stagnation experienced since 1990. Although profits have fallen, short of a threat of total collapse of the economy these dominant enterprises are not compelled to restructure radically and change their mode of operation.

Conflict and contradictions

Critiques of economic liberalism's claim that the mutual advantage and interdependence of market exchange was an effective basis for social order helped to define the sociological understanding of modern capitalism. Attention has focused on two characteristics of capitalist exchange relations not captured by this model of the market: inherent conflicts of interest and power struggles, and the existence of unintended negative and potentially destructive consequences of free markets.

Conflict

Unlike the competitive market model, which assumes an equal distribution of bargaining power, the classical sociological conception identifies capitalism as a system based on institutional inequalities that create a continuous – if at times, subdued and suppressed – struggle between economic interests. Most attention has focused on the fundamental capital and labour conflict, but, as we shall see, other struggles exist and have recently become more prominent – for example, those between management and shareholders in the corporation, and between consumers and monopoly producers.[10]

Markets in human labour, as Marx insisted, are not natural. Only with the expropriation of almost all the material means of production and subsistence by property-owning classes is the majority of the population compelled to sell its only resource – labour power – as a commodity. However, labour power is a human attribute and, unlike the sale of other commodities, the sellers remain able to exercise a degree of control over what they have sold. This renders the wage contract qualitatively and quantitatively indeterminate. Hours of work, levels of skill and exertion and so on cannot be as completely controlled by the buyer of abstracted labour power as they might be if the whole person were to be bought, as in slavery. In capitalism, the supply of the commodity of abstracted labour power remains to a significant degree under the control of its possessors and, consequently, its qualities and properties are determined in a continuous struggle with the owners and controllers of employing capital.

Workers use two strategies to control the supply and, therefore, the price of labour power. First, they attempt to maintain the scarcity of the supply of skill and technique by erecting barriers to entry in an occupation, as in the mediaeval guilds. Indeed, the range of tasks and competencies that define occupations and the occupational structure of an economy are, to a significant extent, the outcome of such

struggles between capitalists and workers over the organization of work and the introduction of new technologies (Collins
1986: 131). Workers' control of their labour power is greatest
where the supply is restricted by the costs and difficulty of
acquiring the skills. The maintenance of such scarcity in order
to achieve a degree of monopolization of market opportunities is most obviously seen in modern professions such as law
and medicine (see Collins 1986: 126–7); but successful control
of the supply of wage labour also occurs quite widely. For
example, printers' unions in many countries were able to
restrict entry to the occupation and resist the introduction of
the information technology that threatened their market
power during the 1980s. In Britain, the newspaper printers'
control of the supply of labour and the work process was
eventually broken by Rupert Murdoch's News International
Corporation with assistance from the Thatcher government's
assault on the power of trade unions. As we shall see in
chapter 6, it has been argued that throughout the history of
capitalism the organization of work by management in the
large modern enterprise has involved a gradual strategic
'deskilling' in order to reduce workers' power to control the
supply of labour in this way (Braverman 1974).

   The second means used by labour for controlling its supply
is 'collective bargaining' by the occupations organized into
trade unions across an industry or sector of the economy.
Armed with the threat of a withdrawal of labour, trade unions
negotiate the price of their work and the rules that govern
the employment relationship. One of the most significant
changes in capital–labour relations brought about by collective bargaining was the transition from short-term 'spot'
work contracts, by which labour is hired by the day or
week, to longer-term employment contracts which specify
hours and conditions of work, rates of pay, redundancy procedure and compensation for unemployment due to factory
closure, and so on. In short, workers strive to 'de-commodify'
their labour by establishing property rights over opportunities for employment, whereas capital seeks to maintain 'flexible' labour markets in which workers are reduced to a readily
dispensable cost of production.

   However, it should not be assumed, as it is in much
neo-liberal economic analysis, that collective bargaining

necessarily results in labour market 'rigidities' in which high labour costs impair economic efficiency.[11] Leaving aside Keynes's contention that wage flexibility does not necessarily ensure full employment, the existence of clear negotiated employment contracts can make capital–labour relations more transparent and, consequently, the costs of production more calculable. As Weber argued, a balance of power brought about by institutionalized strife might bring economic benefits. On the one hand, dominance by one or other side can lead to an intensification of the struggle and a severe disruption of economic activity. For example, if the state suppresses trade unions at capital's behest the struggle can take covert and more damaging forms – for example, industrial sabotage and the deliberate production of defective goods. On the other hand, a high level of worker power can disrupt production and output, as in the British motor car industry in the 1970s. Conversely, the stability of Swedish industrial relations and low level of strikes over many decades is widely attributed to the high level of institutionalized collective bargaining (Fulcher 1991). Indeed, trade unions have been portrayed by the radical left as 'managers of discontent', unintentionally depoliticizing class conflict by redefining workers' potential opposition to the capitalist system as narrow wage-bargaining, within terms largely set by employers.

However, although workers can achieve some degree of control over the supply of labour, the inherent inequality of the capital–labour relation is evident in the fact that the *demand* for labour remains, largely, the prerogative of the owners and controllers of the enterprise's capital. Indeed, capital's power to make the decisions to invest and thereby determine the very existence of paid employment could be said to define capitalism, and lies at the very heart of the struggle for economic existence. In essence, the issue turns on whether there can be the *right* to work in a capitalist economy. That is to say, if full employment were to become an institutionalized social right, then it could be argued that capitalism had been – at least, in part – superseded.[12]

With the political commitment to full-employment policies in most mature capitalist democracies after 1945, workers, as voters, were able, for a time, to exercise a degree of control

over the demand for labour. The shift away from full employment to the control of inflation as the primary goal of macro-
economic policy will be discussed further in chapter 8. Here
we might note that it has resulted in the reassertion of the
prerogatives of capital in and a decline in workers' ability to
control both the supply and demand for their labour. This
weakness has been exacerbated by structural changes in the
mature economies wrought by increasing global competition.
As a consequence, income inequality has increased as real
wages have stagnated and security of employment has diminished as employers impose short-term contracts and casual
work on those outside the elite of educated knowledge
workers (see Glyn 2006; Duménil and Levy 2004; Alderson
and Nielson 2002; Askers and Wilkinson 2003).

However, global competition from low-wage economies
only partly explains today's wage stagnation in the mature
economies; and, moreover, it cannot account for the increased
share of the surplus taken by capital – especially money
capital and finance (see chapter 9). These recent changes are
entirely consistent with the classical sociological understanding of capitalism's fundamental inequalities. The owners and
controllers of all forms of capital have the power to decide
when and where investment, production and, consequently,
employment will take place and to exert the more powerful
influence in determining the distribution of the surplus. In
short, as Weber emphasized, the formal equality of the contract between buyers and sellers of labour is accompanied by
an inherent substantive inequality. At best labour is a countervailing and defensive power.

The intensity and frequency of manifest conflict between
capital and labour has diminished in the mature economies
in the recent past, but it has not been eliminated, and there
is no reason to reject the possibility that the increasing
inequality of global capitalism might yet reignite the classic
capitalist confrontation. Without reading Marx's *Capital*, the
Financial Times recently asked, how could one explain why
the world's richest 2 per cent own more than 50 per cent of
global assets (*Financial Times*, 28 December 2006: 13)?

In addition to capital–labour conflict in the process of
production a further set of opposed interests is to be found
in capitalism's distinctive monetary and financial system. The

financing of production by bank debt is the site of a struggle between creditors and debtors over rates of interest, terms of debt contracts, the provisions of bankruptcy law and so on. Economic theory, following Smith, holds that the rate of interest is objectively determined, in the long run, by the supply of and demand for money-capital. Demand for money capital will be determined by the profitability of the factors and means of production and their ability to meet interest payments. A high level of demand at a given level of interest signals that profits will easily cover the cost of capital, and interest rates will rise to the point where demand falls off. That is to say, this view contends that there exists a 'natural', optimally efficient, rate of interest, produced by the 'invisible hand'. Assuming effective competition between lenders and perfect information on the profitability of enterprise, the price (interest) of the supply of bank-produced money will, in the long run, approximate this rate of profit from the production of commodities.[13]

However, the creation of money does not conform to the competitive market model. As Keynes and Schumpeter argued, the supply of credit-money in capitalism becomes highly 'elastic' – that is, easily produced. With the abandonment of precious-metal currency, there is no natural scarcity and costs of production are negligible. Furthermore, the production of money by bank lending does not simply involve a transfer of existing funds from savers to borrowers; the act of lending creates deposits of entirely 'new' money. Consequently, there is a potential power struggle in the formulation of the rules governing the creation and supply of money (see chapter 4). We have already noted that banks and credit-rating agencies have the power to 'ration' bank credit-money, but this is part of a wider struggle over money creation and its allocation. In general, capitalism's debtor classes (producers and consumers) favour an abundant supply of 'cheap money' (low-interest bank credit) and welcome the reduction of the real value of their debt that any ensuing inflation might bring. On the other hand, creditor classes press for 'tight' money policies in order to maintain a positive real rate of interest (nominal money rate minus inflation). For example, there was acute conflict over the return to the gold standard in the USA in the late nineteenth and early twentieth centuries. Farmers, small business and consumers feared that a gold standard would make money scarce, enhance the power of the banks to take advantage of the restricted supply and ultimately create a recession by starving the productive economy of money-capital (see Carruthers and Babb 1996). Again, conflict over the question of who controlled the supply of money was at the heart of the 'monetarist' experiments in the 1980s (see p. 78).

Contradictions and crises

Critics of the 'invisible hand' point not only to endemic conflict but also to the existence of contradictions that constantly provoke crises that can impair production and lead to depressions. These contradictions are 'systemic' in the sense that they are unintended consequences of the routine activities that constitute capitalism rather than deliberately taken disruptive action. Stagnation in pre-capitalist economies is generally the result of exogenous factors such as war, pestilent disease and population decline, and natural disasters. These continue to exert their effects, but, as Marx and Keynes explained in their different ways, capitalism produces endogenous – or self-inflicted – dislocation.

Although it is widely accepted that market capitalism can be unstable, crisis-prone and the cause of unwanted negative effects, Marx's belief that these 'contradictions' would bring about its demise now commands little or no support. The French 'regulation school', for example, has produced sophisticated Marxist analyses of capitalism's contradictions which do not reach the conclusion that these will be necessarily terminal (see Aglietta 1979; Boyer 1990; Jessop 2001). Today, the main point of contention is whether these problems can be completely eradicated or whether they are chronic but none the less manageable. In other words, the major disagreement is whether the fluctuations in economic activity – business cycles, booms and slumps – are self-correcting, as Smith's economics implies, or whether the economy requires constant remedial action by governments and central banks.

Staunch advocates of the market system are overcome, from time to time, by the optimistic belief that the capitalist system's 'imperfections' (or 'contradictions') have actually been resolved. The more naive interpretations of Keynes's work led to this conclusion for a while after the Second World War, and at the end of the twentieth century it was briefly fashionable to think that information and communication technology would create a 'New Economy', increasing productivity to such an extent that economic crises and recessions would be consigned to history. However, like all such prognoses of the perfectibility of human institutions, both were eventually shown to be hubris – first in the crises of the 1970s and then in the bursting of the 'dot.com' stock-market bubble at the turn of the twentieth century.

Polanyi's *The Great Transformation* (1944) is one of the most influential general accounts of the free market's contradictory capacity for self-destruction which, he contends, led to the near-collapse of capitalism in the economic and political crises of the 1920s and 1930s. Based loosely on Marx and Durkheim, it argues, as we have noted, that economic exchange in all previous economic systems had been 'embedded' in wider social institutions. The regulatory norms of reciprocity and politically controlled redistribution were better able to nurture and preserve society's material resources. By detaching them from these wider social controls the unbridled market transforms them into commodities, a transformation which eventually brings about their depletion and destruction. According to Polanyi, 'disembedded' markets in land, labour and money create, respectively, environmental degradation, human misery, and inflation and financial crises.

Having observed governments' efforts to repair the damage caused by the inter-war crises in the twentieth century, Polanyi rejected Marx's apocalyptic vision. Rather, the market's destructive tendencies lead to dialectical 'double movement' in capitalism between, on the one hand, the continued expansion of the socially and politically 'disembedded' markets and, on the other, efforts to regulate their destructive consequences. Thus by the mid-1930s there was a swing towards the regulation of stock markets, the introduction of employment standards, the beginnings of modern welfare states and, eventually, the adoption of full employment policies.[14] After the crises of the 1970s, the pendulum swung back towards market 'deregulation' (see chapters 8 and 9). Today there are clear signs that this will be reversed with tighter regulation in the wake of the increasingly serious credit crisis that began with the US subprime mortgage defaults in 2007. Some critics believe that economic globalization will eventually bring about a second general destabilization of capitalism and a similar 'double movement' in which attempts are made to re-regulate free markets.

More precisely, capitalism is prone to two kinds of recurrent systemic economic crisis: cycles of over-production/under-consumption, and financial crises caused by cycles of credit expansion and contraction, which might eventually trigger debt-deflation (see chapter 2). The two sources of crisis – that is, deficient demand and credit cycles – have become increasingly interconnected as expressions of capitalism's most fundamental and definitive characteristics – debt-financed production, consumption and speculation.

The extreme fluctuations in supply and demand, seen by Marx in the mid-nineteenth century as the 'anarchy' of the market, resulting in crises of over-production/under-consumption, have since been moderated by macro-economic policy.[15] As Marx and Keynes argued in their different ways, the ultimate constraint on the continuous expansion of commodity production, without which capitalism might easily sink back into stagnation, remains the limit on effective demand that is inherent in the contradictory wage–profit relationship. Incomes cannot be raised indefinitely to finance the expansion of consumption without encroaching on the share of the surplus claimed by profits. If profits fall to an unacceptable level, investment and production are cut, triggering a downward cycle of falling employment and demand. Consumption was raised after 1945 by government expenditure, but, as we shall see, the inflationary crises of the 1970s led to limits being placed on this attempt at a solution.

Subsequently, deficient aggregate demand (Marx's 'under-consumption') has been held at bay, as we have noted, by the extension and expansion of consumer credit and a fundamental shift in savings–income ratios. Private consumption financed by private indebtedness to banks and credit-card companies has reached unprecedented levels and has become a prominent feature of the increasing dominance of the financial sector in modern capitalism (see chapter 7). However, this does not resolve the over-production/under-consumption contradiction. On the contrary, it is widely believed that it creates potential for a further crisis if the point is reached where the debts cannot be serviced and repaid, triggering debt-deflation.

As Schumpeter and Minsky explained, the entire capitalist system is held together by an enormous credit network which can be quickly unravelled by defaults on debt repayment, triggering a chain reaction which slows down production and consumption. This process can originate anywhere in the economy – consumers, producers, banks and so on. However, as we shall see, it is widely believed that the expansion of debt-financed dealing in increasingly complex financial markets has increased the risk of defaults in the credit and capital markets which in turn makes banks more 'risk averse' and reluctant to lend. Eventually, as we have noted, these credit 'squeezes' or 'crunches' affect the production of goods and services by lowering investment and consumption.

With debts unpaid, firms go bankrupt and workers are laid off, consumers cut spending, financiers and consumers become reluctant to borrow and banks become even more unwilling to lend as the downward spiral takes hold. As the ultimate source of money, governments and central banks can, as 'lenders of last resort', lend to banks whose position is threatened by defaults. But these measures are not always successful, particularly if trust in the banking system has been seriously eroded and the financial institutions have become wary of lending to each other. Moreover, lending by the central bank in this way runs the risk of creating what economists refer to as 'moral hazard', that is to say the belief that central bank action to preserve the system encourages high-risk lending and speculation, which increases the probability of further credit booms and the almost inevitable 'bust', or 'credit crunch'. These issues will be explored further in subsequent chapters.

Credit expansion also fuels the most potentially volatile crises in capitalism – speculative 'bubbles' in financial asset markets. As I have emphasized, it is a hallmark of capitalism that all material means, resources of production – including the enterprise itself and its capital – are also marketable financial assets. This dual character of capital, as we shall see in more detail in chapter 7, gives rise to financial markets in capital assets which produce two key linked features of capitalist economies: asset speculation and the struggle between money-capitalist 'predators' for control of the enterprise by hostile takeovers.

By increasing price volatility and the risk of crisis, and diverting resources and energy from production, short-term financial speculation has a potentially contradictory relationship with what Keynes referred to as long-term 'business enterprise'. At the present time even the staunchest defenders of capitalism have joined its critics in condemning the general 'financialization' of capitalism. In particular, attention is focused the potential for destabilization created by bank lending to 'hedge funds' for speculation in an ever increasing range of 'exotic' financial assets – especially in the foreign-exchange markets. Again, these will be examined in chapter 7; here we might simply note that the mounting concern echoes Keynes's mistrust of the financial market 'casino' and Minsky's contention that financial instability caused by debt-finance was an inherent and enduring feature of capitalism (for a general discussion of financial crises see Kindleberger and Aliber 2005).

Conclusion

Adam Smith's basic contention that the material advance of human society is made possible by the market coordination of specialized economic functions and competition between producers is indisputable. So far, human society has not developed social and economic institutions that are better able to coordinate complex activity and stimulate economic dynamism. However, a number of important qualifications to this widely accepted assessment should be acknowledged. First, the market is only a part of the capitalism; it is not synonymous with the entire economic system – as much neo-liberal economic analysis all too readily assumes. This tradition emphasizes the formal legal freedom of all classes of economic agents to bargain, compete and thereby produce the prices which act as signals for the spontaneous and impersonal integration of large-scale decentralized economic activity. Some parts of capitalist economies contain markets that do resemble this model, but they are not typical and the general structure of capitalism cannot be understood in this way. Capitalism refers to an economic system in which the ownership and control of capital confers the power to employ wage labour on terms that are determined, as we shall see in chapter 6, by a power struggle in a *non*-market institution – the capitalist enterprise.

Second, market exchange is not merely a functionally efficient mechanism for allocating resources; it is also an arena of conflict. As we have seen, Marx focused on the basic struggle between capital and labour, and more generally Weber viewed the market as the site of the 'battle of man against man' (Weber 1978: 93). Furthermore, it can be argued that concentrated monopoly and oligopoly power is the typical outcome of these struggles, which results in the domination of suppliers and consumers by large enterprises.

Third, the pursuit of material self-interest by competing economic agents produces a wide range of unintended negative consequences. As we shall see in following chapters, states – singly and collectively – are required to intervene to regulate and control the market's self-destructive effects, by making such provisions as welfare to maintain the quality of 'human capital', planning to prevent the depletion and degradation of the environment and, more importantly, the rescue of the financial system whenever defaults and bank failures threaten its collapse.

Finally, it should be emphasized that the market exchanges that link the different parts of modern capitalist economies are not the direct and 'spontaneous' result of some innate human capacity for cooperative bargaining, as is argued in some versions of economic liberalism. Markets in pre-capitalist economies were largely 'marketplaces' – bazaars, market squares, fairs – where barter and face-to-face haggling took place. These bear some superficial resemblance to economic liberalism's conception of the primordial market, but closer inspection shows that the exchanges were governed by elaborate social structure of norms and conventions (see Polanyi 1971 [1957]).[16]

However, markets in modern capitalist economies have a quite different social structure, in which participants are guided by 'the potential action of an indeterminately large group of real or *imaginary* competitors rather than by their own actions alone' (Weber 1978: 636, emphasis added). Here Weber is pointing to the way in which modern states have created anonymous and impersonal social spaces for multi-lateral indirect exchange. The large-scale markets that are typical of modern capitalism are complex social institutions, constituted by standardized weights and measures and money, and regulated by laws and conventions. What is deemed to be fair competition, the rights of the contracting parties, the form of contract and the marketable quality of goods did not emerge spontaneously (see the discussion in part I, and Collins 1986). Large-scale capitalist markets require elaborate procedural and substantive rules. Indeed, as Vogel has shown, deregulation in the late twentieth century to create 'freer' financial markets has paradoxically produced more rules (Vogel 1996). From this perspective, the European Commission bureaucracy is a necessary condition for the creation of such a large 'common' market and does not, as it is widely believed, impede efficiency (Fligstein 2001). Capitalists constantly complain about the costs of 'red tape' without realizing that without basic rules for regulating market exchange their activities would not be possible.

Furthermore, all forms of peaceful market exchange presuppose the existence of an authority – usually a state – effectively to suppress violence and to protect property. Market exchange is risky if rights to ownership cannot be clearly established and safeguarded (de Soto 2000; North 1981). Finally, as we saw in the previous chapter, the most important prerequisite for the existence of market exchange is the very thing that the market *cannot* produce – that is, a stable monetary system for establishing and calculating prices.

6
The enterprise

The large-scale privately owned business enterprise, employing wage labour, is specific to modern capitalism. Work was organized on a large scale in the very earliest city states and bureaucratic empires – such as Babylon and Egypt – three thousand years ago, but it was almost exclusively devoted to building religious, military and infrastructural projects (temples, dockyards, roads, irrigation), using slave labour. Before capitalism most goods were produced for direct use within the household and the community. Production for market exchange was limited in scale and until the nineteenth century took place in domestic households and small workshops. Work and home were integrated and production was financed almost entirely from saved income.

For a time immediately before the emergence of the modern European capitalist enterprise in the early nineteenth century, some domestic textile production was financed and coordinated into integrated chains by merchant capitalist entrepreneurs in the 'putting out' system. Raw wool, imported or collected from sheep farmers, was 'put out' sequentially to different households for the different stages in the production process – washing, spinning and weaving. The finished cloth would then be marketed by the merchant-entrepreneur. Steam powered mechanization enabled the integration of this dispersed division of labour in factories. However, as we shall see, the distinctive property and authority relations of the capitalist firm, including the division of labour and task specialization, were not simply determined by these technological developments.

Although there is a wide variation in types of firm, modern capitalist production typically takes place in large externally financed, bureaucratically organized enterprises in which different specialized stages of production are integrated. Day-to-day control and coordination of work are undertaken by salaried managers who, for the most part, do not have an ownership stake in the business. As we have noted, the modern capitalist enterprise is typically financed with externally raised money-capital in the form of stocks, shares, bonds and bank loans (see the discussion in chapter 7). Consequently, direct operational control of the enterprise is at least partly separated from ownership. Family owned enterprise has not disappeared and continues to play a significant role, but it is no longer as commonplace as it was throughout the nineteenth century.

As we have seen, Weber implied that family ownership and management introduced non-rational loyalties and emotions that could compromise rational capital accounting. For example, household expenditure might interfere with investment and it could be difficult to dismiss an incompetent family member. This tension is a common theme in literature, television and film – for example, the 1980s television sagas *Dynasty* and *Dallas*. In the real world Mario Gucci, the third-generation head of the Italian fashion business, was assassinated on the orders of his former wife for selling his 50 per cent share of the business and depriving his children of their inheritance (for further entertaining examples, see Gordon and Nicholson 2008). On the other hand, however, the long-term survival of some family firms also points to the fact that the motivation to preserve the family inheritance can be a means of projecting the firm through economic recessions and an uncertain future. Dynastic capitalism is more prevalent in continental Europe than in the stock market financial systems of the USA and the UK, where the enterprise is more 'liquid' – that is to say, is more easily bought and sold (on European family capitalism see James 2006).

There are significantly different – but ultimately complementary – accounts of the development of this basic element of the capitalist system. As is the case with the other capitalist institutions, those explanations deriving from economic analysis see the bureaucratic enterprise as the cost-efficient solution to the problems of coordinating and controlling divided labour and specialized economic functions. The sociological tradition, on the other hand, focuses on the enterprise as a locus of capitalist power in which different interests – owners, managers and workers – struggle to increase their share of the surplus that it creates.

This chapter is divided into three parts. First, the general theories of the basic nature and functions of the capitalist enterprise are outlined. In the second section a brief sketch of the development of the enterprise, informed by some of these insights, is presented. Finally, the struggle between owners and managers for control of the surplus generated by the modern corporate form of enterprise is discussed.

Theories of the capitalist enterprise

In 1991 Ronald Coase received the Nobel Prize for his answer to a question that he had posed in 1937 (Coase 1937). If, as economic theory maintains, market exchange is the most efficient means of organizing and coordinating production and distribution, why, he asked, do firms exist? For example, why were all the different elements in the 'putting out' production chain, in which independent domestic producers were connected and coordinated by contractual market relations, drawn together and placed in the large vertically integrated enterprise? Coase's answer was that the organization and coordination of economic activity occur in firms whenever rational calculation reveals that the market mechanism is more costly to use.

In his highly influential *Markets and Hierarchies* (1975) and *The Economic Institutions of Capitalism* (1985), Oliver Williamson developed Coase's conjecture and argued that the firm arises as a response to 'transactions costs' that occur in contractual market exchange. These costs are produced by the existence of imperfect information and unequal bargaining strengths to be found in actual markets, as opposed to the abstract, perfect competition model. Human beings are assumed to maximize their self-interest amorally by taking advantage of these market imperfections – in Williamson's terms, they display 'opportunism with guile'. In short, people are not to be trusted; they will cheat, shirk and take advantage of every conceivable opportunity. For example, the existence of only a limited number of acceptable suppliers of raw materials or components in a production chain ('small-numbers bargaining' and 'asset specificity') enables them to exploit a producer by raising prices or by giving priority to new business and, consequently, failing to supply a promised order on time. The drawing up and enforcement of elaborate legal contracts is one possible solution to this problem of 'transactions costs', but this can be even more costly in legal fees than the exploitation by a supplier that it is intended to prevent.

However, in many circumstances transactions costs can be reduced by the integration of the different parts of a contractually linked production chain ('market' in Williamson's terms) into a single enterprise – or 'hierarchy' – in which command replaces price and contract as the means of economic coordination. For example, an enterprise might decide to 'make' rather than 'buy' components and to integrate vertically a contractually based production network into the bureaucratic authority structure of a single enterprise. Production can be organized by varying degrees of integration of the production chain depending on the level of transactions costs to be reduced – from large vertically integrated bureaucratic firms to looser structures such as franchising, dealerships and a subcontracting market.

Some forms of production, for example large-scale construction projects, for which demand is low and discontinuous, cannot be cost-effectively organized into permanent, integrated hierarchies and, consequently, they are typically undertaken by contractors and layers of subcontractors. But such large-scale construction is also characterized by uncontrollable escalating costs and legal disputes as the independent layers of subcontractors take advantage of their positions – as the British Football Association recently experienced with construction of their new Wembley stadium. 'Transactions cost' theory is also used to explain the transnational firm, for example, in which 'hierarchy' is a less costly form of coordination than using transnational contracts with spatially and culturally distant independent producers and suppliers.

In this theory 'hierarchy' is seen as simply as the efficient solution to the problem of ensuring the effective coordination of the division of labour. Power and authority are considered as purely functional, implying that subordinates submit to commands because it is self-evident that the cost-effective outcome is to everyone's advantage. However, it is by no means clear that the historical development of the capitalist enterprise can be explained in this way. For example, how could the consideration of 'transactions costs' have persuaded hand-loom weavers to abandon domestic production in the early nineteenth century in order to become wage-earners? Integration of the production chain and the elimination of the cottage spinners' and weavers' autonomy most certainly reduced the merchant-entrepreneurs' transactions costs, but it was the *power* of capital and the existence of a supply of property-less wage-labour that made the large textile enterprise a possibility.

Similarly, the explanation of the structural variations in modern capitalist enterprises in terms of transactions costs also assumes rather than explains the existence of an authority structure. It is not simply a question of executives and managers having sufficient information to calculate the relative costs of different forms of economic organization, but also, most pertinently, the *power* to implement them. Moreover, the large vertically integrated hierarchical firms that emerged in the late-nineteenth-century USA were not created simply as an *alternative* to costly market exchange, but as a means of creating a powerful organization that could *supersede* the market in order to make monopoly profits (Arrighi 1994: ch. 4).

Power is at the centre of the classic sociological accounts of the enterprise. For Marx, the capitalist enterprise exists in order to dominate and exploit wage-labour. But the obvious point must not be overlooked: the social categories of capital and wage-labour must first exist for this particular form of exploitation to be a possibility. In Marx's account, capitalism presupposes a property-less proletariat which is compelled to sell its labour-power to the owners of capital. It will be recalled that in his critique of classical economics Marx made a distinction between 'labour' and 'labour-power'. The worker does not sell a fixed unit of labour input for a wage in an equal exchange, but sells 'labour-power' to be organized by the capitalist in such as way as to extract 'surplus value' through exploitation. As we shall see, the organizational and technological design of work is to a significant extent the result of the struggle over how this 'labour-power' is to be used. Submission to domination in the labour process is part of the wage contract. In short, the capitalist enterprise is the *means* by which labour is transformed into capital.[1]

For Weber the capitalist enterprise, like the modern state, is a corporate body whose gradual structural differentiation from household and family enables, as we have noted, the removal of arbitrary non-rational decision-making based on traditional norms and family ties. As the modern enterprise relies on external finance, it is necessary to calculate precisely the returns due to contractually linked outside creditors, as opposed to a share in the common household or family 'pot' (Weber 1981 [1927]: 225–9). Thus modern capitalist accounting is made possible by its separation from traditional and emotional ties. As we have seen, Weber identifies capitalism with the rational accounting of the profitability of returns to capital (Weber 1978: 85–90).

Weber's analysis remains relevant for modern debates. Is oriental family capitalism a viable alternative to the Western model, or is it a form of 'crony capitalism' in which personal allegiances and nepotism interfere with economic rationality? For example, would kinship ties impede the decision to sell a loss-making family firm? Weber appears to agree with conventional modern economic analysis that the joint-stock corporation, owned by outsiders, is the most efficient form of organization. Here, separation from family ownership creates a competitive market in which a firm's market value, based on performance, is a means of monitoring the managerial bureaucracy. However, as we shall see, others would argue that joint-stock corporations are subject to pressures from shareholders to aim for short-term profits at the expense of investment for long-term growth, which a family dynasty would be more likely to favour.

As we noted in part I, this 'formal' rational calculation of profitability has a 'substantive' basis in the power and control that comes with the complete appropriation of non-human means of productions and the formally free labour market. Capitalists and their managers can freely manipulate the production process, and hire and fire workers to maximize returns to capital. In the most general terms, Weber's theory of the modern enterprise is very similar to Marx's – that is to say, the enterprise is where the power of capital operates directly in the control of the means of production and labour. Therefore, in contrast to 'transactions cost' theory, the bureaucratic firm is not an alternative to the market, but the complementary location of economic rationality. For Weber it is a question of markets *and* hierarchies, not markets *or* hierarchies. From this Weberian standpoint, 'efficiency' and 'power' explanations of the existence and functions of the capitalist firm provided by orthodox economic theory and Marxism are not as opposed and incompatible as their adherents appear to believe. The calculation of efficient ratios of inputs and outputs has a basis in the inequality of the distribution of power in the enterprise.

Each theory captures an aspect of the capitalist enterprise and its development. Modern enterprises are a rational means of reducing 'transactions costs' associated with decentralized contractually coordinated chains of production – that is to say, market exchange. With regard to the discussion of the market in chapter 5, it is significant that the most telling instance of 'market failure' is the market's inability to produce a result that is acceptable to the owners and controllers of capital. The history of capitalism, as Marx emphasized, can be written in terms of the progressive subordination of labour. In other words, the reduction of transaction and other costs presupposes the existence of a definitive feature of capitalism: all means of production are the private property of the enterprise. This confers the power to devise and implement in the production process the organizational and technological changes that minimize costs.

Capital's constant effort to reduce all types of costs is part of the ongoing struggle between owners, creditors, managers and workers for the enterprise's surplus, which, as we shall see, is the major force in shaping the structure of the enterprise.

A short history of the development of the capitalist enterprise

Arrighi's history of the capitalist enterprise takes the form of an analysis of how the various 'costs' that arise in the control and coordination of chains of production and capital accumulation have been dealt with. In addition to the 'transactions' costs of market exchange, his historical sketch also considers the important question of the costs of providing the coercion necessary to maintain a level of pacification that permits the operation of decentralized market capitalism. Unlike slavery and the manorial household, for example, the domination of capital in the autonomous enterprise relies on the 'externalization of coercion costs' in the state (Arrighi 1994; Arrighi and Silver 1999).

Three major historical forms of capitalist enterprise are identified, and each is associated with successive capitalist state hegemonies: (i) Dutch and English joint-stock chartered companies in the seventeenth and eighteenth centuries; (ii) British family enterprise capitalism in the nineteenth century; and (iii) US multi-divisional, multi/transnational corporations from the late nineteenth century onwards.

(i) External finance of enterprise by money-capital in the form of joint-stock companies originated in Italian mercantile city states such as Venice and Genoa during the sixteenth and seventeenth centuries as a means of spreading the risk of long-distance trade – posed by the weather, pirates and enemy powers – by splitting the capital to finance the ventures between wealthy individuals (*commenda*). This form of enterprise was the first in which there is a clear separation between external ownership interests and the direct operation of enterprise. As the merchants were also the political ruling class in these bourgeois republics, economic power and political power were very closely linked and, consequently, states provided all the necessary protection for the trading ventures. With the decline of the Italian bourgeois city states, economic power shifted to the monarchies of northern Europe, where mercantile capital and the state were in competition for control of profitable opportunities. For example, the attempt by Charles II of England to monopolize trade in certain commodities was an important factor in his downfall. Eventually, the north European states and their mercantile bourgeoisie achieved, as we have noted, a mutually beneficial accommodation in the 'memorable alliance'.

In addition to the monetary and fiscal arrangements of public banks and national debts discussed in chapter 4, the other important products of this alliance were the first great externally financed joint-stock capitalist enterprises – the English East India Company (1600) and Dutch East Indies Company (1602). As their respective states were not financially strong enough either to undertake or adequately to protect the ventures, they granted monopoly charters to the merchants to trade in the East. This solution created a hybridization of capital and coercion in which the enterprises 'internalized' their 'protection costs' by raising armies. However, 'transactions costs' remained 'externalized' in the organization of long chains of independent domestic producers in foreign lands. Unlike the economic strategy of states and empires, these 'company states' did not merely extract tribute and taxes, nor did they impose direct controls on an economy. Rather, they financed and co-ordinated indigenous workshop or communal production into a chain, as in the European 'putting out' system. These were considerable organizational achievements, involving coordination on a large scale. During the eighteenth century the English East India Company organized a dynamic Indian cotton industry which exported to Europe.

Two contradictions gradually undermined these 'company states'. First, the coercion costs, borne by the company, escalated as the exploited indigenous populations began to resist. Second, repatriated profits helped to transform the domestic British textile industry, which opposed the East India Company's monopoly. With some intellectual assistance from Adam Smith's texts on the virtues of free trade, this monopoly was consequently abolished in 1813.

(ii)   Nineteenth-century British family capitalism was based on the protection of global trade networks, undertaken by imperial state powers, in which production became linked to the exploitation of the empire's primary products. In the cotton textile industry, for example, the relationship with India was now reversed as its raw cotton was processed by

British enterprises which had been transformed by mechanization and a supply of wage-labour after the enclosure of agricultural land and the collapse of domestic production. Reorganization of the proto-capitalist 'putting out chains' into factories reduced transactions costs by subordinating workers to rigorous exploitation which enabled their productivity to be precisely controlled and calculated. Marx and Engels's classic exposition of early capitalism and the condition of the proletariat is a description of 'machinofacture' in small- and medium-size family enterprises. However, some family businesses were organized on a large scale, with their bureaucratic management hierarchies and the vertical integration of divided labour and specialized production processes.

Some early family capitalists attempted to extend capital's control over labour beyond their firm's gates. In 1853, for example, Sir Titus Salt built a large textile factory and a small town alongside the river Aire, near Bradford, England, to house the 3,000 workers it employed. Although Salt genuinely wished to better the appalling living conditions of the working class in the new industrial towns, he was primarily intent on improving the quality of his labour force and, most importantly, on countering the growing opposition to capitalism expressed by the Chartist movement. Most ordinary streets in Saltaire contained one or two larger houses for the higher-level management in order that they could keep the workers under surveillance outside working hours. Public houses were prohibited, not so much from an opposition to alcohol but on the grounds that they could be used as meeting places for discontented workers. Recreation was organized in the parks, billiard hall and library built by the Salt family.

However, such local monopolies were atypical and temporary features of mid-Victorian capitalism, which was characterized in Britain and elsewhere by small- and medium-size enterprises and, by today's standards, high levels of competition. And as Adam Smith had surmised and Marx observed, high rates of return on relatively small amounts of money-capital in small-enterprise production attracted many new entrants to the industries. The resulting intensification of competition required the continuous reduction of capital costs through mechanical innovation, which led to falling rates of profit, over-production and a series of deflationary spirals, culminating in the protracted stagnation of the Great Depression between 1873 and 1896. In what was arguably the first global process of 'creative destruction', Britain's capitalist hegemony, based on its family enterprise and workshop capitalism, was partially superseded by a new form of enterprise and market structure.

(iii)   After this Great Depression in the last quarter of the nineteenth century, the modern corporation emerged at the upper levels of all the capitalist economies – but most extensively in the United States. First, family capitalism, incapable of raising enough capital for large-scale mass production technology, was gradually replaced as the main form of enterprise by 'joint stock' corporations – that is, enterprises financed by the public sale of stocks and shares. Second, the vertical integration of production chains in large corporations and horizontal combination in cartels were the means of avoiding the earlier competition that had reduced profits to intolerable levels and induced the Great Depression. Thus modern capitalism assumed its typical structure of large enterprises, organized as oligopolies or monopolies, with a hierarchy of bureaucratic management separated to some degree from owners.

The major capitalist economies pursued somewhat different paths. In Germany, and a little later in Japan, horizontal and vertical integration was accomplished in association with the big banks and was part of a state-sponsored process of development which intensified competition between the leading capitalist states. In both economies, families retained a significant degree of control through their connections with the banks which financed the restructuring (James 2006). This pattern of development was captured at the time in Hilferding's classic Marxist study of *Finanzkapital* (1910).

'Locked in' to the earlier form of capitalism, Britain moved much more slowly and uncertainly towards monopoly capitalism and the corporate form of enterprise. Money-capital and finance, centred on the City of London, remained cosmopolitan and concerned with global commercial and financial activity rather than the creation of a domestic form of monopoly capitalism (see Ingham 1984). However, Britain did produce one successful type of organization which, significantly, was based on a structural form inherited from early capitalism.

Family-owned, London-based investment companies operated like global 'putting out' merchant-financiers, organizing long production chains in the Empire, but, unlike German and US firms, did not themselves become directly involved in multinational production. In domestic industry there were some combinations and vertical integration, but the British move to monopoly and oligopoly capitalism was less extensive and relatively unsuccessful (Chandler 1992 [1984]).

In the United States the bureaucratic, multi-divisional, multi/transnational corporations based on mass production created a 'second industrial revolution'. Large-scale mass production poses three interrelated exigencies. First, it is capital-intensive and requires high levels of externally generated finance. Second, the advantages of economies of scale and declining cost per unit of output can only be fully realized if there is full capacity utilization in a smooth continuous flow of materials into, through and out of the factory to consumers. Third, in order to warrant the enormous capital investment this uninterrupted 'throughput' requires, as we have already noted, uninterrupted mass consumption.

By the late nineteenth century banking systems were sufficiently integrated to support the creation of money by their dense, and increasingly international, credit networks. They provided the foundation for the investment banks that financed the formation of the upper levels of the US economy as a series of oligopolies and cartels. JPMorgan in steel, Rockefeller in oil and DuPont in chemicals were financial–industrial conglomerates centred on a holding company, or trust, which coordinated and directed production and marketing. They were able to wield great control over the economy. For example, the Standard Oil Trust was an association of forty legally separate companies tied to Rockefeller's Standard Oil Company through cross-holdings of stock and credit–debt relations, coordinated and administered by an investment bank. Rockefeller's holding company rationalized the oil industry by concentrating production into three refineries which accounted for about 25 per cent of the world's output of kerosene.[2] The average cost of production fell from 1.50 to 0.45 cents a gallon, whilst profits increased from 0.53 to 1.003 cents a gallon (Chandler 1992 [1984]: 140–1). The whole operation depended on maintaining an uninterrupted daily flow of between 5,000 and 6,000 barrels. The investment necessary for the continuous flow of Standard Oil's gasoline was vindicated in 1913, when Henry Ford completed his Highland Park automobile assembly line. The time to construct a Model T chassis was cut from over twelve hours to about ninety minutes, reducing the price of the car by half. Motoring for the masses had arrived.

Bureaucratic organization is the only effective way to manage the smooth, continuous flow of materials into, through and out of the factory and thereby minimize transactions costs. 'Such coordination cannot happen automatically. It demands the constant attention of a managerial team of hierarchy. Scale is only a technological characteristic; the economies of scale are organizational. Such economies depend on knowledge, skills, and teamwork – on the human organization essential to exploit the potential of technological processes' (Chandler 1992 [1984]: 139–40).

The only relevant organizational practices available at the time were those to be found in the modern state's first bureaucracies – the military. It is difficult to see how the vast US railways, telegraph and, subsequently, large corporations could have been operated had it not been for the recruitment of managers from the ranks of those who, at the time, were the only ones to possess the organizational knowledge and skills – former officers from the USA's Westpoint military academy. The routine operation of the world's first modern large-scale corporations was conducted not by owners but by the ranks of a salaried management hierarchy. As we shall see, this set in train a more complex struggle for control of the surplus than had occurred during the nineteenth-century class conflict between family owners and their workers. To be sure, workers and managers continued to struggle, but, as we shall see, they were later to find a common interest in opposition to external owners who were bent on squeezing every last bit of surplus from the new corporations.

We have already discussed the rise of modern mass markets that consume the output of the modern corporate oligopolies (see chapter 5). Here we might simply note that these were extended across the USA and other advanced economies by new mass-communications industries, which also eventually assumed the same modern oligopoly structure. Newspapers, magazines and, a little later, radio and television linked the giant corporations to mass retailing conducted by department stores and mail-order distributors. The 'democratization of luxury' had truly arrived in 1905, when Sears Roebuck in Chicago began regularly to process over 100,000 mail orders per day taken from its advertisements, and distributed across the country by an integrated rail network (Chandler 1992 [1984]).

Finally, it should be noted that the US enterprises were, from their inception, multinational. By 1914, US direct investment abroad, at 7 per cent of gross national product, was as high as in the 1960s, and by the late 1920s the automobile corporations of Ford and General Motors had opened plants in Britain and continental Europe.

It was essential for the continuation of this mass production–mass consumption regime that market capitalism's 'business cycles' – that is, erratic fluctuations of supply and demand – were eliminated. This was eventually achieved, to a large extent, by Keynesian-style macro-economic policies. Governments took some responsibility for maintaining aggregate demand and also the provision of infrastructure for modern mass production. For example, national electricity networks provided energy for both industry and the new consumer durables that they powered – washing machines, radios, televisions and so on. The Italian Marxist, Antonio Gramsci, referred to this integration of government policy with mass production as the 'Fordist' stage of capitalist development.[3]

The temporary relative decline of the USA in the 1980s led to the conjecture that its organizational form of capitalism was being superseded. In *The Second Industrial Divide* (1984), Piore and Sabel, for example, argued that the dominance of US 'dinosaur' corporations was being effectively challenged by new forms of organization. On the one hand, there was a relative shift away from mass production towards 'flexible specialization' and informal networks and alliances between small- and medium-sized firms in local industrial districts. On the other, east Asian industrial organization, especially Japanese 'relational contracting' and 'just in time' methods of vertically disintegrated production chains, were seen to be more effective. However, large US corporations responded to this competition and the economic crises of the

1970s by cutting wages costs to increase profitability and, as a result, 'stockholder value' (see below). To be sure, capitalist business enterprise in the advanced economies changed to some extent in these directions, but these trends should not be exaggerated. By end of twentieth century, the large multi/transnational US corporations and their counterparts elsewhere had survived to remain the typical dominant form of capitalist enterprise.[4]

The struggle for the enterprise's surplus

The modern capitalist enterprise is a highly developed form of organization for the coordination of the division of labour and efficient exploitation of profitable opportunities, but, as we have stressed, it is also the site of conflicts over the distribution of the revenues it produces (see, for example, Henwood 1997; Fligstein 2001).

In modern legal terms the modern capitalist enterprise is a 'corporation' – that is, a 'fictional' legal entity comprising both legally 'natural' persons (individual shareholders, boards of directors, workers, managers) and also other 'fictional' legal entities such as pension funds, and insurance companies with ownership interests. As a legal entity, the corporation has rights and duties as do 'natural' persons. It can sign contracts, own property, pay taxes and so on. However, matters become complicated by the fact that the legal 'natural' persons who occupy the roles that comprise the legal fiction of the corporation not only have individual rights and duties, but also an 'interest' in the corporation – as a source of income and profit. Other fictional entities also have 'interests' – for example, a bank has an interest as a creditor.

We cannot pursue these issues in any detail here, but simply register how this complex corporate structure produces equally complex disputes which create pressure for continuous procedural and legal changes in response to the shifts in the balance of power between the different interests. Corporate rights and duties are ambiguous and constantly disputed. For example, shareholders are generally considered to be the legal owners of the corporation, but the individual shareholder does not actually 'own' the right to dispose of that part of the enterprise's *physical capital* represented by the share. Rather, the shareholder has the right to sell the share which in itself only represents a right to a share of the profits (dividend). However, the directors and incumbent managers decide, under pressure from these external ownerships interests, what the amount of dividends will be. In addition to this legal duty to create a profit for distribution to shareholders, corporate directors also have legal responsibilities to employees, regarding health, safety and pension rights, which are determined in continuous constant struggle. (As we shall see, financial entrepreneurs – 'corporate raiders' and 'private equity' – attempt to avoid this complexity and potential compromise of the pursuit of maximum profits by taking the publicly owned corporation back into private ownership, thereby placing it outside the constraints of public corporation law.)

In the modern corporation shareholders, bank creditors, managers and workers all strive to maximize their claim on the enterprise's assets and profits; if the conflicts are not resolved, or if one group gains overwhelming dominance and extracts too much revenue, the enterprise's capacity to produce a surplus can be impaired. Today these issues are generally referred to as the question of 'corporate governance' – that is, the system by which firms are controlled and operated, the rules and practices that specify the relationship between workers, managers and shareholders, and the overall process by which investment capital is allocated. 'Corporate governance' refers to the ongoing quest to produce an acceptable, but not necessarily equal, balance of power between the constituent interests that comprise the corporation (see the general discussion in Gospel and Pendleton 2004).

The struggle for control of the 'labour process'

The balance of power between capital and labour and the conflict over wages and salaries of workers and lower managerial levels within the enterprise are determined by external and internal factors. At a most basic level, the struggle over the enterprise's surplus is influenced by conditions in the wider product and labour markets. On the one hand, the enterprise's willingness to accede to wage demands depends on its ability to pay, which is, in turn, conditioned by the level of competition and the capital–labour cost ratio. Wages tend to be relatively higher in enterprises in monopolistic competition and in highly capitalized firms where wage costs are a small proportion of total costs – for example, in the petrochemicals industry. On the other hand, as we noted in chapter 5, the success of collective bargaining in raising wage levels obviously depends on the levels of unionization in an industry or sector.

Within the framework of these exogenous conditions, there exists a continuous struggle, between the managerial representatives of capital and workers, for control of the 'labour-process' – that is to say, how work is organized. In the discussions of Marx's fundamentally important distinctions between 'labour' and 'labour-power', we have noted that capital uses its power to control and manipulate the organizational and technological structure of work in order to increase the level of worker productivity – or, in Marx's terms, the rate of exploitation.

Braverman's celebrated elaboration of Marx's analysis, *Labor and Monopoly Capital: The Degradation of Work in the Twentieth Century* (1974), argued that division of labour and task specialization in the capitalist firm, especially the division into managerial functions and shop-floor labour, had involved a progressive separation of 'hand and brain' and a 'deskilling' of work. In this view, the way in which the production is organized is not simply and directly determined by available technology (see also Marglin 1974). Rather, technological development is driven by the need to control and subordinate workers by removing their autonomy and discretion. The more workers come to resemble readily interchangeable parts of the machinery that they operate, the more powerless they are to influence what is considered to be a 'fair day's work for a fair day's pay'. Thus 'scientific management', developed by F. W. Taylor in the early twentieth century, introduced 'time and motion' techniques by which all work tasks were reduced to the most simple and speedy movements and rigorously enforced by management. Subsequently, capital assumed total control of the pace of work with the continuously moving assembly line, first introduced on a large scale in Henry Ford's automobile plant, and epito-mizing the complete subordination of the worker.

Labour and Monopoly Capital stimulated an important debate on the nature of work in modern capitalism in which, for example, some critics argued that modern technologies such as computers have 'reskilled' rather than 'deskilled' workers. But it should be noted that these same technologies are a means of more intensive impersonal surveillance and control of the pace and quality of work in, for example, call centres and supermarket checkouts.

The fundamental dilemma for the capitalist enterprise of trying to reconcile the contradiction between the exercise of capitalist power and worker motivation is highlighted by this kind of control by technology. Management power is enhanced, but workers resent the loss of autonomy and they respond with strikes, industrial sabotage and a general with-drawal of cooperation. If the level of unemployment is high enough, managers can attempt to deal with this opposition with the threat of dismissal. Otherwise, depending on the levels of hostility and interference with production, managers are forced to modify this strategy for control. On the one hand, some control and discretion is returned to the workers by a modification of technology or an easing of the techno-logically determined pace of work. On the other hand, there is often a shift towards the use of ideologies which focus on the cooperative nature of work. In Burawoy's words, worker consent has to be 'manufactured' (Burawoy 1979).

For example, in reaction to overtly authoritarian 'Tay-lorism', the 'human relations management' conception of the enterprise as a socially interdependent system was introduced during the middle of the twentieth century in an attempt to foster a sense of work-group solidarity and identification with the firm. Such ideological control is most clearly evident in large Japanese and east Asian corporations, where the day can begin with the company song rendered by workers wearing insignia that display their level of productivity. As we have noted, it has been argued that modern capitalism is characterized by a 'new spirit', in which the critiques of capi-talist work have been paradoxically appropriated by manage-ment texts and used in an attempt to persuade workers that their labour is a source of fulfilment (Boltanski and Chiapello

2005; see also critiques of the organization of work in modern capitalism in Sennett 1998; 2006).

Corporate governance and the struggle between ownership and management

The emergence of large enterprises in the late nineteenth century, with their managerial bureaucracy and increasing reliance on external finance from bank loans and equity shares, brought about a degree of separation of ownership from day-to-day control. There have been two divergent interpretations of this development (see the discussion in Scott 1997). On the one hand, it was concluded that this expressed the dominance of capital in a more extreme, pure form of finance capitalism. On the other hand, others believed that share ownership was becoming so fragmented and dispersed into myriad holdings that it left managers in de facto possession of the corporation and diluted the dominance of money-capital.

Early investigations in the USA claimed to uncover an increased concentration of economic power. Attacks on the undemocratic character of the new 'big business' were endorsed by the US Senate's Pujo Committee (1913), which concluded that six closely connected New York banks had gained control of the major corporations (see Scott 1997: 105–14). A populist political backlash based on a complex alliance of rural conservative interests, the working class and small business led to legislation which was aimed at curtailing the power of the Wall Street banks and their links to the corporate monopolies (Roe 1994).

Following the further erosion of Wall Street's legitimacy after the 1929 crash, an alternative influential interpretation of corporate capitalism was proposed by Berle and Means in their classic study *The Modern Corporation and Private Property* (1932). Here it was argued that shareholding in the modern corporation was becoming so fragmented and dispersed that there could be no concentrated dominant external ownership interest. Consequently, the managerial hierarchy was left with considerable autonomy and de facto control of the day-to-day operation of the enterprise. Despite somewhat equivocal supporting evidence, it was nevertheless concluded that managers without a direct ownership stake in the corporation would act as the disinterested guardians of the 'people's' capitalism' that widespread shareholding was bringing about.[5]

However, this 'managerialist' attempt to re-legitimize capitalism continued to be challenged by Marxists and other critics, who approached the question differently by looking behind the data on dispersed shareholding. They claimed to uncover the existence of closely linked networks of banks, large majority shareholdings and some families, which continued to exercise a great degree of *strategic* control as opposed to day-to-day *operational* control of the modern corporation (Scott 1997; Stearns and Mizruchi 2005). As we shall see, developments in the 1980s clearly show how external money-capital is indeed capable of intervening in the routine operation of corporations if their interests are thwarted by management.

In continental Europe the 'managerialist' interpretation of the modern business enterprise was less influential due to the more obvious reliance on large bank finance – as portrayed in Hilferding's Marxist classic, *Finance Capital* (1981 [1910]). As we shall see below, bank-based external enterprise finance is also related to the persistence of family ownership to a greater extent than in the USA and a quite different configuration of interests and balance of economic power.

On balance, however, research in the USA during the 1960s and 1970s tended to support the 'managerialist' contention that control of the typical large corporation had shifted significantly away from outside financial interests – families, stockholders, banks – to the managers. A further indication that external financial and creditor interests had lost power during this 'Golden Age' of 'managed' monopoly capitalism after the Second World War was their falling share of the corporate surplus (Henwood 1997; Fligstein 2001). Echoing Keynes's 'euthanasia of the stockholder', J. K. Galbraith argued in his *New Industrial State* (1967) that the modern corporation was controlled by a managerial 'technostructure'. Unlike owners with a direct financial stake, managers did not pursue profit maximization, but, rather, focused on growth, sales and prestige in order to consolidate their power and security. The implicit message in such analyses was that this was a more socially responsible and effective way of organizing capitalism, as it ensured the steady production of goods and services and maintained high levels of employment.

During the 1950s and early 1960s, in a transformation of Marx's depiction of the classic capital–labour confrontation, an implicit 'producers' alliance' had developed between workers and managers for the maintenance of the long-term survival of the corporation and satisfactory levels of wages and salaries. Of course, conflict inside the enterprise did not disappear, but it was significantly diminished by the easing of the pressure ruthlessly to pursue profit-maximization and siphon off generous dividends to shareholders. At the time, this 'withering away' of strikes was attributed to the 'institutionalization' of industrial conflict – that is, to the collective-bargaining institutions (see the discussion in Ingham 1974). But it now seems just as likely that workers and managers in Western capitalism's large corporations had reached an acceptable deal based on a common interest – stability of employment and production and greater control of the surplus. This deal was also reinforced by governments' pursuit of full employment in the major capitalist economies (see chapter 8).

'The revenge of the rentier'

By the mid-1970s, however, a combination of falling profits, inflation, global recession and eventually a collapse of the stock market spurred money-capital interests to attempt to recover their lost dominance. This 'revenge of the rentier' involved a rebalancing of power between owner interests (creditors and shareholders), managers and workers (Smithin 1996; see also Glyn 2006; and the discussion in chapter 4). This shift was most apparent in the stock-market financial systems in the USA and the UK, where money-capital can more easily gain control of a publicly owned corporation through the purchase of its shares on the open stock market. But, as we shall see, as stock market finance becomes more widespread, similar changes are also beginning to take place in those continental European economies where bank debt has hitherto been the main source of external finance (see Lane 2003).

Since the 1980s pressure on the incumbent managers to 'unlock shareholder value' has come from a new class of 'financial entrepreneurs' who borrow heavily to purchase the number of shares necessary to gain effective control of publicly owned enterprises – that is, in a 'leveraged buyout' (LBO).

These entrepreneurs search for corporations which under-perform in relation to their assets and whose consequent falling share price makes them an attractive prospect for later resale at a large profit, after performance has been improved by rigorous cost-cutting by the new owners. In other words, as we have already noted, financial markets transform the enterprise itself into financial asset to be traded like any other commodity. These developments will be examined in more detail in the following chapter on the capital and financial markets; here we will focus on the consequences of their effect on the internal struggle over the enterprise's surplus.

Once a corporation has been brought back into concentrated private ownership in this way, an effort is made to align managers' interests with those of the new owners and shareholders by the use, among other methods, of 'stock options'. In addition to their salary, top-level executives are given the option to purchase their corporation's shares at an agreed fixed price. Consequently it is in their interest to strive to increase the stock-market price of their corporation's shares, exercise their option to buy the shares at the fixed price and sell them at a profit. With the top executives on side, the resulting private companies fell under the financial discipline of the new owners and controllers.

In the long term, profits and dividends to shareholdings and, as a result, the market price of the shares can all be increased through investment in physical capital and increased efficiency. But in the short term, financial entrepreneurs can achieve greater profitability by cutting labour costs and increasing what Marx would have called the 'rate of exploitation'. Workforces are 'downsized' and middle management 'de-layered', and the increased profits are channelled to stockholders, including the top executives. Finally, the consequent rising share price enables the financial entrepreneurs to sell their acquisition at a profit. In other words, 'an LBO (leveraged buy out) is a form of class struggle' (Henwood 1997) (see also the discussion in chapter 7).

During the second half of the twentieth century the pattern of share ownership in the mature economies had changed from individuals to the so-called 'institutional' investors – mutual funds pension funds and insurance companies. Like the financial entrepreneurs, they were also intent on maximizing returns, and 'shareholder activism' from this quarter further increased pressure on management and added complexity to the struggle for the corporation's surplus. On the one hand, the investment funds found a common interest with the financial entrepreneurs, but, on the other, some investors, especially pension funds, often opposed the increasingly high levels of top executive pay and the capture by private financiers of the corporations in which they had invested. Their pressure for greater scrutiny and control of executive pay has been reinforced by the corporate scandals in the early twenty-first century – Enron, Worldcom and others. In the USA companies are now required to report all aspects of executive remuneration to the US regulatory authority, the Securities and Exchange Commission. However, by 2007 fewer than 10 per cent of the largest had done so, but they provide a representative sample. Top of the list so far is Ken Lewis of Bank of America with total pay of $114.4 million in 2006 (*The Economist*, 24 March 2007). Given that real wages in the USA have stagnated over the past decade, there are concerns amongst capitalist elites that this growing inequality could damage 'social harmony' (*The Economist*, 20 January 2007).

There is considerable debate about the extent and significance of variations in the structure of corporate governance across the major capitalist economies and, by implication, the nature of the struggle for the surplus between the contending groups with an interest in the enterprise – workers, managers, banks, shareholders, private owners and so on (Coates 2000; Woolcock 1996; Gospel and Pendleton 2004; Story 2000; Goyer 2002; Vitols 2001; Lane 2003; see also the discussion of 'varieties' of capitalism, pp. 214–22). The details need not concern us here, but, as we have noted, the main differences in corporate governance are related to the mode of external finance – stock market or bank lending. The further question – whether a process of convergence towards the equities and securities of the Anglo-US model of corporate governance – will be considered briefly in our concluding chapter. Here we need simply to reiterate the main points of contrast.

In many economies where bank loan finance predominated, the struggle for the enterprise's surplus became stabilized in long-term settlements between labour and management. In a similar way to the temporary 'producers' alliance' in the post-1945 stock-market systems, both sides agreed that the major objective was to meet the interest payments on existing loans and to finance any expansion out of retained revenue, thus avoiding further indebtedness. In return for moderation in wage claims that might squeeze profits, workers are offered considerable employment protection in settlements by which both sides endeavour to secure the long-term survival of the enterprise to provide acceptable wages and salaries. This strategy is complemented by an emphasis on the maintenance of a highly skilled labour force to enable the enterprise to retain its market share (Estevez-Abe, Iverson and Soskice 2001). Germany exemplifies this mode of corporate governance in which the main interests – labour, management and finance – are formally represented on supervisory boards in enterprises with 2,000 or more employees (Lane 1989). Although there are significant differences which make simple classification difficult and possibly misleading, a similar structure is to be found in Japan and France (see, for example, Dore 2000; Amable 2003).

The ownership of capital and the political struggle

These differences and historical changes in corporate governance are related to variations in the wider political struggles that are common to all major capitalist societies (Roe 2003; Estevez-Abe, Iverson and Soskice, in Hall and Soskice 2001; see the debate in *Socio-economic Review* (2005) 3: 311–89; Dore 2000; Coates 2005).[6]

The Anglo-American type of large corporation, where diffuse stockholding has separated ownership from management control, would appear to coexist uneasily with the kind of social democratic politics which has brought about the high levels of employment security and welfare to be found in most continental European countries. So-called 'flexible' labour markets – that is, where workers have a low level of job security – gives shareholders confidence that, if market conditions dictate, costs can be cut and profits and dividends maintained by firing workers. Conversely, job security legislation which makes this more difficult inhibits extensive share ownership. However, this is not to say that all workers in 'flexible' employment systems are powerless. Under certain circumstances, as we have noted, diffuse and fragmented stockholding owners can be outflanked by an alliance of managers and workers in the large corporations of the modern oligopolies. Both benefit from the maximization of growth and employment rather than the maximization of profits and dividends, as occurred in the period after 1945 when managers and workers increased their share of the surplus. However, stock-market financial systems open up the possibility that the interests of shareholders and management can be aligned, as they were in the United States and Britain in the 1980s. This shift in the balance of power is also reflected in the politics of the wider society as governments, such as Thatcher's Conservatives in Britain, systematically reduce the workers' control over employment and job security, further giving confidence to shareholders that wage costs can be cut and dividends maintained.

On the other hand, the high levels of welfare, job security and controls on the capital market to prevent hostile takeovers in continental European social democracies encourage management to avoid conflict with labour and to define their interests in terms of security and the avoidance of risk and radical change in the company's activities. In France, Germany and Italy, as a counter to this implicit alliance of management, workers and social democratic governments, ownership has been more concentrated in the hands of banks and families (Roe 2003). For example, Germany's 'codetermination' representation of workers on the boards of German enterprises coexists with the exercise of strategic 'behind the scenes' control by informal networks based on banks, families and large shareholders (Roe 2003: 71).

Furthermore, the broader structure and balance of class interests and power have an impact on development of the different modes of external enterprise finance. In the USA, as we have noted, popular opposition led governments to curb the integration of banks and big business in the late nineteenth and early twentieth centuries, which stimulated a more widespread use of stock-market finance. Moreover, race and ethnic divisions, together with the anomalies of regional support for the Republicans and Democrats, meant that neither party would have been able to prosper with an electoral programme that appealed specifically to working-class interests by promising job security and social welfare (Roe 2003: 104–6). Consequently, once it was established, widespread shareholding could be maintained with the confidence that profits and dividends could be readily achieved if necessary by cutting labour costs.

Conversely, the rise of organized working-class politics in continental European countries during the twentieth century led to the decline of stock-market finance. For example, in 1913 stock-market capitalization in France, at 0.78 per cent of GDP, was greater than the USA's 0.39 per cent. However, by 1990 the figure for France had fallen to 0.24 per cent and that for the USA had risen to 0.54 per cent (Roe 2003: 69). The ascendancy of left-wing politics in France after the victory of the Popular Front in 1935 and the reconstruction of a popularly acceptable form of capitalism with extensive job protection, both here and in Germany, after the Second World War created a conception of citizens as 'stakeholders' in the enterprise. This is inimical to stockholder capitalism (Roe 2003: chs 7 and 8).

However, as we shall see in chapter 7, financial globalization, involving such developments as 'private equity', is exerting pressure on the social democratic pattern of employment rights and concentrated ownership by banks and families. Following the lead of the USA and the UK in opening up their economies to an inflow of capital during the 1970s and 1980s, the other major capitalist countries became involved in a process of 'competitive deregulation' of their capital markets in order to gain access to the supply of finance from global investment funds. Foreign investors look less favourably on those economies where workers continue to have significant property rights in employment and where concentrated bank and family ownership continues to exert a strong influence over corporate governance. With the intensification of global competition, global financial interests exert pressure to replace employment security and social welfare with economic 'flexible' labour market policies. The struggle over the fate of the post-1945 political settlement with labour has dominated politics in France and Germany since the 1990s. However, there is no inevitability about the outcome and both governments understandably continue to show equivocation and inconsistency in the face of these conflicting pressures (Held and McGrew 2007; Hay 2006).

Conclusion

The struggle for control of the capitalist enterprise between owners, managers and workers has changed in the advanced economies over the last fifty years or so. Direct confrontation between enterprise capital and workers over the distribution of profits and control of the organization and pace of work has abated and given way to more complex conflicts which have followed the increasing power of money-capital to buy, sell and restructure firms and corporations in order to extract a greater share of the surplus. In the past, these 'waves' of mergers and acquisitions have occurred in distinct phases – in the 1890s, the 1920s and the 1960s. However, since the latest began in the 1980s, the pace of corporate mergers and acquisitions has barely slowed, and it would now appear that continuous change of enterprise ownership is a routine feature of capitalism. The successful reassertion of money-capital's dominance of capitalism has been the driving force behind this secular trend and is both cause and consequence of the reduction of the power that organized workers in the major economies had gained during the twentieth century. Moreover, these shifts in the distribution of power have coincided with the intensification of global competition and the struggle by enterprises to maintain their market share through mergers and the acquisition of competitors. As we shall see in the following chapter, the so-called financial 'intermediaries' make vast profits from these deals. For example, the British mobile phone company Orange has changed ownership so many times that the fees generated for the banks and advisors involved have exceeded the company's historic revenues (Chancellor 2001a; 2001b).

Once the buying and selling of corporations reaches a certain momentum, any given company is increasingly forced to participate either to pre-empt being acquired or in order to compete with any newly merged rivals. In many ways, this transformation of the enterprise itself into a marketable commodity expresses the very essence of capitalism – that is, the ultimate subordination of all economic activity to the power of pure money-capital.

7
Capital and financial markets

Private property and wage-labour were present to some extent
in earlier economic systems, but, as I have emphasized, the
financing of production by capital markets and the existence
of large-scale speculative markets in financial assets are specific to capitalism (Schumpeter 1994 [1954]: 78).[1] Both activities are made possible on a large scale by the supply of
credit-money – that is to say, the ready availability of bank
created 'money-capital' by which capitalism is distinguished
from other types of economy.

Over the last twenty-five years or so financial sectors have
grown considerably in relation to the rest of the economy at
both national and global levels. Since the 1970s the US stock-
market valuation of financial corporations has increased
from less than 10 to almost 30 per cent of the valuation of
non-financial corporations. Over the same period, aggregate
financial corporations' profits in the USA have grown from
around 20 to over 50 per cent of those of non-financial corporations (Glyn 2006: 52). In the twenty-five years between
1980 and 2005, the stock of global financial assets grew from
109 per cent ($10 billion) to 316 per cent ($140 billion) of
global GDP, prompting discussion of 'financialization' as a
new stage of capitalism (Glyn 2006; Krippner 2005; Epstein
2005; Erturk et al. 2008; Wolf 2007; Morris 2008; see also
Blackburn 2006).

This expansion of the financial sector has been accompanied by a bewilderingly arcane complexity. Even participants struggle to comprehend the astonishing proliferation of specialized markets by which money is mutated, by what is known as 'financial engineering', into a complex array of ever-changing tradable financial assets and instruments. It is no longer simply a matter of stocks and shares, but also futures, options, 'swaptions', credit-default-swaps, derivatives and so on (for an accessible survey see Valdez 2003). The important 'derivatives' markets will be examined later; here we might briefly note that they are essentially forms of organized speculative gambling on price changes. The 'derived' financial asset is a contract (or wager) between two parties that the price of a commodity or asset (for example, copper or the dollar–euro exchange rate) at time x will be $y. The contracts are also traded; that is, they are bought and sold by third parties. Profits and losses are the result of the divergence, at the designated time, between the derivative contract price and the actual price of the commodity or asset from which it is 'derived'.

In attempting to unravel the complexities of modern capitalism's financial system, it is helpful to distinguish between 'money', 'capital' and 'financial' markets. The money market, as discussed in chapter 4, comprises the institutional creditor–debtor links between the state, the central bank and the banking system which coordinate the supply and demand for money – that is, a means of payment denominated in a money of account. This is the fundamental source of the money that fuels capitalism. The capital market comprises the institutions and organizations – stock markets, investment banks and so on – for transforming this supply of money into money-*capital* to meet the demand from producers for the financing of the production of goods and services. These are the *primary* markets in the sense that they are the basic means for generating the fundamental supply of money-capital for enterprise – that is, with the supply of the first 'M' stage in Marx's (M)oney $\rightarrow$ (C)ommodity $\rightarrow$ (M)oney$_1$ notation of the capitalist process.

As we have already noted, there are two main ways in which 'primary' money-capital for enterprise can be raised – by stocks and shares (equities) or debt in the form of bank loans and bonds on which interest is paid. Owners of stocks and shares receive revenues in the form of a 'dividend' from a 'share' of the enterprise surplus. In addition, as we shall see below, they may look for a profit from selling stock if the price on the secondary stock market increases. In this way, as we have noted, stock markets also transform the enterprise itself into a tradable commodity. By bidding for shares, it is possible to gain control of an enterprise even against the wishes of the incumbent management and directors – that is to say, by means of a 'hostile takeover' carried out, for example, by 'corporate raiders' and 'private equity' groups.

Money-capital can also be raised directly by a bank loan at a rate of interest that varies according to market conditions and the credit rating of the borrower. (However, as we saw in chapter 4, the rate of interest in modern capitalism is ultimately dictated by the rate at which the banks can borrow from the central bank to finance lending and balance their books.) Enterprises can also raise capital by the issue of debt in the form of a bond which specifies the date of repayment and usually fixes the rate of interest to be paid during the term of the loan. The increasing plasticity of fungible forms of money-capital in modern capitalism is apparent in the way in which enterprises can now raise capital by 'securitizing' their prospective revenue or profits.[2] Money is raised by selling the enterprise's future income – for example, a relatively dependable projected revenue stream such as rents, or interest payments on mortgages – as a 'security'. This form of finance has grown dramatically; for example, between 1998 and 2006 securitized issuance in Europe alone increased from 30 to 450 billion euros (*Financial Times*, 16 August 2007). (As we shall see, the securitization of US 'subprime' mortgages led to the global financial crisis during summer 2007.)

It has been suggested that such methods of raising finance have reduced the role of bank lending as the powerhouse of the capitalist system. Whilst it is true to say that *direct* bank lending as a primary source of finance might have declined relative to these alternative forms (for example, 'securitization'), it is entirely misleading to construe this as the 'death of banking' (Stearns and Mizruchi 2005). In the first place, the purchase of 'securitized' assets and other alternative finance is made with bank loans. But, more importantly, the banks' privileged access to central bank money – the ultimate source of the means of payment by which debts are settled – maintains their pivotal position. Central banks' links with their banking systems are the bedrock of capitalism. At times of financial crisis, money – that is, 'liquidity' – can be pumped into the banking system by central banks, as 'lenders of last resort', to prevent the total disintegration of the credit networks that hold the capitalist system together. This occurred in 2007 when the collapse of the UK mortgage bank, Northern Rock, was prevented with loans of over £30 billion that were underwritten by the UK Treasury (see pp. 167–9).

As we noted in the previous chapter, capitalist economies have varied quite considerably in the relative mix of stock-market (equity) and bank (debt) finance. One group of economies – comprising the USA, the UK, and those countries that were part of the British Empire – rely largely on the stock market. In contrast, continental European capitalist economies and late starters such as Japan use bank loans to a greater extent. The two modes of finance are, as we have seen, related to different enterprise structures of ownership and control and, consequently, different configurations of the struggle for its surplus between owners and incumbent managers.

As I have emphasized, it is a definitive characteristic of capitalism that all property, including raw materials, money-capital and physical capital, has a *dual* character – as a means of production and as a marketable 'financial' asset. *Secondary* markets are those in which these financial assets are traded with a view to making profits, not through the production and sale of goods and services, but from speculation on anticipated changes over time in the price of the asset – that is, $(M)oney \rightarrow (M)oney_1$, or the trading of pure exchange values. Profits can also be made by exploiting price differences between spatially separate markets – that is, by arbitrage. In 1995 the trader Nick Leeson famously brought down London's old elite investment bank Baring Brothers with the losses on his arbitrage trades between the Tokyo and Singapore foreign exchange markets.

Routinely, the shared expectations and strategies of the market participants in these secondary markets – arbitrageurs and speculators – maintain relatively stable prices for financial assets. However, speculative 'bubbles', in which large and rapid price rises are followed by precipitous falls, are an inherent and frequent feature of secondary financial markets in capitalism. Early financial crises in which asset prices inflated into 'bubbles' which then burst occurred in the Dutch 'Tulip Mania' of 1637, London's South Sea Bubble in 1720, and the Hamburg commodity price crash of 1799. Crises occurred every decade or so throughout the nineteenth century and as capitalism expanded and extended its global reach – 1907, 1929, 1974, 1987, 1990, 2001 and 2007 (see Kindleberger and Aliber 2005). The common denominator in all crises is the fact that 'bubbles' can only occur if easily available credit-money can be produced by a banking system. Crashes and panic occur when, for whatever reason, prices begin to fall and assets are sold to repay the debts that fuelled the speculation and to avoid further losses. As we have already noted, at this juncture central banks frequently step in to provide loans to the major banks in an attempt to keep the system intact.

Orthodox economic theory's 'efficient market hypothesis' maintains that the two markets – 'primary' for financing production and 'secondary' in speculative assets – are functionally integrated in a way that maximizes the efficient allocation of capital. First, on the assumptions of perfect information, perfect competition and rationality, it is argued that share prices in the secondary market accurately represent the prospective profitability of the enterprise (see the discussion of perfect competition in chapter 5). Thus money is drawn towards successful companies, driving up their share price and increasing their capital. Conversely, a falling share price acts as a spur to improve performance. In this conception of the capital and financial markets, 'bubbles' that disturb this orderly process are attributed to unexplained psychological traits – for example, 'irrational exuberance', as Alan Greenspan, the charismatic chairman of the US Federal Reserve, famously put it during the 1990s 'dot.com' boom (see Shiller 2000; Pixley 2004). However, as we have seen, both Keynes and Minsky argued that speculative bubbles were an inherent consequence of the normal functioning of capitalism. Secondary speculative capital markets are made possible by uncertainty – that is, the absence of perfect information about an enterprise's future profits.[3] Thus, as Keynes argued, capital markets have an inherent tendency to become unproductive 'casinos', diverting capital from enterprise and creating unnecessary price volatility and 'bubbles'.

Second, the 'efficient market hypothesis' implies that competition between capital market intermediaries – investment bankers, brokers, securities traders and so on – keeps their profits at a level that represents no more than their functional contribution to the process by which savings (money) is transformed into (money-)capital for productive enterprise. If brokers and investment bankers were to extract too much in the way of fees and commissions, they would be undercut – as the deregulation of the stock markets in the 'big bangs' of the 1970s and 1980s intended.[4] However, as we shall see, the actual structure of today's capital and financial markets does not conform to this model; rather, they are dominated by an oligopoly of investment banks which are able to use their power to control opportunities for profit in ways that some would suggest impair efficiency in the supply of capital (Augar 2006; Chancellor 2001a; 2001b).

Third, as we shall see shortly, modern economics' finance theory also argues that futures and other derivatives markets harness speculation with 'hedging', which creates price stability and, therefore, performs a positive function for the economy.

In what follows these general issues will be pursued in discussions of three important features of today's capital and financial markets: the stock market and the investment bank oligopoly; the new financial developments of 'hedge funds' and 'derivatives' markets; and a further examination of the buying and selling of the corporation in the mergers and acquisitions market. Finally, we shall take a brief look at the case of Enron's rise and fall as an example of how these new financial markets have become closely entwined in modern capitalism with the large business enterprise.

Stock markets and the investment bank oligopoly

Since the early development of markets for government shares in the early eighteenth century, stock markets have undoubtedly become one of society's most effective economic institutions for channelling finance into productive enterprise. But throughout the history of capitalism it has been persuasively argued that bankers, stock brokers and share dealers are not simply economic theory's 'neutral intermediaries' for the coordination of the supply and demand for capital. Since their appearance on the capitalist scene, it has been alleged that their position gives them the power to manipulate the market to their advantage (for a penetrating sociological analysis of the early-eighteenth-century London stock market, see Carruthers 1996; for a sociological study of Wall Street in the late twentieth century see Abolafia 1996).

There are two sources of profit-making for stock market intermediaries. First, stockbrokers and dealers charge commissions on the purchase and sale of stocks for clients – today, for example, the 'fund managers' of the large insurance and pension funds.[5] Second, investment banks can trade stocks and shares on their own account. These activities present the obvious potential for market manipulation. For example, dealers might buy shares cheaply, promote them and ramp up the price, or use information on imminent price changes that is not available to the public. In order to maintain trust in the markets, regulations and conventions have been developed to prevent such manipulation by the 'insiders'. However, stock market 'deregulation' during the 1980s and the growth of investment banks which combine the whole range of financial activities, including stock and share trading on their own account, would appear to have weakened these controls.

In the first place, as we shall see, dealers and investment banks are in a position to encourage and stimulate a high turnover of stocks and shares ('churning') in the secondary market purely for their own advantage, regardless of the wider economy's demand for primary capital (see Augar 2006). Since the 1960s the rate at which the US financial fund, in pursuit of short-term speculative gains, turns over (or 'churns') its entire portfolio has increased from once every five years to once a year (*Financial Times*, 18 October 2006).

'Insider trading' involves the use of privileged information – for example, the impending news of a takeover bid, or the declaration of an increased profits by a firm – by the market intermediaries to purchase shares, on their own account or through an accomplice, before they rise in price. Intentional 'insider trading' is universally prohibited, but for obvious reasons the regulatory authorities, on the 'outside', find it difficult to monitor and control. Britain's Financial Services Authority estimates that 'insider trading' is present in over 30 per cent of transactions on the London Stock Exchange (Dubow and Monteiro 2006). Such manipulation of the stock market has been a ubiquitous feature of capitalism, especially during investment booms when there is the greatest opportunity for profit-making – for example, in the South Sea Company 'bubble' of 1720, in the USA during the 1920s and again in the late 1990s 'dot.com' and 'new economy' bubble. Throughout the history of capitalism, the periodic public disclosure of opportunistic predatory manipulation of the financial markets has led to a serious loss of legitimacy of the capitalist system and has invariably set in motion a process of investigation and legislative re-regulation to repair the damage.

In his post-mortem on the 1929 Wall Street Crash, the lawyer Ferdinand Pecora discovered how the oligopoly of Wall Street banks had cooperated to their mutual advantage by ramping up the price of particular stocks (Chancellor 2001a; 2001b). Targeted stocks would be bought at a low price and then recommended by word of mouth and in the *Wall Street Journal*, raising their price and creating a profit for the banks. In addition, JPMorgan, for example, distributed stocks at below market prices to persons on its 'preferred list', including the former president Calvin Coolidge. Pecora's investigations led to the 1930s New Deal legislation which set up the Securities and Exchange Commission to regulate the capital market.

The investigation by the New York State attorney general, Eliot Spitzer, into the late 1990s information technology boom and crash revealed similar market manipulation (Augar

2006). Investment banks and brokers recommended the purchase of stocks to their investment fund clients (pension funds, insurance companies, wealthy private individuals) based on research conducted by the investment banks' own financial analysts. This created what is known as a 'conflict of interests' – or more prosaically, the possible exploitation of investors. Analysts' remuneration is determined by the amount of fees from the sale of stocks that they are able to generate for their own investment bank. Aside from 'churning', profits can be further increased by producing favourable reports on the investment potential of the shares of the investment bank's own corporate clients. A 1992 Morgan Stanley memorandum, for example, wished it to be 'fully understood by the entire firm, including the research department, that we do not make negative or controversial comments about a client as a matter of sound business practice' (Chancellor 2001b: 30). During the build-up to the information technology bubble in the early 1990s, the ratio of 'buy' to 'sell' recommendations made by analysts to investors rose from 6 to 1 to nearer 100 to 1 just before the bubble burst in 2000.

The late 1990s 'dot.com' bubble was also inflated, and with it the investment bank profits, by the promotion of new 'start-up' companies in which the banks had invested before they were offered in a public flotation of shares. These offers were again accompanied by their analysts' 'buy' recommendation. Chase Manhattan's disposal of its equity in an internet software company, Infospace, following flotation, realized a 7,000 per cent profit. As entirely new ventures, such internet companies had no histories on which to base sound judgements and, of course, many failed, bursting the bubble. But by this stage the investment banks had already realized their capital gains in addition to fees and commissions. The small investors, who had no access to the shares before their flotation and were not part of the insider network that received an allocation of shares at the point of issue, experienced the biggest losses when the market turned (Chancellor 2001a; 2001b).

Investigations into serious 'bubbles', such as 1929 and 2000–1, routinely uncover malpractice in the financial system – insider trading, false accounting and so on. And, without fail, it is concluded that this is the work of deviant individuals.

In other words, it is very strongly implied that the system is fundamentally sound and that any minor defects that permit malpractice must be corrected and the perpetrators must be severely punished. It is imperative that trust is restored in the 'headquarters' of the capitalist system. After Spitzer's investigation, remedial legislation was introduced and individual transgressors were successfully prosecuted. As if to show their serious intent, the icon of American respectable middle-class domesticity – the TV lifestyle presenter, Martha Stewart – was imprisoned for a relatively minor infringement of the rules for sales of stock. The Sarbanes-Oxley Act, 2002, introduced a requirement of greater transparency in the publication of information and measures to prevent the use of inside information. However, no attempt was made to deal with the concentration of power in the Wall Street bank oligopoly which many observers believe places them in a position to monopolize opportunities for profit-making, enrich themselves and, some would argue, exploit investors (Augar 2006).

However, the concentration of power at the upper levels of capital and financial markets is such that the major investment banks actually have no need to resort to illegal manipulation. As elsewhere in modern capitalism, these markets are dominated by an oligopoly whose constituent firms, by virtue of their large share of market activity and vastly superior information about investment opportunities, are in a structurally advantageous position. Even if all the rules and regulations that prohibit deliberate manipulation and insider trading are scrupulously observed, investment bank intermediaries have an edge over other participants.

> Wall Street's edge is knowledge and integration. The large investment banks know more than any other institution or organization about the world's economy. They know more than their clients, more than their smaller competitors, more than the central banks, more than Congress, more than Parliament, more than the Chancellor of the Exchequer and more than the Secretary of the United States Treasury. (Augar 2006: 107)

In addition to their own research departments, the flow of information from their clients to the tiny group of dominant

US investment banks – Goldman Sachs, Morgan Stanley, Merrill Lynch, Citigroup, and JPMorgan Chase – enables them to anticipate the direction and level of demand for investment assets (Augar 2006: 11). In other words, the oligopolists cannot avoid very quickly becoming aware which assets are about to trigger wider demand and therefore rising prices or, conversely, which are about to fall. (As investment banks are on both sides of market transactions – advising both buyers and sellers, they are set to gain whichever way the market moves.) Their structural location puts these dominant banks ahead of the other market participants. Arthur Levitt, chairman of the US regulatory authority Securities and Exchange Commission, likened the capital market to an auction in which the auctioneer bids whilst conducting the auction, or to a card game in which one player gets to see everyone else's hand (Augar 2006: 115). The pro-capitalist journal, *The Economist*, was similarly astonished:

> Goldman Sachs now finds itself on so many sides of a deal simultaneously that the mind boggles. Goldman's merchant bank arm competes with clients (and counts them as customers), and its proprietary arm may trade against them. At the same time as it represents a firm, it could be shopping for its sale, attempting to buy it for itself, or competing for an acquisition on behalf of another client. Occasionally – but only occasionally – these roles become so apparent that the conflict becomes public. (*The Economist*, 29 April 2006: 78).

As one would expect in the inner sanctum of the 'headquarters of capitalism', the profits of the Wall Street financial oligopoly reflect their power. Investment banking has 'outperformed the bulk of American industry by a country mile for over thirty years'; for example, profits in the American securities industry between 1975 and 2000 grew 26-fold, from $804 million to $21 billion – four times the rate of increase in corporate profits and US GDP (Augar 2006: 52). Signifying their dominance, investment bankers' remuneration – comprising salaries, bonuses and stock options – is, by a considerable margin, the largest in an increasingly unequal capitalist world. These 'predators' of Braudel's capitalist 'jungle' are able to control flows of money through the exchange networks and markets in such as way as to make enrichment an almost inevitable outcome (Braudel 1982: 30).

Since their emergence in the seventeenth century Italian city states, the controllers of the supply of money-capital at the apex of the financial markets have been the wealthiest and most powerful of all the capitalist classes. Little has changed since the Medicis and other bankers struck the 'memorable alliance' with the early modern states from which modern capitalism was born. Shortly before Christmas 2006, Lloyd Blankenfield, chief executive of Goldman Sachs, reported to the assembled partners on their company's record performance over the previous year. Earnings had risen by 70 per cent to $9.5 billion, providing for an average annual salary (excluding bonuses) of $620,000 for the staff of 26,000, and over $50 million for Blankenfield himself. Earlier in the year he had succeeded Hank Paulson, who had left the firm to become President George W. Bush's US Treasury Secretary, a position occupied by another Goldman Sachs chief executive, Robert Rubin, in President Bill Clinton's administration between 1995 and 1999. The firm has a long history of supplying the US government with personnel, but in November 2006 'the appointment... of Goldman Sachs's William Dudley to head the Federal Reserve Bank of New York market's group raised to an unprecedented level the number of top positions in public service that former executives from any one company have held during a White House administration' (*Financial Times*, 4 December 2006: 5).[6]

The enterprise as a commodity: mergers and acquisitions

With shares quoted on the stock market, the typical modern capitalist corporation is itself a marketable financial asset to be bought and sold. As we have already noted, the 'mergers and acquisitions' business is a central and growing part of the capitalist system. Once again, we see the same conflicting interpretations of the capital market. On the one hand, it is maintained that the threat of 'takeover' stimulates corporate management to greater efficiency and profitability in order to increase the share price, making the enterprise more expensive to acquire and thus reducing the probability of takeover. There are two counter-arguments, as Keynes implied in his analysis of the stock market (see pp. 45–7). First, it is held that the short-term concern with maintaining profits and share dividends can be at the expense of the longer-term development of technological innovation and efficiency. Second, it is argued that most acquisitions are by predatory financial capitalists who are motivated precisely by this strategy of increasing the short-term stock-market valuation of the corporation for a quick resale and profit. In this view, 'takeovers' and 'leveraged buyouts' are simply expressions of the conflict for the control of the enterprise's assets with no particular significance for economic efficiency.

In the previous chapter we discussed this question with regard to the intra-enterprise struggle; here we will focus on the financial entrepreneurs – the 'corporate raiders'. Fuelled by the availability of cheap bank credit, there were waves of acquisitions during the 1960s and 1980s in the major stock-market-based economies, in which large corporations were restructured and remarketed. Mergers undertaken by corporations wishing to increase their market share by the elimination of competitors frequently created a conglomerate structure comprising sectors and divisions of quite different levels of profitability. These proved to be attractive prey for financial entrepreneurs, such as Slater-Walker in 1960s Britain and T. Boone Pickens in the USA during the 1980s, who would search for those corporations which were potentially more valuable when disaggregated and sold in parts – that is, 'asset-stripped'.

After a lull during the 1990s the struggle for control of the enterprise's surplus has once again intensified with the advent of powerful associations of money-capitalists, known as 'private equity' groups – for example, Carlyle Group, Blackstone, Permira and a prominent 'corporate raider' from the 1980s, Kohlberg Kravis Roberts (KKR). These are consortia of wealthy individuals whose creditworthiness enables them to take out large bank loans in order to gain control of enterprises by hostile takeovers. Once control is achieved the companies become wholly privately owned. The value of these transactions has grown enormously. On 20 November 2006 the ownership structure of entire sectors of the major economies was reshaped in a single twenty-four hour period by a 'fever' of acquisition deals worth over $75 billion, 'highlighting the extent to which private pools of money are coming to dominate vast swathes of the global economy' (*Financial Times*, 21 November 2006: 17). By the end of 2006 the total of private equity buyouts had reached a record of $709 billion, more than doubling the 2005 level (*Financial Times*, 21 December 2006: 17). By early 2007 about 20 per cent of all private-sector workers in Britain were employed by private-equity-owned enterprises – for example, the Automobile Association, Birds Eye Food and Boots, which was bought, for $16.62 billion, by a consortium led by KKR, which also holds the current record for the most expensive buyout – $44.37 billion for the US energy and utilities giant TXU (*Financial Times*, Special Report, 'Private Equity', 25 April 2007).

Typically, private equity groups aim to increase the profitability and market value of an acquired company over a period of three to five years in order to sell it at a profit. It is claimed that between 1995 and 2005 private equity generated annual returns which were roughly double those from dividends in UK equities and also compared favourably with the other high-performing assets such as property (Froud and Williams 2007). Having bought out the shareholders and broken any alliance with the enterprise management, the increased profits remain entirely in the hands of the financial entrepreneurs, further increasing the trend towards the redistribution of the surplus away from wages and salaries to money-capital. For example, in 2006 the rate of return on capital in Britain rose to 15 per cent – the highest since data were first collected in 1965. In contrast, the share of national income received by workers is the lowest since the early 1980s (*Prospect*, May 2007: 9).

Private equity differs from the 1980s 'corporate raids' in that the acquisitions extend beyond the publicly owned corporations whose shares can be acquired on the stock market. Family businesses, not only in the USA and the UK but also in continental Europe, including Germany, are also targeted. This has led to suggestions that the historic differences between the stock market and bank-based financial systems might be further eroded by this latest shift in the perpetual struggle to extract and capture value from the capitalist process (Froud and Williams 2007).

This move towards private concentrated ownership represents a break with the twentieth-century trend towards management-controlled and publicly owned corporations in economies such as the USA and the UK (see the discussion in chapter 6). Supporters argue that it represents a return to a 'very pure form of capitalism' (*Financial Times*, 24 August 2004), which is 'in many ways a superior form of capitalism' (*The Economist*, 27 November 2005). The concentration of ownership and its reintegration with control that private equity brings is considered to be more efficient because it is no longer necessary to 'heed the demands of a wide range of stakeholders, employees, management, lenders, unions and politicians', which, it is contended, impedes the efficient allocation of capital (*Financial Times*, 3 February 2007: 15). In other words, power in the wholly privately owned is less diffuse and the prerogative of maximizing returns to capital can be ruthlessly followed. This is consistent with the classical economic liberal defence of private ownership as the means by which individual interest is harnessed to the public good. In support, an analysis of the thirty largest private equity deals carried out during 2003–4 claims that they resulted in an overall increase in employment (*Financial Times*, 2 April 2007: 3).

On the other hand, trade unions and other opponents of this concentration of power in the hands of private capitalists argue that any overall creation of work is merely a temporary departure from the general trend in which value is extracted in the short term by laying off workers and increasing the rate of exploitation in order increase the resale price of the company. The British GMB trade union points, for example, to CVC Capital and Permira's £1.7 billion acquisition of the Automobile Association in 2004 and the loss of 3,000 jobs, leading to a poorer service and a demoralized workforce (*Financial Times*, 2 April 2007: 3). Other opponents are concerned that the acquired enterprises become burdened with the massive bank debts with which they had been bought. By mid-2007 private equity had become a prominent political issue in Britain. Discontent was focused not so much on the consequences of highly concentrated ownership and the loss of the accountability of publicly quoted companies, but rather on the particularly favourable tax breaks enjoyed by private equity firms. Interest payments on the large debts used to finance the deals are tax-deductible, leading to charges that the private equity groups were paying less tax than the workers who cleaned their offices.

This shift towards more concentrated ownership is the latest episode in the fundamental three-cornered power struggle between (i) money-capital's drive to monetize profits in the shortest possible time-frame; (ii) the interests and demands of those engaged directly in the operation of enterprise; and (iii) the social need for goods and services. Each side has its theoretical support. On the one hand, it is argued that the flow of capital to where it will yield the greatest returns will produce the necessary dynamism and efficiency to ensure the continued production of the wealth of nations. On the other, it is claimed that this threatens security of employment and impedes the longer-term development of socially useful production.

However, the greatest danger posed by this development lies in the Achilles heel of the capitalist system – the enormous expansion of debt to finance the acquisitions and the ever present possibility of default. Although the alternative raising of finance by the sale of new shares on the stock market carries the risk that profits might not be sufficient for dividends to be paid, the company's existence is not necessarily under immediate threat; moreover, publicly quoted companies have only limited liability to their shareholders. However, the debt taken on by the company that is taken into private ownership involves a fixed monetary contract in which an inability to maintain interest payments can bring about the enterprise's demise. The recently acquired British company Boots, for example, might have struggled from time to time to distribute dividends and, consequently, lost some stock market value. But because it was bought with borrowed money, a lean period could now spell disaster for the company if it were unable to make its interest payments.

Financial risk management and speculation

We have already noted that a large part of the recent enormous expansion of the financial system has been due to the astonishing growth of speculative 'derivatives' markets and the volume of debt by which they are financed. Thirty years ago the global value of derivatives trades was less than $10 million, but by the early twenty-first century trading on these markets was estimated to be over $400 trillion and to be growing at 30 per cent per annum. To put this in perspective, the annual value of trading is now about thirty times greater than the gross domestic product of the US economy, which was $12.41 trillion in 2005 (Bank for International Settlements 2007).

Derivatives, in particular 'futures', developed out of techniques designed to reduce exposure to losses in commodity markets where the supply and, consequently, prices were subject to unpredictable fluctuations – for example where the supply of agricultural crops is determined by the vagaries of the weather. In response to this uncertainty, markets in agricultural commodities became organized around 'forward' and/or 'option' contracts to buy or sell a particular crop, ahead of the harvest, at an agreed price. For example, an orange-juice producer might contract with an orange grower to buy oranges at a certain price in order to be able to produce the juice at a calculable cost and to deliver it to the retailer at an agreed price. With changes in weather conditions, the anticipated, contractually agreed 'future' price could diverge from the actual price at harvest. Consequently, the original contract of the 'future' price becomes marketable as a speculative asset during the period up to the actual harvest. Eventually, these assets were organized into futures markets – such as the Chicago Mercantile Exchange and Board of Trade (1849) – in which the futures contracts to buy or sell a particular commodity at a certain price at a stated date were traded. In short, speculators were, in effect, gambling on the rise or fall of commodity prices and their deviation at the stated date from the price specified in the futures contract. However, such speculation is only possible in markets with a particular organizational structure.

In the simplest terms, futures markets comprise three players – *hedgers*, *speculators* and the intermediary *market-makers* who organize the trades in the contracts between hedgers and speculators at the commercial exchange. The market enables the producers of orange juice, who have agreed to supply orange juice at a certain price, to hedge the risk of a rise in the price of oranges by buying an orange futures contract which specifies a conjectural 'future' price of oranges at the time of the harvest. Speculators buy futures contracts in the expectation of price changes. If the price of actual oranges rises above the contract price, the hedging juice producer's potential loss in selling to the supermarket at the agreed price is offset by a precisely compensating gain when the futures contract is settled. Conversely, if the price of oranges falls, the hedger's loss on the futures contract is offset precisely by the ability to produce juice more cheaply than anticipated because of the orange's fall in price.

The largest of all derivative markets is now in foreign exchange, where importers and exporters can hedge the considerable risks which accompany rapidly increasing levels of international trade in a regime of floating exchange rates. Exchange-rate fluctuations and interest-rate changes present an enormous potential for speculative derivative trading. In the space of twenty years these markets have grown from a marginal position in the capitalist system to a volume of business that is equivalent to six times the value of the global gross product (*Financial Times*, 19 June 2007: 13). The expansion was triggered by the enormous increase in economic uncertainty unleashed by the collapse of the Bretton Woods semi-fixed exchange-rate regime in the early 1970s (see pp. 209–11). The subsequent floating and rapidly fluctuating exchange rates created both the need for hedging and the opportunity for speculation. Advances in computerized information and communication technology have further accelerated the development of these basic techniques of risk management.[7]

It is widely held that these markets harness otherwise unproductive speculation to the effective management of 'market risk' – that is to say, the unpredictable price changes that disturb the calculation of costs and profits. Without the willingness of speculators to buy derivative contracts, producers and traders would not be able to hedge the 'risk' and, therefore, it is argued that speculation plays a positive function. As a means of dealing with the consequences of the uncontrollable uncertainty, derivatives markets could be considered, from this perspective, as an example of the progressive rationalization of economic life that Weber identified as one of the central characteristics of modern capitalism.

On the other hand, it is contended that high levels of speculation increase price volatility and can also distort the market for commodities. During 2006–7, for example, energy prices for consumers remained high despite falling wholesale spot prices because energy suppliers had bought heavily in the futures market. In other words, energy suppliers were not merely hedging but also speculating (see the discussion of Enron below). Speculation in the oil futures market during 2008 would appear to have accelerated considerably the rate of increase in the price of crude oil (*Financial Times*, 21 May 2008). More importantly, hedging and speculation, like all capitalist activities, are financed by borrowing which carries the danger of 'credit risk' – that is to say, default and the failure to honour the futures contract. It is feared that a large default might trigger a chain reaction, causing disruption not only to the financial markets, but also to the wider economy if a process of debt deflation sets in. In 1998 such fears prompted the US Federal Reserve to put pressure on Wall Street banks to rescue the hedge fund Long Term Credit Management after its collapse following Russia's default on its sovereign debt.

However, the possibility of default is also dealt with in the arcane world of modern capitalist markets with the same financial technology. 'Credit risk' – that is, the risk of default – is also 'commodified' with its own 'credit derivative'. A 'credit-default-swap' (CDS) enables banks to sell the risk of default by a borrower to a speculative investor. As the buyer of risk protection, the bank pays the seller of protection (speculator) a periodic fee in return for the seller's contract to pay its borrower's debt in the event of default. To spread the risk further, such credit derivatives are sold on to other investors as 'collateralized debt obligations' (CDO). Selling on risk in this way lowers the banks' own risk profile, permitting them to lend even more, further increasing the amount of credit in the system to finance more derivative speculation. These financial assets were virtually unknown a decade ago, but midway through 2006 their amount outstanding had grown to $26 trillion (*Economist*, 23 September 2006: 83–5).

As we have noted, the rapid growth of derivatives markets has been driven by 'hedge-fund' investment.[8] Typically, like their private-equity cousins, these consist of small private associations of extremely wealthy individuals which are constituted in such a way as to operate largely outside the range of financial regulatory authorities, such as the US Securities and Exchange Commission and the UK Financial Services Authority. The creditworthiness of the wealthy members enables them to borrow up to more than twenty times the value of their own stake from commercial banks to finance speculation. Although difficult to estimate, the hedge funds' pool of assets placed on the derivatives markets has grown at truly astonishing speed to an enormous size – from $257 billion in 1996 to $1.2 trillion in 2006 (*Economist*, 1 July 2006).

It is not perhaps surprising that hedge fund managers, dealing in such enormous sums of money, are able to award themselves commensurate salaries. In 2005, the average annual salary of the top twenty-five hedge fund managers rose by 45 per cent to $363 million; at the top of the list were James Simons of Renaissance Technologies ($1.5 billion), T. Boone Pickens of BP Capital Management ($1.4 bn) and George Soros of Soros Fund Management ($840 million) (*Financial Times*, 26 May 2006). In contrast, a typical chief executive officer of a top-500 US corporation in 2004 earned a mere $10 million (*US Institutional Investor Magazine*, 2005).

As in the primary capital market, discussed earlier, finance for derivative trading comes not only from newly created bank debt but also from existing pools of savings to be found in the large private pension and insurance company funds of the mature capitalist economies. The greater demands placed upon them by the increasing average human lifespan and the growing propensity for damages litigation have led these institutions to make a relative shift from equities and bonds to the higher yielding, but more risky, derivatives. This linkage connects the everyday lives of the mass of the population to capitalism's very apex and is considered, as we shall see, to present an increased possibility that a serious contagious systemic financial crisis could permeate the entire economy with the loss of savings and pensions (Blackburn 2006).

As ever, opinion is sharply divided on the question of the net balance between the positive and negative aspects of speculation. Does financial speculation create destabilizing price volatility and uncertainty, or is it, somewhat counter-intuitively, a vitally important tool for risk management in an uncertain world? Defenders of the markets point to the reduction of deep financial crises since the 1970s and 1980s and the fact that hedge funds have collapsed and defaulted on their debts without causing serious dislocation. In short, this view believes that economic techniques can solve the fundamental problem of economic uncertainty. It is conceded that spectacular losses can lead to the collapse of individual market participants – the bankruptcy of Orange County, California, in 1994 after a loss of $1.6 billion on derivatives trading, Nick Leeson's loss of $1.4 billion on currency futures and the demise of Barings in 1995, and the collapse of Long Term Credit Management in 1998. Such events are to be expected, it is argued, but, as a consequence of increasingly sophisticated credit-risk management, the defaults did not spread contagiously throughout the financial system and into the economy as a whole. On the contrary, the most serious casualty at the time of writing, Amaranth, lost over $6 billion in natural gas speculation in 2006 and left the scene with debts of perhaps $30 billion without causing anything more than the slightest ripple in the financial markets.

None the less, the regulatory authorities in the USA and the UK show increasing apprehension, shared by the otherwise staunchest supporters of capitalism, that the size of the debts incurred in derivatives speculation does pose a serious threat. Were 'hedge funds the flawed product of a freakish cycle', the *Financial Times* asked in 2006 (*Financial Times*, 14/15 May 2006). A US Republican senator has called them 'the "Wild West" of the financial system' (*Economist*, 1 July 2006), and in his 2002 annual report Warren Buffet, the charismatic head of US investment company and hedge fund Berkshire Hathaway, referred to them as 'financial weapons of mass destruction'. Financial authorities are concerned that the hedge funds' debts are becoming too large to manage and that the level of concentration in the banking oligopoly makes it especially vulnerable to a large default. Over the past twenty years the five largest US banks, for example, have doubled their share of the total banking system's assets, to 45 per cent. Moreover, the banks are not only the source of the finance for hedge funds banks but also the holders of derivative contracts in which one party must lose as the price of the underlying commodity changes. The largest five US banks hold 95 per cent of the total stock of derivatives and JPMorgan Chase holds more than half the total; this 'changed financial landscape may be eroding resistance to systemic risk' (*Financial Times*, 16 February 2005).

Credit-derivatives *manage* risk, but they do not and, indeed, cannot *eliminate* the possibility of default; rather, they merely spread and move the debt around. In essence, the avoidance of a chain reaction of defaults and possible systemic crisis leading to an economy-wide debt-deflation depends, as always, on the availability of further credit-money to bail out the failing debtors. Ultimately, this can only be provided successfully, directly or indirectly, by the state's central bank, as has occurred in recent times, for example, during the UK's secondary banking crisis (1973), the USA's Savings and Loan collapse in the 1980s, Long Term Credit Management's rescue in 1998, and, most recently, in the US 'subprime' mortgage crisis and its spread to the mortgage bank Northern Rock, causing the first 'bank run' in Britain for over 150 years.[9]

During August 2007 asset prices fell dramatically on the global capital and financial markets as a result of defaults on credit derivatives and securitized loans on the US 'subprime' housing mortgage market – that is to say, loans to high-risk borrowers. Lenders hedged their credit risk in the derivatives market and also securitized and sold on their mortgage contracts. This encouraged even greater risk taking by the extension of loans to progressively lower-income groups. Again, we see the contradiction between individual rationality and system instability, as observed by Keynes in his analysis of the stock market. The lenders were rational in selling their individual risk of debtor default, but this increased the aggregate threat to the financial system. As the securitized mortgages had been widely trading on impenetrably complex global markets, it was almost impossible to identify which banks and financial enterprises had been left holding the defaulted debt. This further reduced confidence in the markets, and investors in such instruments tried to divest themselves of the risk by selling the assets. Consequently, the credit derivatives and securitized mortgages became 'illiquid' (unsaleable) and the contagion spread to other asset markets, including the major stock markets, and eventually to the very core of the financial system – that is, to the money markets in which banks lend to each other. Banks became reluctant to lend for fear that the borrower might be holding vulnerable credit derivatives and securitized mortgages. Consequently the rate of interest on these inter-bank loans increased significantly and the supply of credit-money – the lifeblood of the capitalist system – began to dry up in a credit 'squeeze' or 'crunch'. To avoid a deflationary impact on the economy, the major central banks (the US Federal Reserve, the European Central Bank and the Bank of England) extended loans to their banking systems. Many major banks reported having to write off bad loans and announced large losses. At the time of writing the crisis has produced only two major casualties – the British mortgage bank Northern Rock and the Wall Street investment bank Bear Stearns. But almost all the major investment banks had suffered large losses.[10] By early 2008 a significant slowdown was being forecast for those mature capitalist economies most closely linked to the credit crisis, and the emergence of a full-scale debt deflation was by no means discounted.[11]

The 'financialization' of modern capitalism in the sense of the increasing dominance of financial practices and the fusion of business enterprise with 'financial engineering' was evident in the spate of corporate scandals that occurred around the turn of the twenty-first century at the time of the collapse of the 'dot.com' boom. As usual, the subsequent investigations offered the public a rare glimpse into the upper reaches of the capitalist system.

The Enron affair

The fall in disgrace of the US Enron Corporation in 2001 gives us some idea of the complexity of the relations between the investment banks and corporations and of the way in which derivatives markets have begun to blur the separation of the spheres of production and purely financial transactions.[12] With the successful prosecution of the chief executives for fraud, Enron's demise was widely portrayed as the result of the corruption and dishonesty of individual 'bad apples'. However, as we have noted with regard to the Wall Street investment banks, it is important not to lose sight of how the structure and practices of the financial system in which these individuals operated enabled their particular kind of malpractice to occur at the very highest levels of the US economy.

Enron was named 'America's most Innovative Company' by *Fortune Magazine* for six consecutive years in the 1990s, and, until the loss of jobs and pensions, its 21,000 employees were in one of the magazine's list of '100 best companies to work for in America'. Enron recorded revenues of over $100 billion in 2000, but eventually it was revealed that the company, with the connivance of its auditor Arthur Andersen, had been able to keep its staggeringly high losses and enormous debts off its published balance sheet. On this disclosure, the price of Enron's stock dropped from $90 to 30 cents and it filed for bankruptcy on 2 December 2001 with over $40 billion of debts. Inquiries not only revealed insider trading, bribery and corruption; they also showed how some investment banks operate and the resulting pervasive influence of financial practices.

Enron was formed in 1985 as a Texas-based corporation involved in buying and distributing gas and electricity and in the construction and operation of energy infrastructure – pipelines, power plants and so on. Like other suppliers, Enron hedged its trades in the new energy derivatives markets, but it did so to such an extent that by 1999 its original pipeline business had been drastically reduced and the company had set up its own web-based energy derivatives trading system, Enron Online. By the time of the collapse, Enron was trading over 800 commodities and derivatives – metals, forestry, weather risk management, sugar, coffee and, most significantly, credit-risk management and the buying and selling of corporations in the 'mergers and acquisitions' business. In effect, Enron had left the sphere of production and distribution and had transformed itself into a financial firm, pursuing 'liquidity' in 'M-M' deals. 'Monetize. That was the buzzword', a senior Enron executive later explained to the investigators (*Financial Times*, 1 March 2002: 28).

After Enron abandoned its energy distribution pipeline businesses and lost their cash revenues, it required vast loans from the Wall Street investment banks to finance its derivatives and mergers and acquisitions business. In 2000 alone, Enron paid more than $250 million in fees – in addition to the interest on loans – to banks, including Credit Suisse First Boston, Merrill Lynch, Chase, Citigroup, and JPMorgan. According to one of them, Enron was the 'golden goose' (*Financial Times*, 1 March 2002: 28).

The key to Enron's continued expansion, and with it, of course, the profits of the Wall Street investment banks, was the continuous rise not only of its own stock-market valuation but also, after the deals had been done, of the shares of the corporations it had acquired for resale. Not surprisingly, Enron's investment bank creditors consistently recommended these stocks as 'strong buys'. Indeed, brokers at Credit Suisse First Boston and Lehman Brothers continued with their positive recommendation to the markets until only a few days before Enron filed for bankruptcy (*Financial Times*, 1 March 2002: 28). As Enron's stock price rose to its peak of $90 in early 2001, its executives, who knew of the hidden losses, began to sell their stock and, at the same time, reassured the public that any falls were temporary and that prices would rise to the $130 to $140 range. The investing public and Enron's employees suffered the consequences of the deception.

Further malpractice was revealed after the collapse of other large US companies – such as Worldcom – in the wake of the bursting of the 'dot.com' financial bubble in 2000. As we noted, scandals set in train a process of re-legitimization, including the Sarbanes-Oxley legislation which was intended to increase the disclosure of company accounts and executive activities in order to repair the damage to public trust in US capitalism.

Conclusion

Typically, the initial phase that inaugurates the capitalist production of commodities is the raising of finance in the primary capital market. On the basis of an assessment of the prospects of enterprise profitability in accordance with accounting conventions, banks have the power to create the supply of money-capital for its finance, either directly in the form of bank loans or indirectly for the purchase of equities. In capitalism, whether or not production takes place rests largely on the decisions made by Schumpeter's 'merchants of debt'. Of course, their power is not absolute and ultimately depends on the continuation of a steady flow of revenues from profitable enterprises to cancel the debts. None the less, it is the capital market, not merely retained profits, which inaugurates and fuels the dynamic expansion of the system.

All opportunities for the realization of profits – that is to say, prospective profits – from all forms of capitalist activity can be transformed into speculative financial assets. Pure speculation adds nothing directly to the production of commodities, but, by providing the capital and financial markets with a supply of money, it confers the liquidity and fungibility of all assets. In turn, liquidity and fungibility give capitalism a flexibility which reinforces its inherent dynamism. Capital can be transformed into money and switched to whatever and wherever the prospects of profit seem greater. Sustained, long-term economic expansion has never taken place without the existence of extensive capital and financial markets (Rousseau and Sylla 2006).

However, the relation of money-capital with production is not simply a matter of the smooth functional transfer of finance to the most profitable destinations, as it is in the economic 'circular flow' model. There is also a negative side to the links between these two fundamental elements of the capitalist economy. First, the power of money-capital and the quest for liquidity can result in the extraction of capital from the production of goods and services and employment and the pursuit of pure, particularly speculative, financial transactions. The profitability of pure financial exchange might divert money-capital from the production and sale of goods and thereby deplete the revenues which are necessary to service the debt that finances the production, as we have seen in the 'private equity' debate. Second, the dynamism and flexibility provided by capital markets and readily produced credit money is necessarily accompanied by the possibility of collapse and stagnation. In other words, the corollary of debt-financed expansion is default and the unravelling of the credit networks that sustain it. Speculative derivative markets have been harnessed to the attempt to avoid this outcome, but the credit-default-swaps and other instruments cannot resolve the contradiction. This supposed solution involves an infinite regress in which further debt is created to finance the credit derivatives. As we have noted, the effects of defaults in the US subprime mortgage market that began in summer 2007 were still being felt in summer 2008. Billions of dollars of financial assets were being written off by US and European banks as the securitized mortgages and credit-default-swaps became 'illiquid' – that is to say, unsaleable depreciating assets. This reduced the banks' capital base and impaired their capacity to lend to each other and to their borrowers. Moreover, the anonymous, impersonal nature of the securitization market made it difficult to ascertain which banks were most affected, which further reduced trust and confidence.

Capital and financial markets comprise the powerful nerve centre of the capitalist system in which the creation of money-capital and its deployment is controlled by the investment banks and financial enterprises. However, these markets cannot be seen simply as channels for the efficient transmission of savings to the most profitable destinations and their operators merely as neutral 'intermediaries'. From sixteenth-century Italy to the City of London and Wall Street today, bankers and financiers have been the wealthiest and most powerful members of the capitalist classes.[13] As a result of record hedge fund investment in 2006, 'the combined earnings of the world's top 25 hedge fund managers of almost $15bn exceeded the national income of Jordan'. Three individuals took home more than $1 billion and average earnings of the top twenty-five more than doubled between 2004 and 2006 to $570 million (*Financial Times*, 24 April 2007: 1). There is no evidence to suggest that this level of remuneration is determined exclusively by their functional contribution to 'transactions efficiency' in the financial markets. That is to say, the current trend towards 'financialization' once again raises the question for which there is no clear answer. How are developments in the structure of capitalism to be explained? In this instance, do financial asset markets simply represent the solution to economic problems for which their operators receive a commensurate reward (see Rajan and Zingales 2004)? Or do money and finance capitalists have the power to create instruments and practices of self-enrichment? Regardless of any other consideration, Adam Smith's argument that private individual profit-seeking resulted in the public benefit of economic growth depends on the existence of a high level of market competition. And, as we have seen, this condition scarcely applies in modern capitalism.

Discussions of the emergence of 'financialization' as a new stage in the development of capitalism tend to overlook the fact that the guiding principle of capitalist activity has always been 'liquidity' – that is, the sequential transformation of all assets into money, back again into assets and so on (see the discussion in Arrighi 1994: 2–4). Previous eras have also seen rises in the relative dominance of finance, but they have never before been on such a scale. On all these occasions and especially today, the expansion of finance in relation to production has been accompanied, as we have noted in passing, by a significant rise in inequality, which has reversed the egalitarian trend of the second half of the twentieth century (Phillips 1993, 2002; Duménil and Lévy 2004a). This question will be taken up in our concluding chapter.

8
The state[1]

The two logics of power

One of capitalism's distinctive characteristics lies in the particular historical coexistence and mutual dependence of two kinds of power: private economic power from the control of property and opportunities for profit-making, and the coercive territorial power of states. The question of the proper relationships and boundaries between the two has been continuously disputed since the moment in early modern Europe when this private economic power, having been nurtured and protected by the developing states, became sufficiently strong to demand greater freedom in its pursuit of profit. *The Wealth of Nations*, it will be recalled, was Smith's rebuttal of state-centred mercantilist economic doctrines. He argued that the material advance of civilization required the liberty to pursue commerce without interference and competition from the state.

Relations between market-capitalism and the state express the interaction of these two interdependent, but different, 'logics' of power and space (Arrighi 1994: 32–5; Tilly 1990). On the one hand, power can be based on the direct control of the territory in which human and material resources are to be found. After a calculation of the costs of acquisition in relation to the putative benefits of possession, power can be increased through conquest of the space which contains the resources, followed by their direct extraction, using forced labour and taxation in kind or money. On the other hand, power can be increased by the use of money-capital to control, exploit and expand chains of production and commerce without acquiring the territory in which they are to be found. This can be undertaken by private interests, by states or by close cooperation between the two. In mercantilism, 'the state is handled as if it consisted exclusively of capitalistic entrepreneurs' (Weber 1981 [1927]: 347). However, a state's mercantilist policies can and frequently do conflict with private capitalism's pursuit of profit as an end itself. As long as the world is pacified to the degree necessary for pursuing profits, capitalists place self-interest before statecraft and nationalism.[2]

As we shall see in the following chapter, current debates on globalization are essentially about the latest intensification of the ongoing conflicts and mutual dependence between capitalist controllers of economic resources and the states between and through which the resources are situated and flow. To take a simple example: transnational corporations sometimes prefer to locate in states with low levels of taxation, yet at the same time expect them to have sufficient revenues to maintain social order, security, the quality of human capital and infrastructural services.

As Weber astutely observed, empires which aim closely and directly to control economic activity within the conquered territory are inimical to dynamic capitalism. Whilst the British exploited their imperial possessions, they did so by allowing private capital to develop their economies. In this regard, for example, Hitler's failed imperial project was anachronistic. The German Reich was to control directly all the resources of the conquered states, not with the primary intention of expanding and developing them, but rather to extract their wealth in order to strengthen the Fatherland.

Today there is much discussion of whether the world's capitalist superpower has an 'empire' (Mann 2003; Ferguson 2005; Hardt and Negri 2001; Wade 2003). The USA's territorial possessions are very small compared with those of Rome and Britain, but its domination of the global economy is arguably even greater. In particular, the use of the US dollar as a de facto world currency gives the USA, its Wall Street investment banks and transnational corporations great wealth and power (Gowan 1999; Wade 2003). However, because the two spheres of the US state and private capital remain relatively autonomous, their interdependencies are potentially contradictory. For example, Wall Street investment banks might take opportunities to make profits on the foreign exchange markets which result in an unwelcome dollar exchange rate, and global outsourcing by US transnational corporations can perturb domestic politics.

The power of private money-capital emerged out of the particular geopolitical conditions in early modern Europe which had produced a delicate balance between these two logics of power, both *within* and *between* states. The 'memorable alliance' was forged at the pivotal point in time when, on the one hand rulers, in pursuit of their state-building, had need of, but were not capable of controlling or expropriating, the merchants' wealth, and, on the other hand, when the early merchant-capitalists calculated that protection costs were best borne by states. Moreover, the territorial competition that produced the early modern European state system was a basic driving force behind the adoption of national debt as a means of financing military expenditure (see chapter 4). As we have already noted, this gave each side – state and capitalist bourgeoisie – an interest in the long-term survival of the other and, eventually, created the capitalist banking system. In return for their investment in the state debt, the capitalists received protection for their ventures and interest payment on their loans. Marx's conclusion that the state was now owned by bourgeoisie is an exaggeration, but the new 'fiscal constitution' did represent a dilution of the power of monarchical feudal states.[3]

These developments produced capitalist society's typical social structure of two relatively autonomous but interdependent spheres – state and economy.[4] In general terms, the state supports and maintains the economy which, in turn, produces the wealth which supplies the loans and taxes with which the state provides the support. This relationship between the state, its creditors and, eventually, its taxpaying and enfranchised citizens is specific to capitalism and remains an axial link between state and society. On the one hand, as we have seen, the state's creditors fear that state spending will fuel inflation and erode their investments, whilst the state agencies and the government need to finance their activities and, after the advent of mass representative democracy, retain popular support. On the other hand, although inflation reduces the real value of their debt, the pursuit of an inflationary strategy would soon be counterproductive. Creditors would withdraw financial backing, weakening the state and causing it to lose legitimacy, as the history of many Latin American democracies clearly shows.

There are three main areas of state activity in relation to the economy. The first and least contentious role is to provide physical security and a degree of social order which permits peaceful economic activity. Second, states implement and enforce the legal rights by which the different economic agents are constituted (as property owners, employees and so on) and the procedural rules by which they conduct their exchanges. Despite their differences, Smith and Marx were agreed that the safeguarding of property rights was a linchpin of the capitalist system. Third, the state's direct participation in the economy is its most contested activity. As we have seen, Smith argued that the market economy was self-regulating and required very little direct involvement by the state. It should provide only those goods that for one reason or another private enterprise was unwilling or unable to undertake – that is, 'public goods'. However, capitalism has proved to be a chronically unstable form of economy – prone to crises and stagnation, as Marx, Keynes and others explained. Consequently the state's involvement in the economy has gradually extended in scope to include macro-economic stabilization (growth and employment), attempts to deal with 'market failure' and so-called 'externalities', and – most importantly – to act in concert with its central bank as lender of last resort to control financial crises.

The neo-liberal 'public goods' theory implies that the level and scope of state activity can be optimally fixed by economic cost–benefit analysis (see chapter 5). In effect, it is argued that state intervention in the market economy can and should be determined by its 'marginal efficiency' – that is to say, state involvement in the economy should continue to the 'margin' where costs and benefits are in balance. For example, the level of state expenditure on welfare and education should be assessed in terms of its impact on the quality of 'human capital' and the efficiency of the labour force. Aside from the enormous technical difficulties that this poses for economic analysis, there are more fundamental reasons for rejecting this understanding of the state's role. First, given the existence of finite resources, this exclusively economic logic presupposes a consensus on the rank order of the whole range of 'public goods' and 'externalities' – education, defence, welfare, transport, environment pollution and so on. Each public good, for example, would then be provided to the point at which costs and benefits were in balance. This is not unattainable in principle, but such agreement is highly unlikely in the context of the competing claims in a modern representative democracy. But, more importantly, the ends pursued by states can become ultimate values which cannot be determined by cost–benefit analysis. For example, education, health and social welfare do not merely have an impact on the economic efficiency of 'human capital', but are intrinsically desirable human wants. In short, the question of state–economy relations is not merely a technical economic question; politics is involved at every juncture.

Furthermore, economic liberals maintain that the state can be 'captured' and used by economic classes and agents to pursue sectional interests which increase government expenditure beyond its 'marginal efficiency', impeding the private sector's creation of wealth. For example, 'public choice' theory argues that state officials have an interest in maximizing their sector's bureaucratic power by expanding the scope of state activity and that this leads them to support demands for the goods and services that they provide – transport, welfare and so on (Tullock 1987a). More generally, economic liberals believe that democratic politics can place too many demands on the state to the detriment of the economy. Investment in private enterprise can be 'crowded out' – that is, depleted – by government demand for finance to fulfil promises made to the electorate. As we saw in chapter 4, the neoliberal critique of the social democratic welfare state attributed the inflation of the 1970s to excessive government expenditure (see the survey of neo-liberal critiques of the political economy of social democracy in King 1987; for a concise analysis of the neo-liberal restructuring of the state in the UK see Hay 1996; for the USA see King and Wood 1999; Glyn 2006; Duménil and Lévy 2004; Harvey 2007).

For Marxists, the 'capture' of the state by capitalists is normal – it is, after all, their 'executive committee' (Marx and Engels 1968 [1850]). Capitalist control of the state is achieved in a variety of ways – through ideology, direct participation in government and influence through ruling-class networks (see Dunleavy and O'Leary 1987; Jessop 1990; 2002). But, most importantly, it is secured by the state's structural dependence on the capitalist class's wealth and their control of the capital markets. As we have seen, if capitalist investors fear that inflation will erode the value of government bonds, demand for them will fall, pushing up the rate of interest that the government must pay.

These divergent views reflect the constant political struggle over the scale and scope of the state's role in capitalist society which might bring about the two possibilities which in Weber's view could bring capitalism to an end: capitalist tyranny or socialist sclerosis (see the discussion of Weber in part I). If the state were to become nothing more than the instrument of the capitalist class this would lead to ruthless exploitation, rising inequality, political disorder and the possible overthrow of the state by revolutionary socialists, as Marx envisaged.[5] However, if this were to occur, or if democratically elected socialists were to gain power, dynamism would be lost in the planned economy, eventually leading to economic stagnation. Capitalism will only remain dynamic if the struggle between economic interests persists, but not at a level that threatens the system. In this view, the state's most important roles are to maintain an acceptable balance of power and to ensure that the operation of the economy and the distribution of its wealth are seen as legitimate. As we shall see, it is widely believed that this is most effectively accomplished by liberal representative democracy.

The extent and scope of the state's role in capitalist economies has varied as a result of particular historical circumstances and the balance of political and economic power between the classes and interests (see the discussions in chapters 6 and 9). For example, government expenditure on health and welfare in Scandinavian democracies has been greater than elsewhere, the French state has taken more responsibility for infrastructure than Britain, the Japanese state has been more involved in directly managing the trajectory of its economy, but has spent less on social welfare than most Western economies. Expressing the fundamental divergence of views on the nature of the relationship between the state and capitalism, there is a continuous and inconclusive debate between neo-liberals and social democrats and socialists on the relative efficiency of the different variants (Zysman 1983; Coates 2000; Hall and Soskice 2001; Glyn 2006).

We shall return to this important debate in the concluding chapter; here the focus is on the three general roles that all capitalist states perform to varying degrees: maintenance of social peace, the reproduction of capitalist social relations and the correction of the market's 'failure' sufficiently to maintain an adequate level of employment and its propensity to financial crisis.

Social peace: coercion and legitimacy

Without social order sustained economic activity is not possible. This is accomplished by a combination of force and legitimacy – of might and right. States use their monopoly of coercion not only to resist external threats, but also to eliminate the private use of force in the domestic distribution of resources. So much is obvious; but it should not be overlooked that until recently economic violence was widespread in many of the major capitalist states and, although now marginalized, it is not entirely absent. For example, the Mafia continued to exercise extensive coercive control over labour markets and the distribution of goods and services in many large US cities until well into the twentieth century. Indeed, the suggestion that it might be regaining power as the resources of the Federal Bureau of Investigation (FBI) are diverted to countering the threat of global terrorism points to the fact that violence does not simply disappear, but has constantly to be suppressed.

Organized violence continues to play a significant part in the conduct of economic activity in many emerging capitalist economies, obviously impeding the development of peaceful contractual economic exchange. In the power vacuum that followed the collapse of communism in and the break-up of the Soviet Union, violence played a prominent part in the struggle for control of former state property (Varese 2001; Galeotti 2002). Contract killings in Russia rose from around 100 in 1992 to over 500 by 1994, replacing the law courts as a way of settling disputes. It is even suggested that the assassinations are part of the struggle, referred to earlier, in which Putin's state attempts to regain control of the economy and reduce the power of the oligarchs (*Financial Times*, 14/15 October 2006:7). During 2006 the deputy chairman of Russia's central bank, the chief engineer of Russia Petroleum, the manager of a branch of a state-owned bank, and the journalist Anna Politkovskaya, investigating economic corruption in Putin's regime, were all shot dead.

Marxist accounts of the development of capitalism draw attention to the use of state coercion to dispossess the peasantry and create a property-less class of wage labour. Violent clashes between capital and labour continued throughout the early stages of capitalist industrialization in western Europe and are now being repeated as the process continues its global spread. Although the struggle between capital and labour is, for the most part, now conducted peacefully, physical confrontation has not been eliminated entirely from industrial relations in mature capitalist economies. In the UK during the 1980s, for example, there were large-scale violent clashes between workers and police – especially in the year-long miners' strike in 1984–5. However, in most capitalist economies the state's monopoly of physical coercion is now mainly employed in the economic sphere in the maintenance of property rights and as the last resort in the enforcement of the laws that prescribe the peaceful bargaining procedures, which are now the typical institutional means by which economic conflict is conducted.[6]

The debate on the legitimacy of capitalism is enormously wide-ranging and its complexities can only be touched upon in this discussion (see, for example, Abercrombie, Hill and Turner 1980; Jessop 1990; Held and Krieger 1983). There are two main issues. First, is it possible to isolate a distinctive set of beliefs that explain and justify capitalist social relations – that is, property relations and contractual market exchange? Second, how far is the state involved in the propagation of these ideas?

Most contributions to the debate on the role of ideas and beliefs in the legitimization of capitalist society centre on the questions posed in the broad Marxist tradition. From this perspective, the apparent general acceptance of the inequality and exploitation that capitalism inevitably produces is a puzzle that requires explanation. Three general answers have been given. First, it is held that the combination of political and economic liberalism as found in the classical political economy is bourgeois ideology that masks the reality of exploitation in capitalism. Adam Smith's 'perfect liberty' of individuals to engage in contracts as legal equals is a deception that obscures the power of property. The argument that the impartial 'invisible hand' ensures that rewards are fairly determined by the functional contribution of the different parts to production is similarly seen as a distortion. A corollary of Smith's contention is that failure to achieve success in the competitive market cannot be attributed to the system, but rather to individual error or lack of effort.

The second argument is not concerned with ideas that specifically offer an explanation of capitalist exchange relations and their outcome, but rather with those which deflect attention from the injustice and unfairness. Inequality is made tolerable by various kinds of displacement – for example, in the conception of religion as the 'opium of the people', promising reward in heaven as compensation for earthly discomforts. Of course, the 'opium' is not necessarily merely a metaphor! And heaven can be found on earth in the guise of mass consumption and the distractions of the mass media, as the Marxist Frankfurt School argued (Held 1980; see also Jameson 1991).

The third answer similarly points to the increasingly pragmatic and instrumental nature of the legitimacy given to the capitalist system after the Second World War (see Mann 1970; Abercrombie, Hill and Turner 1980). Evidence strongly suggests that the continued acquiescence of the masses was conditional on the commitment to full employment and social welfare and the promise of uninterrupted increases in income by the major democracies. However, the partial retreat from these policies provoked only muted protest. None the less, there is much to be said for this argument, that capitalism and its inequalities are not accorded positive legitimacy, but merely accepted in the absence of both alternative visions and the power to make changes. In the Italian Marxist Gramsci's terms, the stability of capitalist society is maintained by 'hegemony'. That is to say, the mass of the population do not actively support capitalist ideology; rather, they implicitly 'consent' to the present system as the natural, normal state of affairs because they have been disabled, in one way or another, from conceiving of an alternative (see also Boltanski and Chiapello 2005).

How far the 'state' as such is directly involved in creating and maintaining capitalist hegemony is an even more difficult question. Any answer depends on what is meant by the state. In French Althusserian Marxist theory, the question of the state's role in legitimizing capitalism was dealt with by arguing that as the state was the means by which the working class was suppressed and ideologically duped, then any institution that performed this role must be part of the state. Consequently, the educational system and, less plausibly, the family were designated 'ideological state apparatuses' (see Jessop 1990). There is no doubt that democratic governments are involved in the legitimization of the capitalist economy in the presentation and explanation of their policies. This became clearly apparent in the ideological shift from the commitment to full employment and the advocacy of the virtues of the market that began during the 1980s and continues to spread through all the Western liberal democracies (for a survey of these ideas see King 1987).

Indeed, the legitimacy of capitalist economies is to a large extent a consequence of the fact that they are conjoined to political systems that are based on individual liberty, democratic rights and what Weber referred to as rational-legal legitimacy.

Capitalist social relations and liberal democracy

States produce and maintain capitalist social relations through the laws which prescribe (i) the legal and customary rights by which all classes of economic agents are constituted – employers, employees, consumers, shareholders and so on; and (ii) the procedural rules and norms that govern their relationships. For example, states maintain competition by attempting to control monopoly power, regulate capital–labour relations and employment rights, enact consumer protection legislation, and attempt to safeguard shareholders and pensioners from corporate fraud. In other words, states provide the rules of the capitalist 'game'. (In one view, based on Smith and neo-liberal analysis, it does so objectively and on grounds of efficiency; and from the other generally Marxian perspective it simultaneously weakens workers and maintains the power of capital to exploit.)

These legal rights and procedures have been produced by liberal democratic states, and, by and large, they are based on a distribution of power in which no one group or class is able fully to seize the state and turn it to its advantage. (However, this is not to say that there exists an equal balance of power.) Liberal representative democracy did not appear anywhere until the development of capitalism, and this has led to widespread agreement that there is an affinity or even a necessary connection between them. Lenin, the founder of Russian communism, went so far as to say that representative democracy was capitalism's 'best political shell', in which the spurious equality of democratic citizenship acted to mask the fundamental underlying inequalities of class and economic power (Lenin 1963: 296). Supporters of capitalism view the association more positively and argue that Adam Smith's 'perfect liberty' of market exchange cannot be sustained outside a free and democratic polity (Wolf 2005); contracts cannot be accomplished without legal equality and personal freedom (Friedman 1962). However, the relationship between capitalism and democracy is not as direct and straightforward as implied by some of the more triumphal Western arguments that became widely accepted after the collapse of communism (Fukuyama 1992).

In the first place, the historical association between the two does not logically preclude the possibility that other political systems could coexist with a capitalist economy. It could be argued, for example, that the twentieth-century German and Japanese deviations from the capitalism–liberal democracy norm were cut short by military defeat rather than any inherent incompatibility between capitalism and fascism. In this regard, it would be premature to foreclose the possibility of a wide range of new 'hybrid' linkages between capitalism and authoritarianism in post-communist societies (King and Szelényi 2005). In particular, there is considerable disagreement over whether China can continue to develop a form of capitalism within the framework of state communism (Hutton 2007; Nolan 2004).

Furthermore, the insistence on a necessary functional connection between capitalism and liberal democracy tends to obscure the historically contingent nature of the links between three separate elements – economic liberalism, political liberalism and democracy (Moore 1966; for a survey of the literature see Rueschmeyer, Stephens and Stephens 1992). The creation of the individual liberties which were the foundation for capitalist property rights and freedom of contract in the West was not in any way democratic (see the classic account in Macpherson 1973). In early modern Europe property was a precondition for political representation, and the mass of the population lacked both. Indeed, proponents of political and economic liberalism, such as Mill in the nineteenth century, have always feared that representative democracy could pose a threat to private property and market capitalism. In the first half of the twentieth century there was widespread fear that mass democracy might lead to the capture of the state by the workers and, as Marx believed, a transition to socialism. From this perspective it is, in fact, somewhat surprising that mass representative democracy ever developed within the framework of capitalism (Therborn 1977).

However, if the liberal and the democratic elements of modern political systems are disentangled, it is possible to see that representative democracy was a largely unintended consequence of the 'contradiction' of political liberalism. The very same appeals to universal human rights of freedom of speech and association – used by the mercantile bourgeoisie in their opposition to the claims of absolutist monarchs and their arbitrary rule – were, in turn, adopted by the masses of early industrial capitalism to demand representation. However, there was no simple and straightforward route to democracy, and the eventual outcome was dependent on the particular balance of power and political alliances in different societies (Moore 1966; Therborn 1977). Indeed, as we have noted, the fascist interludes in the mid-twentieth century in Germany, Italy and Japan suggest that different forms of mass democracy other than its representative liberal guise are possibly compatible with capitalist industrialization.

Liberal democracy is the more likely outcome if there is a balance of power among a plurality of dominant classes and elites which prevents any one of them from capturing the state. Under these circumstances, and given the existence of some kind of representative assembly, the franchise was very gradually extended by the competing elites to other potential supporting groups and classes in society. In the classic British case, the universal franchise took almost a century to complete after the first significant extension in the 1832 Reform Act had given the vote to large sections of the middle class (Therborn 1977).

Once established, workers' political parties – in both opposition and government – were the means by which the regulation of capitalist social relations in a framework of 'collective bargaining' was adopted by the major capitalist economies. There are, of course, quite large variations in these institutional arrangements, but it is clear that, by and large, the most extensive legal rights to bargain collectively are to be found in those societies which have had social democratic political parties with strong links with the labour movement (see Fulcher 1991).

However, these links between class and party were never so close as to mount effective challenges to capitalist property relations. Lenin's judgement would appear to have been vindicated, with the gradual institutionalization of the class struggle into 'collective bargaining' by procedural rules. As we noted in chapter 5, these have separated the economic struggle over wages and conditions from political movements which aimed to bring about a socialist transformation of the economy. Trade unions' legal rights restrict bargaining to wage negotiations and universally prohibit the use of strikes for political ends. By these means, some would argue, labour leaders have been transformed from opponents of capitalism into 'managers of discontent' and trade unions, as Lenin argued, have been reduced to mere 'economism'.

Sweden provides support for the view that democracy is, depending on one's view, capitalism's best 'political shell', or the natural consequence of economic freedom (see Fulcher 1991). A survey in 2005 in the British *Guardian* newspaper concluded that it was probably the most successful society the world has ever known. Although Sweden has fallen a little in the OECD's per capita income rank order, it has been able consistently to combine very high levels of economic growth and high levels of employment with the world's most generous levels of spending on health, education and welfare, and, perhaps not surprisingly, social peace. But this epitome of the Scandinavian model of social democracy has also remained thoroughly capitalist, exhibiting one of the highest levels of concentrated and family capital ownership in the world (Roe 2003: 94–7). Over 90 per cent of corporations with capitalization of over $500 million have a concentrated block of shareholding of 20 per cent or more; whereas the figure for the USA is a mere 10 per cent (Roe 2003: 53).

On taking power in 1920 the Swedish Social Democratic Party became the world's first democratically elected left-wing government, and found itself embroiled in a period of intense industrial conflict that resembled Marx's vision of capitalism's 'two armed camps' of the bourgeoisie and proletariat. From the late nineteenth century to around 1930, both the frequency of strikes and number of days lost were far higher than in Britain, France and the USA (Fulcher 1991; Ingham 1974: 30–1). The conflict steadily escalated into a pattern of workers' general strikes and employers' lock-outs until a settlement, brokered by the Social Democratic government, was reached in the Basic Agreement of 1938. All sides realized that a self-destructive stalemate had been reached and created a framework for peaceful collective bargaining. By the 1950s strike activity in Sweden had fallen to less than 5 per cent of the levels in Britain, France and the USA (Ingham 1974; Coates 2000; Fulcher 1991).

There exists a great deal of debate about how the different varieties of capitalism have dealt with class conflict (Coates 2000), but fundamentally these are all variations on a basic model that evolved during the twentieth century. Political and economic conflicts are separated in their respective spheres of state and economy, with their own institutional norms and rules which are determined through democratic representation. Sweden and the other Scandinavian democracies exemplify one extreme position where the state has not only forged very robust procedural rules, but has also overseen a more general substantive settlement between the social classes involving one of the more equitable divisions of the social product and high levels of welfare. At the other end of the spectrum – in the USA, for example – the institutions of collective bargaining remain limited and rudimentary, and democratic representation has done little to modify the unequal distribution of wealth and income (Coates 2000; Phillips 2002). The differences are the result of historical circumstances and the different balance of political and economic forces. For example, the ethnic, religious, regional and economic heterogeneity of the USA inhibited the formation of a strong working-class movement and party that produced both the class confrontation and the social democratic solution that occurred in Sweden (for the classic analysis of the absence of socialism in the USA see Sombart 1976 [1906]; Lipset and Marks 2001). Most other mature capitalist societies can be placed somewhere between these two extremes in terms of the way in which the conflicts between capital and labour are managed.

The state in the economy

There is considerable variation, over time and between different countries, in the extent to which states have participated directly in shaping their capitalist economies (Zysman 1983; Coates 2000). Some of the reasons for these differences will become apparent in the course of the following discussion, and these 'varieties' will be considered again briefly in the concluding chapter. Here we shall be concerned only with the basic scope of the involvement that is common to all states that combine representative democracy and market capitalism. The issue has been addressed in passing in previous chapters; here the main points will be reiterated.

As we saw in part I and again in chapter 5, there are two quite different conceptions of the links between the state and the economy. These provide the intellectual foundations for a continuous and frequently intense debate. On the one hand, as we have seen, economic liberalism asserts that the market mechanism is largely self-regulating and that the state's intervention should be restricted to the residual role of providing 'public goods' and attending to the exceptional instances of market failure. Moreover, it is held, states will distort the market and cause it to malfunction if they stray beyond this limited remedial role. For example, it was argued in the recrudescence of neo-liberalism in the 1980s that government expenditure can 'crowd out' inherently more efficient private enterprise if it exceeds the level which can be justified on strict public goods grounds. This kind of analysis reflects the fact that although there is a mutually interdependent, or symbiotic, relationship between states and private capital, they are also in potential competition for economic resources – as they were more obviously in the seventeenth century when the memorable alliance was concluded. For example, the nationalization of the failed British mortgage bank Northern Rock in February 2008 immediately elicited outraged cries of unfair competition from other banks.

On the other hand, as I have emphasized, a wide and diverse range of views holds that market capitalism requires continuous crisis management by the state to deal with the two basic endemic threats to the economy: the market's inability to resolve serious periodic mismatches between supply and demand that produce crises of over-production and under-consumption, and financial instability which brings the possibility of debt-deflation. Although it is deplored by many economic liberals, it is simply a matter of fact that all modern states are by far the single largest consumers of goods and services in their economy and, as a consequence, they are a fundamental source of the supply of money (see chapter 4). In 2000, government expenditure in the major capitalist economies varied between around 30 per cent of GDP in the USA and 50 per cent in France (OECD *Annual Economic Surveys*, various years). Consequently and inevitably, states have the economic leverage to stabilize their economies and attempt to deal with crises, as Keynes and others advocated.

However, as I have argued, the extent of the actual use of this factual capacity to become directly involved in the economy cannot simply be determined by narrow economic calculus. In a representative democracy, demand for intrinsically valuable 'public goods' such as health care and education, for example, will not be limited simply by a calculation of the optimum level of state expenditure on human capital in relation to GDP – even if this were possible. Furthermore, economic liberalism's claim that supply and demand and, consequently, employment will reach equilibrium in the 'long run' is not a hypothesis that can be put to the test in modern democracies in which economic security is the electorate's greatest concern. Keynes understood that abstract economic models were inadequate for dealing with immediate exigencies and their political consequences: '[T]he long run is a misleading guide to currents affairs. In the long run we are all dead. Economists set themselves too easy, too useless a task if in tempestuous seasons they can only tell us that when the storm is long past the ocean is flat again' (Keynes 1924).

The following discussion will focus on the two most important kinds of direct economic intervention which are common, in varying degrees, to all modern capitalist states: the maintenance of the 'public good' of 'human capital', and the management and stabilization of the economy.

The state, human capital and welfare

The vulnerability of labour to periods of poverty is not an incidental feature of capitalism. As Weber explained, the profitability of the enterprise can only be calculated with maximum 'rationality' if capital is not responsible for the cost of maintaining the quality of labour (human capital). In contrast to slavery, for example, labour costs for the individual capitalist enterprise can be adjusted to market conditions by firing workers if demand for its output production falls. However, in relation to the long-term performance of the economy as a whole, it is better that labour is kept in good working order during periods of unemployment caused by recession. But, in general, competition between capitalists inhibits their provision of welfare for their own workers. Unless there is a collective agreement, payment of wages during a recession will put an individual employer at a cost disadvantage. Moreover, with legally free labour, there can be no guarantee that workers will not leave an employer who has invested in their welfare. Consequently, it has largely fallen to states to maintain the labour force in a satisfactory condition.

Exceptions to this general state of affairs can occur where there is a low level of competition between capitalists. The high level of concentration of capital into the *zaibatsu* and, later, *keiretsu* conglomerates in Japan has enabled a highly managed form of oligopolistic competition in which welfare has been based on the security of 'lifetime employment' (Dore 2000). And as we noted in chapter 6, during early industrialization in regions where there was a single employer and a labour shortage, employers sometimes provided housing and welfare for their labour force in 'model villages' and took responsibility for the maintenance of the labour force during a recession.

However, the typical operation of capitalism requires the state to ensure that the quality of human capital is not degraded by the intensity of capitalist competition to cut labour costs and abandon workers during recessions. As Marx observed, the nineteenth-century bourgeoisie were unable to prevent themselves from 'digging their own graves' by the exploitation of their most valuable resource. Consequently the state stepped in, first to regulate the length of the working day and then progressively to provide welfare for workers and their families.

This provision increased as international competition intensified during the late nineteenth century – that is, before social democratic political parties were able to introduce welfare provisions. In Germany, for example, Bismarck saw clearly that the condition of labour was of fundamental importance in the creation of a strong state to challenge Britain's hegemony (Esping-Anderson 1990). In response to this pressure, and shocked by the poor physical condition of recruits for the Boer War (1899–1902), Britain soon followed suit. If the country's young men were unfit for fighting, it was concluded that they must also be unfit for work. Significantly, advances in welfare have accelerated during the twentieth century's 'mass' wars, involving citizens' armies and bombed civilians. Such warfare presents two exigencies – the need to maintain and secure commitment to the war effort and the maintenance of the working class's 'human capital'. Britain's plans for a comprehensive 'welfare state', comprising unemployment insurance, public health care and housing, were presented in 1942 during the most critical period of the Second World War. To be sure, other less instrumental motives were involved and there was also political pressure from the electorate. Variations in these factors influenced differences in the kind of welfare systems adopted across the capitalist world during the twentieth century, but the fundamental exigency of maintaining human capital, posed by the operation of the capitalist system, is common to all (Esping-Anderson 1990).

Although, with important exceptions such as Japan, it is not generally in the interests of capitalist employers directly to provide comprehensive welfare, it does not follow that it need be both financed and supplied directly by the state. Indeed, private health insurance is the norm in the USA and, as we shall see, there has been recently a move in the other advanced capitalist states towards the privatization of welfare and health care (Hacker 2002). However, in no modern capitalist economy is welfare provision wholly supplied by private enterprise. It remains a 'public good' in the sense that it has not proved profitable for private capital to deliver to *all* strata in society the levels of welfare deemed to be necessary by the state, acting in its capacity as the 'collective capitalist' for the overall maintenance of human capital. Quite simply, those most in need, from both an individual and societal standpoint, are the ones least able to afford it.

However, even if it were to be agreed that welfare should be determined exclusively on cost–benefit economic grounds, the actual level cannot be precisely established. Clearly, public health measures to deal with high mortality rates during epidemics have calculable economic effects, but unless there is a serious shortage of labour, the basic maintenance of human capital does not necessarily require the most advanced and expensive medical techniques. However, with the gradual adoption of the universal franchise in the early twentieth century in the advanced capitalist states, these questions soon became a central part of the politics of social democracy. By this time, the condition of the working classes was not only a matter of the economy's efficiency; it had become a central part of the political struggle for greater social and economic equality. Workers demanded and eventually were granted increasing levels of welfare by successive governments in attempts to secure their electoral support and to deflect the attractions of socialism.

As the twentieth century progressed, the political struggle and circumstances such as the Second World War shifted the balance of class power and drove social welfare beyond the level that might be acceptable to the political elites and capitalist classes on narrowly economic grounds. In the economists' terminology, welfare was not only a 'public good', but had also become a 'merit good' – that is, something intrinsically desirable. In Britain, by the late 1940s, there were serious attempts to conceptualize the welfare state as the final stage in the gradual evolution of democratic citizenship (Marshall 1963 [1949]). Legal equality, developed in the eighteenth century, had enabled the gradual extension of the universal franchise, which, in turn, it was now argued, had made it possible to establish universal rights to the standards of health and material well-being that a society could sustain.

A critical point was soon to be reached, as we shall see, in the tension between the exercise of private economic power and the egalitarian claims pursued in modern social democracy. The nub of the issue was, and remains, employment: in capitalism, can there be a right to work? If so, who decides and on what criteria? This dilemma is at the centre of what Marshall has referred to as the 'war' between class and citizenship.[7]

Many capitalist states have not only financed 'public goods' but have also owned the enterprises which supply them – particularly energy, communications and transport. This has occurred most often in 'developmental states', where the aim was quickly to establish the infrastructure for private capitalist enterprise – as in Germany and Japan in the nineteenth century, followed by other south-east Asian states in the twentieth (Wade 2003 [1990]; Woo-Cummings 2005). State ownership of industry and infrastructure was extended even in some 'liberal-market' economies at times during the twentieth century (Hall and Soskice 2001). Although this was frequently motivated by socialist ideology, the nationalized industries were generally those which were crucial for overall economic efficiency but had been neglected by private investment.

In general terms, however, capitalist interests oppose the state ownership of business enterprise if it is perceived that would be profitable for it to be undertaken privately within a reasonable time frame. The extent of state ownership always entails a struggle between public and private interests. How these are defined and the understanding of the relative efficiency of public and private enterprise is framed by economic analysis which tends to change with shifts in the balance of power between the two sides of the economy. For example, in the mid-twentieth century, when states were called on to reconstruct and revitalize their economies, as in the USA's New Deal and in the UK after the Second World War, it was widely held that transport, communications and energy were 'natural monopolies'. A 'natural monopoly' was a special case of 'public good' in so far as the most efficient scale of production was sufficiently large to allow for only one producer – for example, railways and utilities. There was, of course, wide variation in the extent of state ownership, which was related to the power and influence of social democratic and socialist political parties and governments, but, to a large extent, the case for public ownership was, nevertheless, made on economic grounds.

Management of the economy: counter-cyclical stabilization, financial crises

As we saw in part I, Keynes believed that he had devised the means to counter the cycles of expansion and contraction in capitalist economics – especially sluggish recovery and chronic unemployment. If private capitalists did not have sufficient 'animal spirits' to invest with confidence in production, the state should not take on directly the role of employer as the socialists demanded. Rather, the government's stimulation of aggregate demand by increased expenditure would achieve the same end without compromising market capitalism and individual liberty. Moreover, opposition to spending on welfare, based on the fear of inflationary consequences and the need for higher taxation, could be countered by this strategy. In Keynes's scheme, full employment and social welfare could be symbiotically linked in a positive feedback: employed workers would require less welfare and their taxes would help to pay for whatever was needed.

In effect, Keynesian economics also promised to resolve the fundamental conflicts that the fiscal problems of capitalist democracy constantly threatened to provoke. His theories were aimed not only at his academic critics, but also at the state's creditors and taxpayers. Could the holders of government debt be persuaded that the value of the interest revenues from their government bonds would not be eroded by inflation induced by an increase in government expenditure and, thereby, the money supply? Would the population accept higher taxation to pay for the state's increased role in the economy? For a relatively short time after the Second World War both questions were answered positively, and a balance in the pivotal relationships between the major classes in capitalist democracy was achieved in many Western states. An implicit settlement between the state, its creditors and its citizens was forged. It was associated with – and, some would argue, caused – a coincidence of economic growth, low inflation and full employment (see Smithin 1996; Coates 2000; Glyn 2006).

However, as we saw in chapter 4, this 'golden age' was shattered by the crises of the 1970s, which had the effect of discrediting Keynesian economics and ushering in economic 'neo-liberalism'. The post-war economic boom not only stagnated, but was combined with hyper-inflation to produce the theoretically unexpected phenomenon of 'stagflation'.[8]

Marxists believed that the 1970s was simply the latest expression of capitalism's tendency to overproduction and falling profits (Brenner 2002). Committed Keynesians pointed to the external shocks – such as the oil price rises imposed by OPEC – that had destabilized the essentially sound domestically managed economies (Marglin and Schor 1990). But economic neo-liberals attributed the crises to the distortions of the market mechanism brought about by powerful trade union monopolists and unsustainable and irresponsible demands on the economic system by governments, transmitted through the competitive party system in representative democracy (Friedman 1962; Buchanan and Tullock 1962; Tullock 1987a; 1987b). Governments should attempt to cut expenditure to balance their budgets and thereby reduce the supply of money to the economy (see chapter 4). With less need to finance expenditure taxes could be reduced, which would increase savings and restore incentives for both capitalists and workers to work harder and longer without having their rewards confiscated by profligate governments. Markets were to be made more competitive through 'deregulation' – especially the labour market, which, it was contended, had been distorted by the greater security of employment and control over hours and conditions of work that had been introduced after 1945.

In general, the state should withdraw from direct participation in the economy – 'rolled back' in Thatcher's terms – and, in particular, its enterprises were to be privatized. There was an overarching ideological shift from the advocacy of the collective provision of a universal standard of social welfare and secure employment rights to the emphasis on individuals' responsibility for their economic destiny in a competitive system. Without endorsing the neo-liberal critique of Keynes, its diagnoses of the 1970s crises and its prescriptions for efficient capitalism, it could none the less be argued that Keynesian economic management was unable to operate effectively in the face of changes in domestic and international circumstances. As we saw in chapter 4, full employment empowered trade unions to press for wage increases that helped to create inflation, and governments' control over their domestic economy was weakened by the disintegration of the Bretton Woods international monetary system (see chapter 4, note 13, pp. 233–5).

By the end of the twentieth century Keynesianism appeared to have given way to neo-liberalism, first in the USA and the UK and later in the more managed economies of continental Europe (see Glyn 2006; Duménil and Lévy 2004). Whilst not denying the significance of these changes, it is important to understand that it has not involved such a radical shift in macro-economic management as is widely believed. The basic underlying structural linkages between the democratic state and capitalism have not been altered in any fundamental way. Rather, the point at which governments begin to increase public expenditure to deal with the slowing of cyclical economic activity has been moved as a result of the rebalancing of power between creditor and industrial and labour interests, as outlined in chapter 4. Details aside, the fundamental shift has been in the relative priority given to the goals of economic management – from full employment to inflation control – and in the fiscal and budgetary rules and norms that govern the level of government spending. But states have not been 'rolled back' as far as was intended and, in general, government expenditure has been trimmed, but not drastically cut. This is not to deny the effect of these changes on the higher levels of unemployment that have been the norm over the past twenty-five years. But, despite the rhetoric, states have not totally abnegated responsibility for employment or counter-cyclical spending, nor have they ceased to provide public goods. In democracies in which the majority continues to vote, this kind of economic management cannot be abandoned. In the very broadest sense, Keynesian macro-economic stabilization continues to exist in all but name.

Furthermore, the neo-liberal advocacy of 'deregulation' betrays a significant ideological misrepresentation of the way in which markets operate. 'Deregulation' implies that the economy will be more efficient if there is a quantitative reduction in rules and regulations – 'red tape'. These are seen as impediments to the operation of the 'natural' and 'spontaneous' market. However, all markets are constituted by 'regulation' which specifies the rights of the participants and the rules of exchange. Furthermore, as we noted in chapter 5, the creation of more competitive markets and the reduction of government controls almost invariably results in more rules and regulatory bodies (Vogel 1998). For example, in the 'big bang' of 1986, the London Stock Exchange introduced greater competition by eliminating fixed commissions on transactions and removed barriers to Stock Exchange membership (Ingham 2002). Simultaneously, however, the Financial Services Act introduced a system of regulation that was infinitely more complex and bureaucratic than the one that it replaced (Vogel 1998).

The operation of the market-capitalist economy requires the state to create and maintain continuously the conditions by which they will both prosper. States are dependent on private wealth creation for tax revenues and credit; markets are not self-regulating, and without a state they become chaotic and self-destructive. Weak states have weak economies. Examples may be drawn from all economic activity, but perhaps the state's role in the monetary and financial systems is the most obvious and important. All the evidence of the past three centuries shows conclusively that the state is the ultimate source of the monetary linchpin of capitalist activity. Without the constant vigilance of states' central banks and regulatory authorities, currencies soon destabilize, followed by turmoil in the capital and financial markets and, soon afterwards, the stagnation of production and trade. Of course, monetary systems can become unstable for a wide variety of reasons, but unless a state can issue and maintain a trusted unit of account and means of payment, then its monetary system and, consequently, the rest of the economy will be impaired. Furthermore, as we have seen, once financial crisis takes hold the only possible – but not foolproof – remedy is the provision of 'liquidity' by the state and its central banks to prevent the 'evaporation' of money in a chain reaction of defaults.

Conclusion

There are two are distinct 'logics of power', pursued by states and capital, which are organized and operated quite differently. Regardless of economic liberalism's more extreme claims, the state cannot be organized and run exclusively as a business enterprise, and market exchange cannot replace the relations of domination and authority that constitute the state. On the one hand, whilst states rationally calculate the consequences of their actions, they cannot abandon their territorial integrity and security on the basis of cost considerations alone. The maintenance of sovereignty is an absolute imperative – an end in itself. Capital, on the other hand, can sell an enterprise on the basis of cost–benefit calculation, in order to switch production or even opt out of economic activity altogether for a time by liquidating assets and storing wealth in the form of money. Furthermore, there can be no single optimum relationship between the state and market capitalism and their respective 'logics'. Given constantly changing market conditions and political circumstances, it is inevitable that the imperatives of one side will sooner or later clash with, or contradict, those of the other. State and capital are at one and the same time mutually dependent and antagonistic. Disputes over free trade and the geopolitics of markets in energy are obvious examples. Democracies risk losing legitimacy if exposure to foreign competition brings about an intolerable level of domestic 'creative destruction' in which businesses fail and unemployment rises. Consequently, governments in powerful states such as the USA constantly contradict their avowed adherence to their liberal economic principles of free trade. Energy industries, in particular, are jealously guarded by states, and foreign ownership is often resisted as not being in the national interest.

However, there are good reasons for agreeing with Weber that capitalism functions most effectively if there is balance of power between the two logics of power and that state and civil society are separated. There is agreement across a wide range of different ideological and academic views that the overwhelming dominance of either capital or the state impairs the operation of the economy and, eventually, can impede its dynamism. Economic liberals have been especially concerned about two such 'imbalances'. First, 'rent-seeking' is said to occur when economic agents are able to use the state to appropriate a greater share of the surplus than they would otherwise gain through competitive market exchange (Tullock 1987a; 1987b). For example, the pharmaceutical and arms industries are frequently criticized for making excessive profits from the state's commitment to medical welfare and defence. The less academic term 'crony capitalism' was used in the late 1990s to describe the close links between government elites and capitalists in east Asia, which, it was alleged, inhibited economic competition and led to financial crises and stagnation. However, critics of Western capitalism consider such close relationships between capitalists and political elites to be the norm. When the US government and Federal Reserve Bank pressed a consortium of Wall Street banks to rescue the failed hedge fund Long Term Credit Management in 1997, even the *Financial Times* detected hypocrisy and asked who the 'cronies' were now. In relation to the other side of the economy, economic liberalism's critique of the welfare state, as we have seen, argues that organized labour, in its alliance with social democratic political parties, has been able to use state power to extract a greater share of the surplus than was warranted by its input to productivity.

The point at which any possible impairment of the economy occurs when the state is manipulated to the advantage of any particular economic group or class is very difficult to establish, and it must be remembered that these critiques are ideologically driven by close links to economic class interests. However, the dangers of a fusion of state and capital are more obvious where political elites use state power to appropriate wealth, economic resources and opportunities for profit – described by Weber as political capitalism of the 'patrimonial state' (Weber 1978: 236–7, 1010–69). Any serious erosion of the relative autonomy of the two spheres – state and economy – usually heralds the replacement of liberal democracy by an authoritarian state or a 'token' democracy with rigged elections – as in many African states (Chabal and Daloz 1999). There are many kinds of modern authoritarian state, but they share one important trait – the expropriation and use of the economy's resources to strengthen the political elite's power. In the modern world, this form of political capitalism often develops where a relatively underdeveloped economy is generously endowed with natural resources. The possession of natural resources, especially large reserves of oil, may be a 'curse' in the sense that the revenues may be sufficient to sustain a political regime and pre-empt an interest in encouraging and supporting a vigorous capitalist economy (see Humphreys, Sachs and Stiglitz 2007). The implied corollary that there is an affinity between the liberal democratic state and capitalism is supported by the historical record, but this is not to say that different patterns could not emerge. The frequently posed question of whether China can successfully combine capitalism with an authoritarian non-democratic state in what would genuinely be a 'third way' remains open (Hutton 2007; Nolan 2004). Will the move away from democracy in Putin's Russia impair the dynamism of the economy, as Western neo-liberals believe?

Although most attention is focused on the ways in which the logic of state power can subvert economic dynamism, it must be emphasized that the application of an economic, purely 'market', logic to the state's activities can also be dysfunctional. Ultra-liberal economic doctrine advocates that wherever possible all the state's roles would be better and more efficiently performed by private enterprise and that bureaucratic procedure should be replaced by contractual, market exchange. This thinking has influenced the privatization of many of the economic activities that were undertaken by leading capitalist states during the second half of the twentieth century – for example, utilities and transport and communications. In some cases the process has been taken even further by the privatization of functions that are more directly related to the state's hitherto autonomous role in maintaining internal and external security. Mainly, but not exclusively, in the USA, prisons and some parts of the military are now run by private enterprise (Avant 2005).

However, the counter-argument maintains that the state's services are provided most effectively by public functionaries, motivated by a sense of honour and duty, rather than by pecuniary gain (Weber 1978: 956–1005). Political legitimacy, which is the ultimate foundation of a strong state, is, according to this thinking, more likely to be granted to such 'public servants' than it is to the employees of private enterprise whose explicit and primary motivation is personal profit.

The complexities of the relationship between the logics of the two sources of power are most apparent at the global level. Capitalism will persist, as Weber observed, in the absence of world territorial sovereignty exercised by a global imperial state which might be able to appropriate and control all profitable opportunities. Capitalism flourishes with the free movement of capital in the interstices between the independent states by being able to invest and/or locate wherever it is considered to be most profitable to do so. On the other hand, however, the absence of a single source of sovereignty and the competition between states for money-capital create difficulties for the regulation and control of global markets.

For example, is the branch of an international bank to be subject to its host's regulatory regime or that of the state in which the parent company is located (Kapstein 1994)? Furthermore, although a world of competing independent states provides fertile ground for capitalism it makes it almost impossible to create a single world currency with which to finance international trade (Walter 1993).[9] Aside from the considerable transactions costs of currency exchange, the absence of a single means of payment can impede economic development, as small, weak countries have difficulty in getting their currency accepted. The demand for 'hard' currencies – such as the dollar and the euro – further enhances the power of the major economies and their banks and financial centres and intensifies global inequalities (on the benefits of 'dollarization' for the US economy see Gowan 1999; Wade 2003). These and related questions on the links between states and capital will be pursued further in the following chapter.

9
Conclusions

Our main concern has been with capitalism's fundamental, or generic, elements, and, consequently, relatively little attention has been paid to the different historical paths of development and diverse cultures that have produced its 'species' or 'varieties' – Anglo-US liberal market capitalism, European or 'Rhineland' capitalism, Asian capitalism, 'transitional' or 'hybrid' capitalism in ex-communist economies. Over the past decade or so, a considerable amount of attention has been devoted to this issue and, by way of a conclusion, I wish briefly to consider two closely related questions that arise from this distinction between 'genus' and 'species'. In the first place, are these differences significant, or merely superficial; that is to say, are there a number of equally effective ways of organizing capitalism? Neo-liberal economics maintains that the 'deregulated' or 'free' market, or Anglo-US form, is the most effective and that consequently it will gradually become dominant.[1] Second, is economic 'globalization' in effect a process of 'natural selection' by which the less efficient 'species' are eradicated and replaced by a single genus that resembles the liberal market type?

Globalization

The debate on the nature, extent and causes of globalization has spawned an enormous literature. While it is contended that all dimensions of human existence – cultural, economic and political – are being 'globalized', there is considerable disagreement on the precise meaning of the term 'globalization' and the extent of the process (for an overview of the measures of globalization and the major controversies, see Held and McGrew 2007). These broad issues cannot be considered in any detail here. Rather, I shall contend that the transformations in question are, at a fundamental level, a consequence of the acceleration in the global diffusion of capitalism which has been driven by transnational flows of money and capital.

In general, economic globalization refers to two distinct aspects of the extension and intensification of economic activity across the world (Hirst and Thompson 1999). On the one hand it points to an acceleration of the flow of goods, money and other financial assets *between* nation states – that is, *internationalization*. For example, between 1870 and 1992 global merchandise exports, expressed as a percentage of GDP, grew from 5 per cent to 13.5 per cent, and capital which was raised on international markets, expressed as a percentage of world exports, increased from 1 per cent to 20 per cent (Maddison 1995). On the other hand new economic processes and forms of organization have developed which *transcend* the territorial limits of states. This is genuine *globalization* in which place, or location, is no longer as relevant for an understanding of what is occurring; the 'space of flows' replaces the 'space of places' (Ruggie 1993). The difference between *multi*national and *trans*national corporations illustrates the distinction. In the former, a company with a distinct national identity and ownership, such as Coca-Cola, establishes clones of the parent plant in different countries. In contrast, transnational corporations, often with multinational ownership, locate different stages of an integrated production chain in different countries. For example, in automobile production engines are produced in one country and floor-pans in another, but final assembly might take place elsewhere. In this case, production is truly 'globalized' and is to be understood in terms of a 'space of flows'. However, it is in the realm of money and finance where economic internationalization and globalization are most developed.

Let us remind ourselves of money's pivotal role. First, production is undertaken in order to realize the exchange value of commodities; that is to say, the *primary* motivation for capitalist production is not the creation of utilities but monetary profit. Second, bank debt creates the money-capital that is the means by which production is both inaugurated and terminated. Third, all property and means of production are 'liquid'; that is to say, capital markets can 'dissolve' physical capital into money and then 'reconstitute' it at a different time and place. This makes possible the 'creative destruction' that gives capitalism its flexibility and dynamism. Fourth, capital's liquidity also endows all material means of production and resources with a second characteristic as speculative financial assets.

It is the money-capital of capitalism and that drives the endless pursuit of profit and gives the system its dynamism and flexibility; in short, the creation and control of money-capital is the locus of power in capitalism. It is here that the decisions about when and where the material provisioning for human wants are taken. Moreover, as we have seen, this component of the capitalist system has become progressively more dominant.

A distinctive consequence of this development is the way that the 'liquidity' and 'solubility' of capital loosens connections between 'physical location' and 'economic process'. For example, factories can be sold and relocated 'offshore', or, alternatively, if market conditions are unfavourable to production, liquidated capital (money) can be held either as an interest-bearing bank deposit or used to pursue profit on speculative financial asset markets.[2] With advances in information and communication technologies, capital and financial asset markets exhibit this de-linking of place and process most clearly. These 'virtual' markets consist of global information networks governing the interaction of supply and demand for capital and financial assets. Segments of these markets are physically located where the computer screens are connected to an electricity supply, but as total systems they exist only in cyberspace (Thrift 2005; Knorr Cetina and Preda 2004).

Furthermore, without the availability of a widely acceptable means of payment – that is, a 'global' money – the international flow of goods and services is impeded. Two periods of accelerating globalization – from the end of the nineteenth century to 1914 and in the late twentieth century – were based upon increased international capital flows and the availability of a globally acceptable currency – first, the gold-sterling standard and, second, the dollar standard.[3] The geopolitical disorder that followed the First World War and the breakdown of the international gold-standard monetary system in the 1920s led to the reversal of an earlier globalization trend that had begun in the late nineteenth century, involving the slowdown of world trade and the subsequent depression of the inter-war years (Hirst and Thompson 1999; Frieden 2006). It should be stressed that both phases of global free-market capitalism were made possible by the securing of global order by the British and American states and their provision of world currencies. (Paradoxically, it is precisely at these times that the ideological belief in the self-regulating market is most strongly held.)

Money is potentially the most mobile of the 'factors' of production; that is to say, it is capable of being transmitted through time and space more easily than physical capital and labour. But money and the markets through which it can move have first to be constructed and maintained. This is true both at the level of nation states and globally. Acceptable, freely available money and global capital and financial asset markets were, to a very large extent, political creations, not the spontaneous results of economic agents' quests for profit. 'Deregulated' global finance is not 'natural'; rather, it has been the work of states. 'Globalization was a choice, not a fact' (Frieden 2006: xvi).

Since the 1970s cross-border flows of money, capital and other financial assets through global markets have increased at a far faster rate than any other measure of economic activity, and have been the most prominent feature of the acceleration of economic globalization (Bryant 2003). For example, as we have noted, foreign-exchange markets for trading national currencies now consist in the 'flows' between interconnected computers rather than the 'space' of the trading floor in a particular location (Thrift 2005; Knorr Cetina and Preda 2004). Turnover on these foreign exchange markets has grown enormously – from US$ 17.5 trillion, or twelve times the value of world exports, in 1979, to US$ 297.5 trillion, or sixty times the value of world exports, by 1995 (Bank for International Settlements, *Annual Report*, various years). Growth in these markets accelerated in the early twenty-first century, and by 2006 the value of annual turnover stood at US$1,000 trillion (*International Financial Services*, 2006). As we saw in chapter 7, the astonishing growth of the global derivatives markets is closely tied to the opportunities for speculation that are presented by the regime of floating exchange rates. The primary economic function of foreign-exchange dealing is to provide producers and traders with the currency needed for their imports and exports, and, consequently, it could be expected that turnover on these markets correlated closely with the volume of international trade. However, over 95 per cent of all foreign exchange transactions are now purely speculative, and daily turnover ($1,880 billion in 2004) on foreign-exchange markets is now over fifty times greater than the value of daily world exports ($33 billion in 2005) (Held and McGrew 2007: 83). 'Financial engineering' has created a vast array of interconnected global capital and financial asset markets – especially in derivatives and securitized credit. There are two questions to be addressed. First, how did these changes come about, and, second, what are the consequences? As in all our previous discussions, there are two main answers – one which attributes economic change to the market's evolutionary impetus to efficiency, and another which contends that markets and money are created and sustained, but not directly operated, by state power.

Much mainstream economic theory views globalization and 'financialization' in a positive and favourable light – as the result of the market's efficiency. It is strongly implied that the global economy might ultimately come to resemble the competitive market of the economic textbook model in which barriers to the exchange of goods, services, and money and finance are removed. The free flow of capital comes about because it is the most effective way to increase the wealth of nations by enabling free trade. Furthermore, as we have seen, the derivatives and futures markets for hedging and specula-tion on price changes of physical commodities, money and financial assets are said to bring about price stability (see chapter 7). Advances in information and communication technology and organization, particularly the Internet, have facilitated and accelerated this process and progression to ever greater levels of efficiency.

The alternative explanation of the growth of global money and financial markets and the general diffusion of capitalism across the world focuses, as we have suggested, on the role of states in pursuit of their interests (Helleiner 1994; Gowan 1999; Gilpin 2001; Porter 2005; Frieden 2006). As we have noted, the two periods of globalization, founded on flows of capital and the existence of an internationally acceptable currency, were brought about by the hegemony of a dominant state and its capitalist classes – the British-led late-nineteenth-century free trade/gold standard regime and the US-dollar-based system after 1945. Although it is not unequivocally the case, the so-called 'level playing field' of open international markets generally favours, on balance, the strongest player, and the use of its currency as global money can bring enormous economic benefits and political power.[4] During the first phase of globalization, from the late nineteenth century to 1914, the City of London drew in vast wealth in interest payments, fees and commissions, and foreign debtors lived in fear of a rise in the Bank of England's interest rate (Walter 1993).

At their meeting in 1944 at Bretton Woods in upstate New York, the USA and the UK had two goals in mind as they set about planning the reconstruction of the post-Second World War global economic order. Both states were committed to economic liberalism, believing that an international division of labour and free trade were the means of achieving world prosperity. The priority was to create an international monetary system to ensure that international trade and consequently production would not be impeded by a lack of a trusted medium of exchange and means of payment, as it had been in the period between the two world wars. Keynes, Britain's representative, pressed for a truly global 'stateless' currency to be called the 'bancor', but US objections led to the adoption of the US dollar, backed by gold, as the international money.

Second, as we have seen, governments wanted to eliminate the external influence of foreign-exchange market speculation on the exchange rate of their currencies, which they rightly considered could compromise the political pledge to full employment that they had made during the war (see pp. 84–6). To achieve this end, semi-fixed exchange rates were to be engineered by currency exchange controls managed by the states' central banks in collaboration with the new Bretton Woods institutions – the International Monetary Fund and the World Bank. These steps virtually eliminated currency speculation on the foreign-exchange markets and placed the provision of currency for international trade under the control of governments and their central banks. Free trade, made possible by the new international monetary system, also enabled the global expansion of the large powerful US corporations, which was also encouraged and supported by the US state.

The Bretton Woods international monetary system was difficult to manage, but this was not the main reason for its disintegration in the early 1970s. Rather, the United States concluded that it was no longer in its interests to maintain the linchpin relation between gold and the dollar, and withdrew support for the system by which exchange rates between currencies were fixed and managed and flows of capital controlled (Helleiner 1994; Frieden 2006). By abandoning the control of money-capital flows – that is, 'deregulating' its capital market – the USA was able to attract foreign finance to fund its mounting deficits brought on by domestic expenditure and the war in Vietnam. The opening up of Wall Street to inflows of foreign capital on May Day 1975 was followed by rounds of 'competitive deregulation' in which the major countries' financial markets abolished all restrictions in order to have access to the newly freed flows of capital from around the world. Global twenty-four-hour trading in stock and foreign exchange markets, based on Tokyo–New York–London–Tokyo links, had arrived.

Arguably, this 'deregulated' regime has enhanced US power, and some have suggested that it was a deliberate US strategy, not simply to finance its deficits but also to increase its global dominance (Gowan 1999). With the collapse of the cooperatively managed dollar standard of the Bretton Woods system, the dollar became the de facto global currency. But now it was under the *exclusive* control of the US Treasury and Wall Street (Wade 2003). This confers considerable advantages on US governments and private financial interests. For example, by manipulating its interest rate, the US government can influence the dollar's exchange rate, either to reduce the price of imports and the deficit or to reduce the interest payment to foreign holders of debt. Private US banks and US global corporations gain profits and a competitive advantage from the global use of the dollar. By 1995, 61 per cent of all central bank reserves were held in dollars, 77 per cent of all bank loans were in dollars and the dollar was used to denominate 48 per cent of all invoices (Gowan 1999). Clearly, the USA is not omnipotent, but, in a real sense, the globalization of money is, in effect, 'dollarization'. Indeed, it can be persuasively argued that 'globalization' is no more than both the expression and consequences of the combined power of the US state, its multi- and transnational corporations and above all its Wall Street investment banks (Gowan 1999; Rosenberg 2000, 2005; Callinicos 2003).

As we have noted, economic globalization elicits two familiar divergent responses (see the survey of the debate in Held and McGrew 2007). On the one hand pro-globalization economists see it as an expression and vindication of their confidence, based on Smith and Ricardo, that an international division of labour based on comparative advantage and the subsequent exchange of goods and services will, in the long run, increase global welfare.

On the other hand it is contended that these developments simply exacerbate the problems produced by market capitalism – instability and inequality. It is widely held that global money markets are a major cause of equally 'global' financial and monetary crises. For example, speculation against the Thai baht in 1997 was the major cause of the east Asian financial crisis and the economic dislocation that followed (Noble and Ravenhill 2000). It led some eminent economists to call for the reintroduction of international capital controls – for example, a 'Tobin tax' to reduce volatile speculative flows (Porter 2005: 39). Others point to the fact that the crisis was short-lived and that the global capital markets were the means by which finance could flow back to revitalize the region (see the debate 'Is global capital out of control?' between Robert Wade and Anatole Kaletsky 2007).

There is also considerable debate on whether currency speculation on foreign-exchange markets exerts an unwelcome influence on the domestic economic and social policies of nation states (see, for example, Weiss 2003; Held and McGrew 2007). Changes in exchange rates have a range of direct and indirect effects on an economy (see chapter 4, note 13). These will vary according to particular circumstances and the structure of the economy. For example, a rising exchange rate might make exports more expensive and less competitive, inducing unemployment; a falling exchange rate might induce inflation by raising the price of imported goods. Economic neo-liberals argue that the markets reflect the rational assessment of confidence in an economy's strength and the profitability of its enterprises. Their opponents contend that this does not simply represent an objective assessment of economic prospects, but rather the preference for arrangements and policies that increase the rate of exploitation and weaken organized labour. National currencies are evaluated in terms of their government's conformity to neo-liberal economic preferences – low levels of government spending, especially on social welfare, low taxation, flexible labour markets, privatization and market deregulation. These policies weaken trade unions and attract inflows of capital to both the state's securities and its corporations (see the debate in Weiss 2003). Moreover, critics of neo-liberal pro-globalization argue that some sociological theories, which present 'globalization' as an irresistible 'juggernaut', constitute an ideological mask that 'normalizes' the advance of cosmopolitan money-capitalist power to dictate the terms of domestic democratic politics (see the critique of Giddens 1999 in Rosenberg 2000, 2005; see also Callinicos 2003; Hay 2006).

For its advocates, global market capitalism not only increases wealth but will also eventually lead to its more equal distribution (Wolf 2005). However, the complex and highly contentious debate shows that, on some measures, inequality has risen both between and within nations since the onset of the second phase of globalization in the 1970s (Held and Mcgrew 2007: 120–1). There is evidence to suggest that (i) there is a trend of increasing inequality of household wealth in the mature capitalist economies which is more pronounced in the liberal market economies, particularly the USA and the UK; (ii) there is a very low growth or stagnation of real income at the lower levels; (iii) the largest and fastest growth of income is very highly concentrated at the top – less than 1 per cent of households; (iv) an increasing proportion of the top incomes comprises revenue from financial and capital assets; and (v) wealth inequality (all forms of property, including capital and financial assets) is greater than income inequality and is increasing at a faster rate (Duménil and Lévy 2004; Osberg 2003: 121–41; Atkinson and Piketty 2007).

There are no clear and agreed explanations for these patterns, but there is reason to believe that they are, to a large degree, directly and indirectly a consequence of 'financialization' and the growing power of global money-capital. First, a large part of the increased inequality is accounted for in a direct way by the rapidly rising earned incomes in the financial sector and the increasing proportion of income in the upper levels of the class system that is derived from property, capital and financial assets in interest, dividends, capital gains and so on (Krippner 2005).[5] As we have seen, remuneration in very top positions in the financial sector – especially in the new speculative derivative markets and in the mergers and acquisitions business – has grown enormously and at a much faster rate than other parts of the economy. Moreover, as we have also seen, there is nothing to suggest that the enrichment of the financial sector is the result of the supply of and demand for expertise and functional contribution to the production of goods and services. Given the great concentration of power in these markets, it is rather simply a matter of their being able to reward themselves (Augar 2006). And this renewed dominance of money-capital has reinforced the downward pressure on wages in order to increase profits and extract 'shareholder value' (see chapter 6).

Finally, the globalization of capital and financial markets has created a truly cosmopolitan money-capitalist class which is not directly dependent on the profits from commodity production that is located in any particular place. Therefore this class has less need to achieve settlements with national labour forces of the kind that occurred in the 'species' or 'varieties' of managed or coordinated capitalism in the post-Second World War European social democracies and also in Japan (see also Krippner 2005: 2003).

'Varieties' of capitalism

Discussion of the importance of institutional variations in capitalist economies was prompted by the question of whether there were different but equally effective paths of economic development. It was observed that following the unplanned emergence of market capitalism in Britain, 'late development' could be sponsored and directed by states, as in Germany and Japan (Gerschenkeron 1962; Zysman 1983). The astonishing growth of Japan and other east Asian economies, the continued success of France and Germany and the eventual relative decline of the USA led many to go further than suggesting that there were merely different institutional paths to economic success and to argue that state sponsored and managed capitalism was more effective than free markets (Shonfield 1965; Albert 1991). This reconsideration of economic liberalism was associated with the shifts in the balance of political power in Western economies that had occurred after 1945, leading to the commitment to full employment and Keynesian macro-economic management.

However, as we have seen, the crises of the 1970s and the subsequent intellectual and political discrediting of Keynesian economics led to a vigorous restatement of the original virtues of Smith's economics. This confidence in the superiority of the market has been reinforced, first, by the collapse of the state socialist alternatives to capitalism and, second, by the protracted economic stagnation in Japan since 1990. It seemed that there was after all only one best way of doing capitalism – by 'free' markets.

Intellectual opposition to this restatement of classical economic liberalism has become centred on two quite divergent traditions – sociological 'institutionalism' and Marxist-inspired 'regulation theory'. The increasingly complicated debate cannot be examined in any detail here, but it should be noted that it is conducted almost exclusively within sociology and political economy. That is to say, there is little direct dialogue between the neo-liberal economists' advocacy of the free market and these opposing schools (Hall and Soskice 2001; Amable 2003; Streeck and Thelen 2005; Deeg and Jackson 2007; for a broader approach that engages economic literature see Coates 2000, 2005). Details aside, the broad 'varieties of capitalism' (VoC) school holds that capitalist economies have significant institutional differences and that there is no reason to believe that there is one best way of organizing capitalism, as is strongly implied by the neo-liberal model of the market.

Leaving aside the complexities and the construction of more elaborate typologies (Coates 2000; Boyer 2005), the classification of the 'varieties' of capitalism into two main ideal types of 'liberal market economies' (LME) and 'coordinated market economies' (CME) accurately presents the major differences in question (Hall and Soskice 2001: 1–68). Economic coordination of firms in LMEs is accomplished by competitive market relations characterized by 'arm's length' – that is, impersonal – market exchange in response to price signals. CMEs rely more extensively on non-market coordination involving networks, strategic interaction and collaboration (Hall and Soskice 2001: 8). LMEs have higher levels of income inequality and lower levels of employment protection than CMEs (Hall and Soskice 2001: 21; see also Atkinson and Piketty 2007).

Capitalist economies can be placed on a continuum between these two polar ideal types – LME and CME. Of the major OECD states, five are classified as liberal market economies (USA, Britain, Canada, New Zealand and Ireland) and ten as coordinated market economies (Germany, Japan, Switzerland, Netherlands, Belgium, Sweden, Norway, Denmark, Finland, and Austria). The USA is taken as an archetypical LME and Germany as the exemplar of a CME. France, Italy, Spain, Portugal, Greece and Turkey fall midway between the two polar types in 'ambiguous positions' (Hall and Soskice 2001: 21).

'Complementarities' are said to exist between the economic institutions of each 'variety'; for example, as we noted in chapter 6, there is a link between the financial system and corporate governance. The provision of finance by bank loans, as opposed to the stock market, is described as 'patient capital', in that it permits a longer time perspective on returns to investment which, in turn, enables the retention of a skilled labour force with significant employment protection, as in Germany. Firms overcome the risks which this commitment entails by cooperation in training programmes and technology transfers in order to strengthen the industrial sector as a whole (Hall and Soskice 2001: 22–3).

After their apparently superior performance after the Second World War, economic growth in the CMEs had slowed by the end of the twentieth century. But Hall and Soskice reject the neo-liberal economic argument that this was the result of interference in markets forces by continental European states and of the 'crony' capitalism of east Asia: 'despite some variation over specific periods, both liberal and coordinated market economies seem capable of providing satisfactory levels of long-run economic performance' (Hall and Soskice 2001: 21).

Aside from issues concerning classification and the range of 'variety', there are two basic and closely related questions in this debate. First, how did the institutional differences come about? Second, is there a process of convergence, as the neo-liberals argue, to a single type, based on the Anglo-US systems and driven by the superior functional efficiency of market coordination?

There are two quite distinct, but not incompatible, explanations of institutional variety – as the result of 'path dependency' (see Arthur 1985) or the product of economic and political conflict. 'Path dependency' refers to the fact that, in the absence of any countervailing force, the institutional framework that is in place at the beginning of capitalist development will persist as a formative influence on the forging of subsequent 'complementary' institutions. For example, London's eighteenth-century market for government stocks and bonds later provided the means for financing capitalist enterprise in the late nineteenth century, setting the framework for the Anglo-US liberal-market type of economy. The second wave of capitalist development, most notably in Germany and Japan, was sponsored by governments as the basis of a wider strategy to create strong, internationally competitive nation states. As we have seen, all capitalist development is dependent on the state, but in Germany and Japan state involvement in the economy was more direct and extensive than in Britain and the USA. In close collaboration with their capitalist classes, they financed infrastructure, sponsored industrial development in association with the large banks and created an educated and skilled workforce (Streeck and Yamamura 2001).

However, as we saw in chapter 6, economic and political conflict can produce quite sharp departures from 'path dependency'. Stock-market finance declined in France in the 1930s in response to the Popular Front socialist government's regulation of the labour market, but flourished in the USA in the face of popular opposition to the emergence of bank-based monopoly capitalism in the late nineteenth and early twentieth centuries (Roe 1994; Phillips 2002). During the 1980s, Margaret Thatcher's Conservative government put Britain back on a neo-liberal path after an uncertain and incomplete deviation towards corporatism and the coordinated market form of economy in the 1960s and 1970s.

In other words much of the institutional variety across capitalist economies is the result of the means by which the Weberian 'struggle for economic existence' has been resolved to the point at which a level of social peace necessary for sustained capitalist production is achieved. In this respect, it is significant that the coordinated market economies are also to a large extent, though not exclusively, those in which 'corporatist' political settlements underpinned the post-Second World War commitments to full employment and social welfare (Goldthorpe 1984). 'Tripartite' negotiations between the three 'corporate' bodies of labour, employers and government aimed to fix wages, prices and government expenditure at a level that was both acceptable to all parties and non-inflationary. Until the 1970s crises, it was widely believed that this form of regulation was superior to the unprincipled labour market struggles in the liberal market economies.

In short, it would appear that there is a range of viable institutional arrangements for organizing capitalist economies and relationships between its constituent classes and the state. Furthermore, it is possible that different 'varieties' or 'species' are relatively successful at different times and under different circumstances. For example, state management and direction of the economy in many east Asian countries has brought considerable success, despite the accusation that this has involved 'rent-seeking' and 'crony capitalism' that contravened the principles of the free market and created inefficiencies (see the discussion of 'rent-seeking' in chapter 8).

Again according to neo-liberal theory, the high levels of taxation and government spending on welfare in Scandinavian social democracies should impair economic performance by creating inflation and 'crowding out' resources from the inherently more efficient private sector. However, between 1990 and 2003 productivity in Sweden's manufacturing industry grew faster than in any other industrialized economy, including the USA (Glyn 2006: 167). Furthermore, Finland and Sweden occupy second and third places in the pro-capitalist World Economic Forum's order of international competitiveness – several places above the USA and the UK (*The Economist*, 30 September 2006).

The second issue in considering the genus and species of capitalism is more intriguing and politically contentious. It involves two interdependent questions that were posed in the discussion of globalization: does the current trend towards the liberalization of the world's major economies herald the eventual convergence to an Anglo-US liberal-market type, and, if so, is this because of its superior long-run economic efficiency? According to this view, the success of coordinated market economies, such as Japan, was inevitably short-lived because the close links, on the one hand between the large corporations and on the other between these and the state, produced an institutional rigidity which, unlike the looser market coordination, was unable to adapt to changing circumstances.[6]

There is reluctance within the 'varieties' school to accept that convergence is taking place, but some exponents have no doubt that since the disintegration of the post-Second World War class settlements and the economic 'golden age' there has been a significant trend towards market liberalization in the coordinated economies (Streeck and Thelen 2005: 1–39).[7] Two closely related institutional changes have occurred in the west European CMEs. First, labour markets have been made more 'flexible'; that is to say there have been reductions in employment protection and job security and a loosening of restrictions on working hours (Glyn 2006). Second, there has been a shift towards the use of stock-market finance and a marked increase in the intrusion of hostile takeovers and mergers, often orchestrated by the highly mobile money-capital of Anglo-US investment banks and private equity funds (see Schmidt 2002 for a comparison with Germany). In France, for example, the value of capitalization of the French stock market grew from a low 5.6 per cent of GDP in the 1980s to 111.5 per cent by 1999 (Schmidt 2002). In Japan, partly as a consequence of the persistent deflation and stagnation, lifetime employment is less prevalent, there is an increasing use of stock market finance and the tight financial links between banks and corporations have been loosened to some extent (Vogel 2006). However, the institutional distinctiveness of the CMEs is not being rapidly swept away. There is evidence that existing ways of operating capitalism in these countries are merely being adapted to take account of the forces for change. For example, the state continues to exert a strong influence on the French economy, but this power has shifted from the traditional *dirigiste* direction of capital and the exclusion of labour from decision-making to the enforcement of market liberalization, accompanied by an attempt to temper the social consequences (Vogel in Streeck and Thelen 2005). Furthermore, French governments resist hostile takeovers by foreign interests, and there has been only partial privatization of infrastructure services and utilities – electricity and air and rail transport. And there is continued support for 'national champions' – for example, the Sanofi-Synthélabo–Aventis merger in pharmaceutical industry to produce a challenge to US corporations (see Schmidt 2002). After over half a century of the post-Second World War social democratic settlement and in the absence of a Thatcher-style revolution, political support and legitimacy in the CMEs remains based to a considerable extent on conceptions of 'stakeholding' and 'economic citizenship'. However, the tensions between capitalism and social democracy continue to dominate politics in many continental European states and to produce ambiguity and equivocation. President Nicolas Sarkozy of France supports the liberalization of the economy, but at the same time appears to be as opposed as his predecessors to the Anglo-American style of capitalism and to insist that strategically important industries should not fall into the hands of foreign finance capitalists.

The 'battle of the systems' has undoubtedly begun, in which global flows of money-capital and transnational corporations, as we noted in the previous section, are placing pressure on the basic institutions of the CMEs – labour protection and security and the provision of long-term capital (Whiteley, Quack and Morgan 2000).[8] In addition, the global spread of capitalism has increased price competition in manufactured goods, placing pressure on wage costs and, consequently, the 'stakeholder' conception of the capitalist social relations of production. However, the strength of this global force should not be overestimated. 'Complementarity' between long-term, or 'patient', capital and a highly skilled workforce gives many CMEs a comparative advantage in the production of high-quality, high-value-added commodities (Weiss 2003). Lower labour costs in the emerging capitalist economies do not pose a direct threat to specialized niche production in mature CMEs such as Germany's Mercedes Benz, Porsche and Audi automobiles. Moreover, the labour intensive, low-value-added parts of production processes can be outsourced to emerging capitalist economies such as China and India, further reducing the costs of niche production of quality goods.

The greater potential disturbance to the CME 'variety' comes from the intrusion of money-capital and financial markets bent on monetization and short-term profits. Although the VoC approach focuses to a large extent on production and industrial relations, it implicitly recognizes that the fundamental difference between the two main 'varieties' lies in the nature of their financial systems. Domestic, 'patient', bank-based capital permits the longer-term orientation in production which enables 'complementary' non-market collaborative coordination between firms and banks and between firms and workers – as in Germany and Japan. However, global 'financialization' involves the penetration of domestic economies by so-called 'footloose' capital with the intention of transforming the enterprise into a financial asset whose value is enhanced by increasing short-term profitability by a reduction of labour costs, threatening the 'stakeholding' mode of governance.

'Liquidity', 'flexibility' and 'creative destruction' are understandably resisted by those outside the money-capital networks and markets – that is to say, those classes directly involved in production – incumbent family owners, managers and workers. These classes have achieved a favoured position in the coordinated market economies. First, the cooperation of capitalist elites and key workers required for the creation of a strong 'national economy' by the late-developing states, was attained, in part, by protecting them from global market forces by means of welfare, long-term employment and government subsidies and contracts. Again this can be seen most clearly in the Japanese and German economies, where the stability and strength of large firms was a government priority during the post-war period as a means of building political stability.

The basic question is whether the liberal market 'variety' will continue to spread because money-capital's search for profits, unhindered by coalitions of producers in the enterprise, is the most effective form of capitalism, ensuring the necessary cost control and 'creative destruction' for continued dynamism (Rajan and Zingales 2003; on the impairment of capitalism by such 'distributional coalitions' see Olsen 1982). Or is the erosion of coordinated managed capitalism the result of the hegemony of the US form of capitalism, as practised by its all-powerful transnational corporations and Wall Street investment banks, and disseminated by the 'Washington consensus' in global capitalist agencies such as the World Bank and the International Monetary Fund?[9]

Aside from the enormous complexity of the question it is, however, not one that that can be answered with any certainty, because whatever the outcome of the 'battle of the systems', it will not be the result of any single pure economic logic of efficiency as neo-liberal economics implies. As we noted in the previous chapter, a basic level of social peace – that is, a settlement between the classes – is a precondition of capitalist production. Consequently, how this is achieved will vary in relation to the complex struggles between shifting economic and political alliances which shape the institutional structure of economies and their performance. The degree to which global capitalism comes to resemble the liberal model will depend on the range of related contingent factors that we have already noted. First, the strength of the 'producers' alliance' within the enterprise and the political unpopularity of economic liberalization will affect the pace of change, as the political history of Japan since the early 1990s has shown.

Second, the dissemination of the liberal market system across the world is conditional on the continued dominance of the US state, its transnational corporations and, in particular, Wall Street's powerful oligopoly.

As we have seen, 'liberalization' of capitalism has been driven to a large extent by global 'financialization'. The world's major capitalist power, the USA, led the way by abandoning the Bretton Woods control of global flows of capital and a little later, in 1975, opening up its domestic capital market, which set in train a process of global financial deregulation. Just as free trade in goods favoured Britain as the strongest manufacturing economy in the nineteenth century, liberal financial markets and the use of the dollar as the world currency brings great benefits to the USA.

First, as we have already noted, the USA and Wall Street gain significant advantages in the world's use of its currency and the banks and financial corporations that create it and disseminate it globally.[10] Second, a 'level playing field' of free trade and markets, including capital and finance, gives an advantage to the strongest players. Since the mid-1970s, the USA, using its dominant position in the General Agreement on Tariffs and Trade (GATT) and the World Trade Organization (WTO), the International Monetary Fund and the World Bank, has promoted rules and practices of global free markets in which there are no barriers to entry or substantial restrictions on the operation of banks and transitional corporations.[11] Third, both the above factors – that is, resistance to and dominance of US capital and its mode of operation – would be affected by serious global financial crises, which have increased with the acceleration of global financial liberalization – 'more between 1980 and 2000 than in any earlier period' (Kindleberger and Aliber 2005: 243). And they have continued with increasing frequency in the twenty-first century. Fourth, any serious weakening of US hegemony that such crises might induce could, in turn, disturb the global geopolitical balance and the level of peace that is the foundation for the diffusion of the US liberal-market version – or indeed, capitalism itself. Finally, as we have noted in passing, China might yet produce an entirely novel form of state capitalism in which control of the economy extends beyond mere 'coordination'.

Will capitalism endure?

The fall of communism in the Soviet empire after 1989 led to serious contemplation that 'the end of history' had been reached in the sense that human society had finally developed, in utter contradiction of Marx's prognosis, a form of economy and society that combined capitalism and liberal democracy which would prove capable of providing for all our needs (Fukuyama 1992). Alternatives to market capitalism had proved to be unworkable. There were few insurrections; rather, 'quiet revolutions' had led to the replacement of state socialist regimes after their economies had finally disintegrated under the weight of their inefficiencies.

Of course, many of those who might subscribe to this general view also acknowledge the existence of persistent sources of instability in capitalism, but these are deemed to be manageable imperfections, not Marx's terminal contradictions. The general tenor of the Austrian school of economics' theoretical defence of the market, discussed in chapter 5, is widely held and has been implicitly and unwittingly incorporated in the 'third way' conception of the relationship between capitalism and democracy. Both theories argue that the liberal political system and market economy, unlike state socialism, have an inbuilt capacity for 'reflexivity', by which the effects of human action are constantly monitored, leading to adaptive behaviour and the correction of malfunction. Indeed, it is very strongly implied in some branches of influential sociological theory that the market is the model for the institutionalized reflexivity which characterizes 'modernity' (see Giddens 1999; Soros 2008; on the connection between the global finance capitalist Soros and modern sociological theory see Bryant 2002). Here, as in neo-classical economics, the possibility of large-scale structural transformation brought about by economic catastrophe and class conflict, as contemplated by Marx, is not considered.

Of course, we have no way of knowing whether history has come to an 'end' in this Hegelian sense, but the last three thousand years of human history provides a basis for scepticism. A thorough examination of the question is far beyond the scope of the present analysis, but we might very briefly reiterate and reconsider the major points of vulnerability that pose threats to the market-capitalist mode of production and exchange.

Although there can be no certainty in such matters, there would appear to be little likelihood that conflict over the distribution of wealth and income will, in itself, bring about fundamental structural change. History is not an infallible guide, but the institutional separation of political and economic conflict during the twentieth century, discussed in chapter 8, would appear to have removed this remote possibility in the major capitalist democracies. As I write, the financial turmoil triggered by the US subprime mortgage defaults has prompted a prominent defender of globalization and market capitalism to suggest that governments should try to control the excessive remuneration in the financial sector (Martin Wolf, *Financial Times*, 16 January, 7 February 2008). Two years earlier, in 2005, Alan Greenspan conceded that rising income inequality was 'a very disturbing trend [and] not the type of thing which a democratic – capitalist democratic society – can really accept without addressing' (Greenspan 2005).[12] At present, however, this no more than the expression of a little disquiet in some quarters of the capitalist elite that the system could be seriously discredited by a combination of blatant greed and financial crisis. But we are clearly a considerable distance from the contemplation of radical change that might attract popular support. With the demise of socialism, there are no grand theories of alternative social and political forms that might command greater legitimacy than the existing order.

However, fault lines in the capitalist system might yet open to the point that they change this state of affairs. Let us remind ourselves of these ever-present sources of crisis. First, as Marx and Polanyi argued, the free market threatens to degrade the physical environment to an extent that seriously disturbs and threatens our existence. It is true to say that global warming, environmental pollution and the depletion of non-renewable resources are not specific to capitalism. Rather, they are consequences of the transformation wrought by the technology of industrialism, and, indeed, it could be argued that the record of state socialism has been worse in this respect. However, the force of the Polanyian critique is directed to the inability of the market to correct these negative consequences. It is less sanguine about the efficacy of 'reflexivity' and recognizes that the situation demands a concerted political will on the part of the major industrial powers. But political and economic rivalry, and the domestic unpopularity of the impact on consumption and lifestyle that measures to control environmental degradation will bring have, so far, prevented effective measures. Such is the hegemony of neo-liberal economics that it is believed that the price mechanism can be employed to resolve these 'externalities'. For example, a market for carbon-emissions credits could make it advantageous for individual enterprises to sell the right to pollute. However, there is widespread scepticism of these strategies, and they have yet to make any significant impact.

Aside from the physical insecurity that capitalism has fostered, there are, as we have seen, three basic and closely interrelated sources of economic fragility in capitalism that exercise the minds of governments, capitalists and economic intellectuals. These are the monetary problems associated with inflation and deflation, cycles of overproduction/underconsumption and financial instability. From both a historical and theoretical standpoint, the most threatening economic source of systemic disturbance, as I have stressed, comes from the inherent fragility of the debt-based monetary and financial system. Twentieth-century history, especially during the 1930s and 1970s, shows that the economic order can be perturbed to such an extent that political instability results. But the crises were managed by those capitalist states that remained powerful enough to implement a combination of political and economic measures that were the result of Keynes's and others' recasting of the theory of the self-regulating market.

From the outbreak of the First World War to the crises of the 1970s there was a gradual decline and reining in of the autonomous power of private money-capital. Capital and financial markets were first disrupted by war and then eventually regulated in response to the first truly global debt-deflation after the Wall Street crash in 1929 threatened to destroy capitalism. The actions of money-capitalists – bankers and rentiers – exacerbated the economic consequences of the crises by pressing for deflationary 'sound money' policies to preserve value of their investments. Even such a staunch supporter of the free capitalist system as Keynes considered that it was necessary to curtail the power of money-capital by placing the financial system under public ownership – the 'euthanasia of the rentier' (Keynes 1973 [1936]: 376). This did not come about, but the efforts during the 1930s to reverse economic stagnation and unemployment were accompanied by controls on money-capital, including, for example, the imposition of ceilings on interest rates in the USA (see Greider 1987).

The Second World War virtually destroyed all private global financial markets and banking networks and further consolidated the collaboration and settlement between states, enterprise capital and their workers in the war effort. Whereas bankers and financiers had been the most influential participants in the reconstruction of the capitalist world after 1918, they were not even invited to the Bretton Woods negotiations in 1944 (Ingham 2004; Burn 2006). As we have seen, since the crises of the 1970s global financial markets have expanded and the dominance of money-capital has gradually been re-established on a far greater scale than ever before in the history of capitalism. As has been shown in the past, unleashed money-capital possesses immense self-destructive power. It remains to be seen whether this will be repeated in the global financial dislocation that has followed the US subprime mortgage defaults and, if called upon, whether states will be able to rescue capitalism. And, in doing so, will they yet again unwittingly create the conditions that sustain the ideological misconception that there exists an 'invisible hand' and that it is best able to regulate humanity's economic affairs?

Notes

Introduction

1   Over the past decade or so the question of the Western origins
of capitalism has become the focus of a heated debate in history
and sociology. On the one hand, the classic nineteenth-century
accounts of Smith, Marx and Weber have been labelled 'Eurocentric' for their neglect of the oriental contribution to the
development of capitalism as a world system (Frank 1998;
Goody 2004). On the other hand, a 'California School' of economic historians has identified a 'great divergence' in the sixteenth century, when China's earlier economic superiority was
overtaken by the West (Pomeranz 2000; Vries 2003; Faure
2006; Arrighi 2008). This fascinating question cannot be
pursued here, but the understanding of capitalism presented in
this book gives clues to my own view of this debate. As the following account strongly implies, I support the view that capitalism originated in the West and that the overtaking of China was
largely due to the emergence in the early modern period in Italy,
the Netherlands and Britain of banking systems that linked the
state and the nascent mercantile bourgeoisie in the production
of credit-money for the finance of production and exchange.
This development was conspicuously absent in China.

1   Smith, Marx and Weber

1   The classical liberal economics of Adam Smith and David
Ricardo argued that free trade based upon 'comparative

advantage' was the best way to increase total world wealth, which in the long run would be to the benefit of all. Countries should specialize in what they could produce most efficiently and then trade it for things others could produce more efficiently. Thus, in aggregate costs of production are minimized. Mercantilist thinking, as we shall see, has not been entirely superseded by Smithian economics. Despite agreement in principle with the collective benefits of free trade, governments are aware, on the one hand, that this might lead to electoral unpopularity if unemployment results from a loss of competitiveness on the world market. On the other hand, certain industries such as energy are protected from foreign ownership because of their strategic importance.

2 Smith had a four-stage scheme: hunting, pasturage, farming, commerce.

3 Polanyi (1957) identified three ideal type systems of organizing production and distribution: by market price, according to norms of reciprocity, and by administrative redistribution. For example, in tribal societies goods are allocated according to customary norms, and in ancient empires and modern state socialism, goods are redistributed by the central authority. See the discussion in chapter 5.

4 We shall return to this important question of the role of money in capitalism in the work of Schumpeter and Keynes and in the discussion of monetary systems in chapter 4. Here we should also note that Smith and other classical economists also made a sharp distinction between bank credit and money. Money was a commodity with an intrinsic value – such as precious metal – that acted as a medium of exchange. Credit, which greatly aided production and exchange, was nothing more than the representation of commodity money or of the wealth that, once generated, would make repayment possible.

5 There is, however, a further incomplete and inconsistent element in Smith's analysis, implications of which were subsequently taken further within the framework of classical economics by Ricardo and others. Exchange establishes and reconciles the natural and market price of goods, but ultimately, according to Smith, the real value of any commodity is equal to the quantity of labour which is required either to earn the wages to purchase it or to hire labour in order that the commodity can be produced (1986 [1776]: 133–4). *The Wealth of Nations* contains the implication that labour is the measure of value. Marx seized upon this and used it as a weapon in his savage critique of bourgeois political eco-

nomy's understanding of a society based on the power of capital.

6 Aside from their academic economic work, both Hayek and Friedman produced more popular defences of market capitalism. See Hayek, *The Road to Serfdom* (1944) and *The Constitution of Liberty* (1960); Friedman, *Capitalism and Freedom* (1962).

7 Marx famously contended that classical political economy begins with the fact of private property, but does not explain it.

8 The nature of money and the relationship between currency and bank credit were the subjects of an intense debate in Britain during the first half of the nineteenth century. Theoretically, Marx tended to side with the 'metallist', or commodity, theories of money that were used to explain the gold standard. Gold could become money – that is, embody value as a 'universal equivalent' – because mining and minting embodied labour time. For Marx, bank credit merely represented 'real' money and Marx focused on its essentially dysfunctional role as 'fictitious capital' that exacerbated crises of overproduction (see Ingham 2004: 61–3).

9 This emphasis on conflict is a significant departure from economic theory which argues that prices express the 'marginal utility' of goods for individuals based on their subjective preferences. Marginal utility is the theory of demand which states that goods will be consumed to the point – that is, margin – at which they cease to give satisfaction. Weber argues, first, that demand is not merely a matter of subjective wants, but rather 'effective demand' based on real purchasing power. Second, he contends that the idea of the 'sovereign consumer' whose wants stimulate production does not apply to modern capitalism, where 'even though the consumer has to be in a position to buy, his wants are "awakened" and "directed" by the entrepreneur' (Weber 1978: 92; see our discussion of 'monopolistic competition' in chapter 5).

10 'Mercantilism' refers to the economic doctrines that were developed by the emerging European states from the sixteenth to the eighteenth century, in which they attempted to include as many sources of wealth and taxable income as possible within their territory. This involved the protection of agriculture and industry with duties and tariffs, the promotion of exports and the hoarding of precious metals. From a theoretical standpoint, the classical economists, notably Adam Smith and David Ricardo, pointed to the self-defeating consequences

if such an economic system were to be universally followed. The overall expansion of the world economy and, consequently, the wealth of all nations depended on the international division of labour and free trade. However, despite the purely logical coherence of classical economic arguments, it can be in the interests of states to use their economic resources as instruments in pursuit of their geopolitical interests. As opponents of the classical liberal doctrine argued, free trade favours the strongest states.

2   Schumpeter and Keynes

1   Schumpeter clearly explained this implicit distinction in economic theory between the 'real' and the 'monetary':

> Real analysis proceeds from the principle that all the essential phenomena of economic life are capable of being described in terms of goods and services, of decisions about them, and of relations between them. Money enters the picture only in the modest role of a technical device that has been adopted in order to facilitate transactions . . . so long as it functions normally, it does not affect the economic process, which behaves in exactly the same way as it would in barter economy: this is essentially what the concept of Neutral Money implies. Thus, money has been called a 'garb' or 'veil' of the things that really matter . . . Not only can it be discarded whenever we are analyzing the fundamental features of the economic process but it must be discarded just as a veil must be drawn aside if we are to see the face behind it. Accordingly, money prices must give way to the exchange relations between the commodities that are the really important thing 'behind' the money prices. (Schumpeter 1994 [1954]: 277)

This does not mean that money is not 'real' in an ontological sense.
2   Furthermore, aside from its misleading depiction of capitalist bank practice as simple intermediation between savers, this financial version of the circular flow also has difficulty in explaining bank profits. The rate of interest could not be a source of profits as it was considered merely to express the 'price' of finance as determined by the supply of savings and the demand for investment that was dictated by the level of

income from the factors of production. At best, banks could make profits from the intermediation service they provided for savers and borrowers.

3 The basic elements of capitalism

1 'How complete the divorce is between the experience of daily life and the teaching of economists can best be seen by reading, for example, Marshall's chapter on capital, with its complicated divisions into national capital, social capital, personal capital etc. Every banker and every commercial man knows that there is only one kind of capital, and that is money. Every commercial and financial transaction is based on this proposition, every balance sheet is made out in accordance with the well-established fact. And yet every economist bases his teaching on the hypothesis that capital is not money' (Innes 1914: 355).

2 The price of financial assets can also vary across spatially distinct markets, creating an opportunity to profit from arbitrage – that is, buying in one location and selling at a higher price in another.

3 See also the discussion of 'mercantilism' and 'political capitalism' in chapter 8. Following Trotsky, some socialists characterized communist Russia as 'state capitalist' (see the discussion in Szelenyi, Beckett and King 1994). Modern China has caused similar debates; see Nolan 2004.

4 A broad school of 'cultural economy' contends that economic systems are best understood as cultural phenomena in the sense that they are produced by 'narratives', which explain how they operate. For example, economic theories of the competitive market can be considered among such narratives of the economy, and they are held to be 'performative' in that they shape how it works (Callon 1998; MacKenzie 2006; MacKenzie, Fabian and Sui 2007; du Gay 1998;). Competition, management practice and financial markets are socially constructed in relation to the theories that are held to explain them. It is true to say that social reality is to some extent constructed in this way – but not entirely so. For example, models of financial markets shape actors' behaviour, which, in turn, reproduces the market; but markets also crash, regardless of the social meanings attributed to them (see Erturk et al. 2008). In other words, complex economic systems cannot be understood entirely in terms of the actors' beliefs about their operation.

5   As Weber later observed, 'the religious root of modern economic humanity is dead' (Weber 1981 [1927]: 386).

4 Money

1   However, these societies did not possess coinage (money 'things'), but used an abstract money notation – 'money of account' – for making budgetary calculations and expressing prices and debts in monetary value (see Ingham 2004).

2   These functions describe – but do not explain – the origins and existence of money (see Ingham 2004).

3   In this theory, the focus of attention is on media of exchange – money 'things' that pass from hand to hand. Less attention is given to other means of monetary transmission. There is an important, but rarely made, distinction between media of exchange and media of transmission. Coins and notes are generally considered to be media of exchange and transmission – or currency that circulates. But credit cards, for example, are not exchanged for goods – that is to say, they are (or should be!) non-circulating media of transmission of abstract value stored in accounts. This of course raises intriguing questions; for example, in a credit card transaction what does money consist of? If coins and credit cards are both money, how do we know this (see Ingham 2006)?

4   If barter cannot produce a stable and uniform measure and standard of value (money of account), the fundamental question of its historical origins remains. The most plausible explanation contends that the concept of a socially accepted general measure of value derives from the elaborate scales of tariffs and penalties imposed by early society as compensation for insult and injury not merely to individuals but also to society as a whole. For example, killing a young man was materially more injurious to society than the murder of an old woman and therefore carried a greater penalty, as did insults to the king as opposed to one's neighbour. Grierson (1979) argues that these *wergeld* ('worthpayment') systems provided the idea of a measure of value (see the discussion in Ingham 2004).

5   As Simmel argues, something may be judged to be more valuable (or longer) than another by direct comparison, but precisely how much more valuable (or longer) can only be established by an abstract measure against which they can both be judged.

6   It is important to note that this theory of money also considers precious-metal coinage to be an abstraction in the sense that a declared weight of metal is considered to be, say, a silver 'penny' of which 12 make 1 'shilling'. Moreover, the abstract purchasing power of precious-metal money can be maintained for long periods even when the silver is debased with base metal, and the abstract ratio of 1:12 remains constant.

7   Of course, money is traded as a commodity on foreign-exchange markets, but it must be first constituted as money – that is to say, as dollars, pounds, yen, euros and so on.

8   Sovereigns could make profits from seignorage – that is to say, declaring that a coin is worth more than its market value in precious metal – and by declaring what they would accept in payment of taxes they could impose their own money.

9   For example, in the early modern period, almost pure gold coins issued by the Ottoman empire were in great demand throughout Europe as a store of wealth, but the Ottoman economy suffered from a lack of finance (Bernstein 2000: 64).

10 Bank of England notes still bear the vestigial and now meaningless words that they 'promise to pay the bearer on demand the sum of £X'; all they could do would be to exchange the note for others to the same amount.

11 Economists are sharply divided on whether central banks should act as 'lenders of last resort' to the banking and financial system in the event of a chain reaction of defaults that threatens to create bankruptcies and makes banks wary of extending loans. On the one hand, it is argued that an injection of state central bank money is the only way of averting a recession in the productive economy caused by this contraction of the supply of credit-money. On the other hand, economic liberals contend that such lending creates 'moral hazard' – that is to say, it encourages banks to make increasingly risky loans in the knowledge that they will be saved if their debtors default.

12 Many central banks are now involved in an attempt to mould 'inflation expectations' by setting an inflation rate target and adjusting interest rates to the level that expert economic analysis believes will achieve it. It is hoped that this will nullify expectations of inflation and consequently make it less likely that producers will raise prices and workers demand higher wages.

13 By its effect on currency exchange rates, speculation on foreign-exchange markets affects domestic economies by changing

among other things the prices of exports and imports. For example, speculative demand for a currency will produce a rising exchange rate; a higher price for exports could make an export industry uncompetitive on world markets and create domestic unemployment. (On the other hand, by making imports cheaper this could help to control domestic inflation.) Conversely, a falling exchange rate could make it difficult for those industries which require imported raw materials. A central bank can attempt to stabilize its currency's exchange rate at a level that is thought to be consistent with a desired level of economic activity and employment in two ways. First, it can try to defend a particular exchange rate by buying or selling its own and other currencies on the foreign exchange market – as the Bank of England spectacularly failed to do on Black Wednesday in 1992 in the attempt to maintain the sterling–Deutschmark exchange rate. Second, central banks can manipulate the domestic interest rates in order either to increase or to reduce demand for its currency on the foreign-exchange markets – for example, raising the interest rate will increase demand for a currency. However, interest rates also affect consumer demand and investment in the domestic economy; raising interest rates to increase demand for currency on foreign exchange markets might, for example, have a deflationary effect on domestic investment and consumption and cause unemployment. The complex relationships between – [1] maintaining a fixed exchange rate for currencies; [2] domestic autonomy in control of interest rates by central banks to influence the level of consumption, investment and therefore employment; and [3] the existence of unrestricted foreign-exchange markets – i.e. free international capital/money mobility, including currency speculation – is known as the 'trilemma' due to the impossibility of maintaining all three conditions simultaneously.

With [3] (unrestricted foreign-exchange markets), it is possible to have either [1] or [2], but not both. For example, with [3] (unrestricted foreign-exchange markets) and [2] (domestic control of interest rates to encourage a desired level of investment, consumption and employment) it is not possible to control a currency's exchange rate. For example, setting a low rate of interest to encourage domestic investment and consumption might drive speculators to sell the currency and acquire other currencies with higher rates of interest. The resulting falling exchange rate could then increase the cost of imported raw materials and other goods and consequently deflate production, consumption and employment. With the existence of unrestricted foreign exchange markets [3], maintaining a fixed exchange rate [1] requires that domestic interest rates are changed in order to either increase or decrease international demand for a currency, regardless of the impact on domestic investment, employment and consumption.

With their commitment to full employment, the Allies decided at the Bretton Woods negotiations to attempt to avoid all the problems that could be caused by the impact of fluctuating exchange rates by introducing exchange controls on international capital and currency movements. Foreign currencies could only be acquired for the financing of trade, not speculation. It was also understood that welfare spending and the government's stimulation of the economy with Keynesian demand management would be seen as inflationary and might cause a loss of confidence in the currency which, with free international money/capital markets, would affect the exchange rate. Thus in order to allow governments to exert the maximum control over their economy, the Bretton Woods international monetary system opted to have both [1] and [2] by preventing [3].

After the disintegration and abandonment of Bretton Woods in the 1970s, the foreign-exchange markets regained their power to influence exchange rates, and now there are two possibilities: either [1] and [3], or [2] and [3]. With [1] (fixed/stable exchange rate) and the existence of [3] (unrestricted foreign-exchange markets), there is the loss of control of [2] (domestic interest rate), because this will need to be changed to influence the level of demand for a currency. With control of [2] (domestic interest rates to influence the levels of investment and consumption) and the existence of [3] (unrestricted foreign-exchange markets), there is a loss of control over exchange rates. This coexistence of [2] and [3] forms the current international monetary regime that has been in existence since the disintegration of the Bretton Woods system of exchange controls in the 1970s. The increased international capital flows and currency speculation are arguably the main factors in economic globalization and place constraints on domestic economic and social policies (chapter 9; and Helleiner 1994; Gilpin 2001: 234–60).

14 In general, inflation has been kept in check by low labour costs in developing countries but this situation will change.

15 Under state auspices in the early twentieth century the Japanese economy was organized into large privately owned blocks of

firms known as *zaibatsu* – later *keiretsu*, or 'enterprise group-ings' (see Gerlach 1992).

5 Market exchange

1 The economic theory of the market is said to be 'performative', in that it provides the rationale and the model for the construction of more competitive markets by privatization, deregulation, competition policy and so on. See Callon 1998; Mackenzie 2006.

2 In this respect it is significant that some of the most notable economic theorists in the early twentieth century had to intro-duce further institutional elements into the model in order to make its operation more intelligible. For example, Leon Walras introduced an 'auctioneer' into his mathematical analysis to make the coordination of the myriad bids and offers more plausible. Alfred Marshall observed that only exceptionally did markets clear in the sense that all goods are sold and all demand is satisfied. Consequently he added a merchant middle-man to the model to hold over some supply and to mediate between producers and consumers and so regulate and balance supply and demand.

3 Weber constructed a sociological interpretation of this argu-ment, which led him to conclude that market struggle is the best known means of establishing the actual scarcity of goods that makes possible money prices and, consequently, rational calculation (see pp. 24–8). Furthermore, competition – or, in Weber's terms, the 'struggle for economic existence' or 'the battle of man against man in the market' – adds the dynamism to the system that would be absent in a planned economy. Weber argued that the Babylonian and Egyptian ancient bureaucratic empires had declined partly as a consequence of their inefficiencies and lack of dynamism.

4 It should be noted that it is the institution of property rights that produces a socially created, not a natural, scarcity.

5 The idea of emissions trading is to harness economic incentives and the market mechanism to reduce atmospheric pollution. An authority – government or governments – places a limit on the amount of a pollutant that can be emitted. Companies or other groups are issued emission permits and are required to hold an equivalent number of credits for the right to emit a pollutant. Companies that need to increase their emissions must buy credits from those who pollute less. In effect, the

buyer pays a charge for polluting, and the seller is rewarded for having reduced emissions by more than was needed. In theory, those that can easily reduce emissions most cheaply will do so, achieving pollution reduction at the lowest possible cost to society.

6 For example, as Akerlof famously explained in his 'Market for "Lemons"', the inability of buyers accurately to distinguish between low-quality ('lemons') and high-quality second-hand cars can keep prices low and, consequently, deter the owners of high-quality cars from putting them on the market (Akerlof 1970). Again, it is possible to remedy this problem, for example by the use of third-party experts to assess quality or by the dealer's offer of guarantees.

7 Of course, not all production and consumption is organized in this way. The small-scale luxury goods sector remains an important way in which elites and upper classes maintain their claim for superior status. However, this no longer consists of independent craft producers. For example, many luxury marques in the automobile industry are now part of large mass-production companies; Ferrari is owned by Fiat and Rolls Royce by Volkswagen. Here the level of competition is also managed by the small number of competitors.

8 Occasionally a successful strategy is found. The high-status German car manufacturer BMW bought the British Rover company in 1994 in order to diversify into different market niches without devaluing its own brand. The investment necessary to make Rover competitive proved prohibitive, and BMW was forced to sell soon after. However, it retained control of Rover's design and production facilities for a new version of the 1960s icon, the Mini, and in doing so BMW seems to have got the best of both worlds. On the one hand, the Mini does not bear the BMW badge and therefore does not directly threaten the existing prestige larger car niche, but, on the other hand, the reputation for high-quality production and covert BMW status has enhanced the Mini's appeal and enabled it to be priced much higher than all the others in the small hatch-back market segment. Of course, the danger is that the continued high volume of sales and the eventual availability of large numbers of cheap high-mileage used cars could dilute the symbolic status of the niche.

9 Furthermore, the capacity of large firms in this type of market structure to offer resistance to the onset of 'creative destruction' may slow the process and add stability to the economy's adjustment (Schumpeter 1942: 90).

10   In Britain the Campaign for Real Ale fought a successful rear-guard action since the 1970s against large brewers' increasing share of the market.

11   The issue is complex; higher labour costs might also, for example, drive firms towards high-quality high-price niches in the product market, as in Germany.

12   Classical economic theory 'depoliticized' the question by arguing that the existence of employment is determined objectively and impersonally by the supply and demand for goods and this is, in turn, determined by the relative costs of employing the different factors of production, including labour. Consequently, it is argued, the level of employment is determined by the willingness of workers to accept the market rate of pay. As we have seen, Keynes challenged this theory by pointing to the fact that labour did not have the power to control the other determinants of economic activity – the rate of interest and, most importantly, the level of aggregate demand in the economy.

13   In essence, this is the circular flow model of the economy with the addition of banks, as mere intermediaries between savers and borrowers, whose revenue for their functional contribution to the process is taken into account in the rate of interest. Again, it should be emphasized that this is a depiction of the long-run outcome in perfect competitive conditions.

14   With the collapse of socialism and communism and Marx's fall from favour, Polanyi's critique of the self-regulating market has experienced a revival following the economic liberalization and globalization of the late twentieth century.

15   Both monopoly capital and governments are now in a better position, using market research and economic forecasting, to attempt to match supply and demand. On this general question see the neo-Marxist French regulation school of capitalism (Aglietta, 1979; Jessop 2001).

16   On the basis of evidence from trade in pre-capitalist economies, it is argued in neo-liberal economic analysis that the rules governing market exchange can develop 'spontaneously' (see, for example, Spruyt 1994). However, two points should be borne in mind. First, these markets were constituted by rules and conventions – not merely the self-interested actions of discrete traders – that governed the exchanges. These regulations were enforced by the private authority of the guilds and associations of traders. Second, these self-governed markets were small in scale and restricted to the margins of their pre-capitalist economies. Large-scale markets which are typical of

capitalism grew in the pacified and regulated spaces created by the modern state.

6   The enterprise

1   The Marxist Stephen Marglin has argued that the structure of the modern firm is not determined exclusively by technology, but is also determined by the exigencies of capital accumulation. The division of labour and the centralized hierarchical organization of the firm are the means used by the bourgeoisie to plays its historic role of controlling and exploiting the workers in order to gain a competitive advantage and, in doing so, accumulating capital and advancing the technological means of production (Marglin 1974).

2   Chandler argued that, as the firms already controlled 90 per cent of the industry, the purpose of rationalization was not to gain monopoly control, but to bring about efficiencies. However, it should be noted that the result of the rationalization was also to double profits and provide a steady stream of revenues for the financiers and Rockefeller's bank (Chandler 1992 [1984]).

3   In an attempt to explain the breakdown of Keynesian aggregate demand management policies in the 1970s, French 'Regulation Theory' developed and adapted Marx's theory of capitalism's contradictions to take account of the ability of capitalist states to 'regulate' – at least temporarily – the recurrent crises (see the discussion in chapter 8).

4   In 2005, eight of the world's ten largest corporations were American ('The FT Global 500', *Financial Times Magazine*, 11 June 2005).

5   This portrayal of modern capitalism as 'people's capitalism' was used by the British Conservative governments during their privatization of the state-owned utilities in the 1980s, in which employees and the wider public were encouraged to buy shares. However, after an early diffusion of ownership, the shares were sold, adding to the holdings of the 'institutions' – pension fund and insurance companies – which led to an increase in the concentration of ownership. The idea that widespread diffuse shareholding by pension funds could become the basis for greater popular democratic control of capitalism has a long history (see Blackburn 2006).

6   Roe's examination of this question is important in two respects (2003: 163–78). First, it shows how patterns of ownership are

associated with social welfare and job security. Second, differences between bank and stock-market financial systems of the major economies are often seen merely as the path-dependent result of the early experience of industrialization; but this work links the differences to changes in the political balance of power between classes.

7 Capital and financial markets

1 Some argue that modern capitalist financial instruments can be traced to the earliest known literate civilizations in Mesopotamia and that there is a direct line of development to modern capitalism (see Baskin and Miranti 1997; and the critique in Ingham 2004).

2 In the context of finance, 'fungible' refers to the ease with which it can be transformed into a wide range of different assets by increasingly complex, but connected, markets.

3 For sociological analyses of how this chronic uncertainty is managed by the actors see, for example, Abolafia 1996; Pixley 2004; Knorr-Cetina 2007.

4 'Big bang' refers to the restructuring or 'deregulation' of the City of London's money and capital markets and the UK financial system in general in 1986. It was intended to increase competition by breaking down the monopolies and 'old boy' networks that controlled the stock market and imposed fixed commissions on trades. In the wider financial system, the clear separation of functions between retail banks, mortgage banks, insurance companies and other financial services was abolished (see Augar 2000). This followed a similar restructuring of the New York stock exchange in 1975 and was part of a global process of 'competitive deregulation' in which major centres vied with each other for a larger share of the rapidly growing global trade in stocks (see Ingham 2002).

5 Fund managers, as the term suggests, manage the assets (stocks, share, bonds, securities and so on) of the large pension and insurance funds of the major economies. In 2006, there were over \$60 trillion in managed assets (*Economist*, 1 March 2008).

6 In late 2006, six ex-Goldman Sachs executives held key positions in President Bush's administration. In *The Global Gamble*, Gowan argues that the alliance between Wall Street and the US government ('Dollar Wall Street Regime') uses the dollar as

tool of economic statecraft for maintaining US power (Gowan 1999).

7 Every conceivable kind of commodity and asset can spawn derivatives from which further derivatives can be derived – that is to say, there are 'derivatives' of 'derivatives'.

8 In a contradictory and confusing use of terminology, 'hedge' funds are concerned primarily with the 'speculation' side of the market.

9 Fearing a collapse of the bank, thousands of depositors queued for hours to withdraw their savings. After some delay and equivocation, the Bank and England and the Treasury stepped in to guarantee the depositors' savings. The incident was a salutary experience for those who believed that such events were no longer possible in a modern financial system, and showed in stark relief the role of the state as the ultimate source of trust in money and the financial system.

10 To a far greater extent than other mortgage banks, Northern Rock had availed itself of the securitization and credit derivatives markets to finance its mortgage lending. Consequently it relied on a continuous flow of receipts from the further sale of securitized mortgages to extend further loans and stay in business. Mortgages were packaged as a security and sold to a subsidiary company Granite, registered in the Channel Islands, which sold them on to investors – such as pension and insurance funds. The investors paid a cash sum and also received interest payments from Northern Rock. Northern Rock benefited in two ways. First, and most importantly, cash was used to extend further mortgages beyond the level warranted by deposits from its own savers. Second, if Northern Rock received 6 per cent interest, for example, from its mortgage borrowers, it could pay 5 per cent interest to the investors. These securities subsequently changed hands numerous times. Defaults on 'subprime' loans (loans to high-risk borrowers) in the USA increased the risk of all securitized mortgages and rendered them virtually unsaleable. Northern Rock experienced a serious disruption of its cash flow. Northern Rock received over £30 billion in loans from the Bank of England which were underwritten by the British Treasury. These proved to be inadequate and Northern Rock was nationalized in February 2008. In March 2008 a lack of liquidity forced Bear Stearns to sign a merger agreement with JPMorgan Chase and to accept a $30 billion loan from the US Federal Reserve. Charles Morris's *The Trillion Dollar Meltdown* appeared too late to be given full consideration. It is an

excellent account of the build-up to the general 2007 credit crisis which emphasizes, as I have done, the way in which the deregulation of financial markets in the late twentieth century gave them the autonomy and power to create the credit bubble (Morris 2008).

11   The celebrated hedge fund financier George Soros believes that the crisis will prove to be the worst since the 1930s (see Soros 2008). As ever, there are two opposed views on the best way to deal with financial crises of this kind. On the one hand it is argued that central bank intervention creates 'moral hazard' in the sense that 'merchants of debt' will persist in imprudent high-risk lending in the knowledge that they will be rescued by the central banks. Furthermore, crises and bank failures are seen as a salutary lesson to the imprudent. For example, Northern Rock should be allowed to go out of business as a punishment and warning to others. On the other hand, it is held that the risk of a large-scale systemic crisis is to be averted at all costs. In short, the contradictions of the capitalist financial system pose insoluble, unavoidable dilemmas.

12   The following account is based on newspaper and magazine articles – mainly the *Financial Times* and *The Economist* – collected at the time. See also Coffee 2005.

13   In addition to their view that theirs is the most important role in the economy, bankers and financiers argue that their high level of remuneration is compensation for the very risky nature of their activity. They point out that when crises occur their sector experiences more severe contraction and greater loss of profits and remuneration than other parts of the economy. Regardless of the accuracy of these claims, the financial sector's far superior average revenues and remuneration is clearly evident in the long run (Augar 2006: ch. 4).

8   The state

1   The question of what precisely constitutes the modern state and its 'boundaries' in relation to the market economy is actually quite difficult to answer and cannot be approached here. For a general survey of theories of the modern state, see Dunleavy and O'Leary 1987; for a sophisticated Marxian analysis of the capitalist state see Jessop 1990.

2   Today it is argued that some states practice 'mercantalism'. For example, the United Arab Emirates, Saudi Arabia, Singapore, Kuwait, China and Norway have accumulated 'sovereign

wealth funds' from their favourable balance of payments which they invest globally and further enhance their state's power (see *Economist*, 10 January 2008). In February 2008 Australia and the European Union announced that they are to tighten the regulations on inward investment from such funds in order to prevent their use for political rather than strictly commercial ends.

3 The taxes and customs duties that were levied to pay the interest involved a transfer of wealth from the lower and middle strata of society to the bondholders. These fiscal arrangements were most developed in England where, by the late eighteenth century, 75 per cent of annual state revenue from taxes, customs duties and tariffs were paid in dividends to 17,000 bondholders (Ingham 1984: 106). As we shall see, the advent of the democratic franchise and the consequent demands for social welfare placed greater demands on state expenditure and, at the same time, extended electoral resistance to regressive taxation.

4 In some respects, this process of separation and mutual accommodation is still under way in the former Soviet empire, especially Russia. The power of the capitalist oligarchs grew during Boris Yeltsin's presidency to the point where they began to wield considerable political power. Putin has striven successfully to redress the balance, taking energy companies back into state ownership and imprisoning those oligarchs such as Khodorkovsky who challenged the political elite.

5 Weber agreed with Marx on the consequences of unchecked rule by capitalists. Lindert (2003), for example, argues very specifically that rule by capitalist elites leads to underinvestment in primary school education and consequently damages economic growth.

6 However, animal rights protestors in the UK have had some success in intimidating employees of and investors in companies which test drugs and other commodities on animals.

7 The dilemma was posed again sixty years later in the starkest of terms by a British chief executive's letter to the *Financial Times*. The leader of the Conservative Party, David Cameron, had suggested that it was the social responsibility of enterprises to employ disabled workers. The executive asked if this applied to top football clubs, teams and pointed out that whilst a decent society looks after the less fortunate, businesses have just one objective – to maximize shareholder returns (*Financial Times*, 18 October, 2006: 14).

8 It had become the accepted economic wisdom that there was a 'trade-off', or negative correlation, between unemployment and inflation, as expressed in the 'Phillips Curve'.

9 The European Union has attempted to overcome this problem with the adoption of a single currency. See Ingham 2004: 188–96; Bell and Nell 2003.

9 Conclusions

1 Following von Mises and other Austrian economists, Weber's 'ideal type' also strongly implies that free-market exchange is the most effective means of establishing predictable prices and rational economic calculation.

2 There are, of course, limits to liquidity. As Keynes pointed out, it is an option for the individual, but not for the community as a whole; see p. 46.

3 The gold standard (late nineteenth century–1914) was an unplanned international monetary system in which the gold–sterling exchange rate, maintained by the Bank of England, was adopted by other countries which pegged their currencies to sterling and consequently to gold at the fixed price. It is, however, more accurate to refer to a gold–sterling standard, as gold was rarely used in international transactions – for one thing, there was simply not enough to finance expanding trade in the first phase of globalization (see Walter 1993).

4 Although it can be advantageous for a country to have its currency used as world money, significant costs might arise. After the relative decline of the British economy in the twentieth century, the efforts to maintain global confidence in sterling with high exchange and interest rates had a deflationary effect on the economy. The Triffin dilemma, named after the eponymous US economist, referred to the fact that the provision of an adequate quantity of dollars to finance world trade in the 1960s might have an inflationary impact on the domestic economy (Gilpin 1987).

5 The reduction of inflation in the late twentieth century has been important in this regard by increasing, for example, the real value of revenue from interest. As we have noted, this was negative for much of the 1970s, but increased to 8 per cent during the 1980s, later hovering around 5 per cent (Duménil and Lévy 2004: 128).

6 However, there are alternative explanations for Japan's faltering performance. These place emphasis on the financially

induced debt-deflation after the speculative boom caused, in part, by the over-valued yen and the liberalization of the financial system that the USA had encouraged during the 1980s (Murphy 2000).

7 It has been suggested that the hegemony of neo-liberal economic analysis in the European Commission imparts a bias towards the liberal-market model in any restructuring of economic institutions in the EEC. European bureaucrats trained in neo-classical economics are an 'epistemic community' whose theoretical models are 'performative' (Quack and Djelic in Streeck and Thelen 2005).

8 A recent empirical test of the relative performance of liberal, corporatist and social democratic models of capitalism with regard to economic growth and social well-being in Europe concluded that there is no evidence to support the claim that market liberalism is superior (Panic 2007).

9 The 'Washington consensus' refers to the preference for neo-liberal policy prescription conditions that have accompanied IMF and World Bank aid and loans to badly performing and developing economies since the 1980s. These include reductions in government spending, privatization, market liberalization and low taxation. It is argued that these preferences derive in part from the dominance of neo-classical economics in the major universities from which IMF and World Bank economists are recruited. As a result of the manifest success of the Japanese and other east Asian economies, and considerable political pressure from these states during the 1980s, the World Bank contemplated publishing a report in which it was to be acknowledged that there were probably different and equally viable developmental paths. However, the Japanese and east Asian crises saved the day for the hegemony of neo-liberalism. The story is told in Wade and Veneroso (1998).

10 By the end of the twentieth century, 61 per cent of all the world's central bank reserves, 77 per cent of all global bank loans and 40 per cent of global bond issues were in US dollars (Gowan 1999).

11 For example, during the 1990s President Clinton's Treasury Secretary, Robert Rubin, an ex-Goldman Sachs executive, successfully worked to open foreign financial markets to US banks. Global capital and financial markets are controlled by US investment banks which now have the freedom to operate in all the major global capitalist centres, including China. Furthermore, the practices and rules by which these global markets operate are created and reinforced almost exclusively by US

interests, including credit-rating agencies, auditors and accountancy firms (Strange 1996; Sinclair 2005).

12 For the general argument that increasing inequality caused by the power of finance is the major cause of political opposition to capitalism in the USA, see Phillips 1993, 2002.

References

Abercrombie, N., S. Hill and B. Turner, 1980. *The Dominant Ideology Thesis*. London: Allen Lane.

Abolafia, M. 1996. *Making Markets*. Cambridge, MA: Harvard University Press.

Aglietta, M. 1979. *A Theory of Capitalist Regulation*. London: New Left Books.

Aglietta, M. and A. Orléan, 1998. *La Monnaie Souveraine*. Paris: Odile Jacob.

Akerlof, G. 1970. 'The market for "lemons"', *Quarterly Journal of Economics*, 84, 488–500.

Albert, M. 1993. *Capitalism against Capitalism*. London: Whurr.

Alderson, A. and F. Nielsen, 2002. 'Globalization and the great U-turn: income inequality in 16 OECD countries', *American Journal of Sociology*, 107, 5, 1244–90.

Amable, B. 2003. *The Diversity of Modern Capitalism*. Oxford: Oxford University Press.

Arrighi, G. 1994. *The Long Twentieth Century*. London: Verso.

Arrighi, G. 2008. *Adam Smith in Beijing*. London: Verso.

Arrighi, G. and B. Silver, 1999. *Chaos and Governance in the Modern World System*. Minneapolis: University of Minnesota Press.

Arthur, B. 1985. *Increasing Returns to Scale and Path Dependency in the Economy*. Ann Arbor: University of Michigan Press.

Atkinson, A. and T. Piketty (eds), 2007. *Top Incomes over the Twentieth Century*. Oxford: Oxford University Press.

Augar, P. 2000. *The Death of Gentlemanly Capitalism*. Harmondsworth: Penguin Books.

Augar, P. 2006. *The Greed Merchants*. Harmondsworth: Penguin Books.

Avant, D. 2005. *The Market for Force: The Consequences of the Privatization of Security*. Cambridge: Cambridge University Press.

Avineri, S. 1968. *The Social and Political Thought of Karl Marx*. Cambridge: Cambridge University Press.

Baskin, J. and P. Miranti, 1997. *A History of Corporate Finance*. Cambridge: Cambridge University Press.

Baudrillard, J. 1988. 'Consumer society', in J. Baudrillard, *Selected Writings*, ed. M. Porter. Cambridge: Polity.

Bell, S. and E. Nell (eds), 2003. *The State, the Market and the Euro*. Cheltenham: Edward Elgar.

Berle, A. and G. Means, 1947 [1932]. *The Modern Corporation and Private Property*. New York: Macmillan.

Bernstein, P. 2000. *The Power of Gold*. London: John Wiley.

Blackburn, R. 2006. *The Age Shock: How Finance is Failing Us*. London: Verso.

Boltanski, L. and E. Chiapello, 2005. *The New Spirit of Capitalism*. London: Verso.

Bottomore, T. 1990. *The Socialist Economy*. Hemel Hempstead: Harvester Wheatsheaf.

Boyer, R. 1990. *Regulation Theory*. Oxford: Oxford University Press.

Boyer, R. 2005. 'How and why do capitalisms differ', *Economy and Society*, 34, 509–57.

Braudel, F. 1984. *Civilization and Capitalism: The Wheels of Commerce*. London: Fontana.

Braverman, H. 1974. *Labor and Monopoly Capital*. New York: Monthly Review Press.

Brenner, R. 2002. *The Boom and the Bubble*. London: Verso.

Bryant, R. 2002. *Turbulent Waters: Cross Border Finance and International Governance*. Washington, DC: Brookings Institution.

Buchanan, J. and G. Tullock, 1962. *The Calculus of Consent*. Ann Arbor: University of Michigan Press.

Burawoy, M. 1979. *Manufacturing Consent: Changes in the Labour Process and Monopoly Capitalism*. Chicago: University of Chicago Press.

Burn, G. 2006. *The Re-emergence of Global Finance*. Houndmills: Palgrave Macmillan.

Callinicos, A. 2001. *Against the Third Way*. Cambridge: Polity.

Callinicos, A. 2003. *An Anti-Capitalist Manifesto*. Cambridge: Polity.

Callon, M. (ed.), 1998. *The Laws of the Markets*. London: Blackwell Publishers.

Campbell, C. 1987. *The Romantic Ethic and the Spirit of Modern Consumerism*. Oxford: Basil Blackwell.

Carruthers, B. 1996. *City of Capital*. Princeton: Princeton University Press.

Carruthers, B. and S. Babb, 1996. 'The color of money and the nature of value: greenbacks and gold in post-bellum America', *American Journal of Sociology*, 101, 6, 1556–91.

Chabal, P. and J.-P. Daloz, 1999. *Africa Works*. Bloomington: Indiana University Press.

Chamberlain, E. 1933. *Monopolistic Competition*. Cambridge, MA: Harvard University Press.

Chancellor, E. 2001a. 'Inefficient markets', *Prospect*, May.

Chancellor, E. 2001b. *Devil Take the Hindmost: A History of Financial Speculation*. London: Plume.

Chandler, A. 1962. *Strategy and Structure*. Cambridge, MA: MIT Press.

Chandler, A. 1990. *Scale and Scope: The Dynamics of Industrial Capitalism*. Cambridge, MA: Harvard University Press.

Chandler, A. 1992 [1984]. 'The Emergence of managerial capitalism', in M. Granovetter and R. Swedberg (eds), *The Sociology of Economic Life*. Boulder: Westview Press.

Chandler, A., F. Amatori and T. Hikino (eds), 1997. *Big Business and the Wealth of Nations*. Cambridge: Cambridge University Press.

Coase, R. 1937. 'The nature of the firm', *Economica*, 4, 16, 386–405.

Coates, D. (ed.), 2005. *Varieties of Capitalism, Varieties of Approaches*. Houndmills: Palgrave.

Coates, D. 2000. *Models of Capitalism*. Cambridge: Polity.

Coffee, J. 2005. 'A theory of corporate scandals: why the USA and Europe differ', *Oxford Review of Economic Policy*, 21, 2, 198–211.

Collins, R. 1986. *Weberian Sociological Theory*. Cambridge: Cambridge University Press.

De Soto, H. 2000. *The Mystery of Capital*. New York: Bantam Press.

Deeg, R. and G. Jackson, 2007. 'Towards a more dynamic theory of capitalist variety', *Socio-economic Review*, 2007, 5, 149–79.

Dore, R. 2000. *Stock Market Capitalism: Welfare Capitalism*. Oxford: Oxford University Press.

Du Gay, P. (ed.), 1998. *Production of Culture/Culture of Production*. London: Sage.

Dubow, B. and N. Montiero, 2006. *Measuring Market Cleanliness*, Occasional Paper 23. London: Financial Services Authority.

Duménil, G. and D. Lévy, 2004(a). 'Class and income in the US', *New Left Review*, 30, 105–33.

Duménil, G. and D. Lévy, 2004(b). *Capitalism Resurgent*. Cambridge, MA: Harvard University Press.

Dunleavy, P. and B. O'Leary, 1987. *Theories of the State*. London: Macmillan.

Epstein, G. (ed.), 2005. *Financialization and the World Economy*. Cheltenham: Edward Elgar.

Erturk, F., J. Froud, S. Johal, A. Leaver and K. Williams (eds), 2008. *Financialization at Work*. London: Routledge.

Esping-Anderson, G. 1990. *The Three Worlds of Welfare Capitalism*. Princeton: Princeton University Press.

Estevez-Abe, M., T. Iverson and D. Soskice, 2001. 'Social protection and the formations of skills: a reinterpretation of the welfare state', in P. Hall and D. Soskice (eds), *Varieties of Capitalism*. Oxford: Oxford University Press.

Etzioni, A. 1988. *The Moral Dimension: Toward a New Economics*. New York: Free Press.

Faure, D. 2006. *China and Capitalism*. Hong Kong: Hong Kong University Press.

Ferguson, N. 2001. *The Cash Nexus: Money and Power in the Modern World*. Harmondsworth: Penguin.

Ferguson, N. 2005. *Colossus*. London: Penguin.

Fischer, D. 1996. *The Great Wave*. Oxford: Oxford University Press.

Fligstein, N. 2001. *The Architecture of Markets*. Princeton: Princeton University Press.

Frank, A. 1998. *ReOrient: Global Economy in the Asian Age*. Berkeley and London: University of California Press.

Frieden, J. 2006. *Global Capitalism*. New York: Norton & Co.

Friedman, M. 1962. *Capitalism and Freedom*. London: University of Chicago Press.

Froud, J. and K. Williams, 2007. 'Private equity and the culture of value extraction', *New Political Economy*, 12, 3, 405–20.

Fukuyama, F. 1992. *The End of History and the Last Man*. Glencoe, IL: Free Press.

Fulcher, J. 1991. *Labour Movements, Employers and the State*. Oxford: Oxford University Press.

Fulcher, J. 2004. *Capitalism: A Very Short Introduction*. Oxford: Oxford University Press.

Galeotti, M. (ed.), 2002. *Russian and Post-Soviet Crime*. Ashgate: Dartmouth.

Gerlach, M. 1992. *Alliance Capitalism*, Berkeley: University of California Press.

Germain, R. 1997. *The International Organization of Credit*. Cambridge: Cambridge University Press.

Gershenkeron, A. 1962. *Economic Backwardness in Historical Perspective*. Cambridge: Cambridge University Press.

Giddens, A. 1999. *Runaway World*. London: Profile.

Gilpin, R. 1987. *The Political Economy of International Relations*. Princeton: Princeton University Press.

Gilpin, R. 2001. *Global Political Economy*. Princeton: Princeton University Press.

Glyn, A. 2006. *Capitalism Unleashed*. Oxford: Oxford University Press.

Goldthorpe, J. H. (ed.), 1984. *Order and Conflict in Contemporary Capitalism*. Oxford: Oxford University Press.

Goody, J. 2004. *Capitalism and Modernity: The Great Debate*. Cambridge: Polity.

Gordon, G. and N. Nicholson, 2008. *Family Wars*. London: Kogan Page.

Gospel, H. and A. Pendleton (eds), 2004. *Corporate Governance and the Management of Labour*. Oxford: Oxford University Press.

Gowan, P. 1999. *The Global Gamble*. London: Verso.

Goyer, M. 2002. 'Anglo-Saxon institutional investors and the focus on core competences: an institutionalist perspective on French and German corporate governance', in C. Milhaupt (ed.), *Domestic Institutions, Global Markets*. New York: Columbia University Press.

Greenspan, A. 2005. www.federalreserve.gov/boarddocs/speeches.

Greider, W. 1987. *Secrets of the Temple: How the Federal Reserve runs the Country*. New York: Simon and Schuster.

Grierson, P. 1977. *The Origins of Money*. London: Athlone Press.

Hacker, J. 2002. *The Divided Welfare State*. Cambridge: Cambridge University Press.

Hall, P. and D. Soskice (eds), 2001. *Varieties of Capitalism*. Oxford: Oxford University Press.

Hardt, M. and A. Negri, 2001. *Empire*. Cambridge, MA: Harvard University Press.

Harvey, D. 2007. *A Brief History of Neo-liberalism*. Oxford: Oxford University Press.

Hay, C. 1996. *Re-stating Social Change*. Buckingham: Open University Press.

Hay, C. 2006. 'What's globalization got to do with it? Economic globalization and the future of the European Welfare State', *Government and Opposition*, 41, 1, 1–22.

Hayek, F. 2001 [1944]. *The Road to Serfdom*. London: Routledge.

Held, D. and A. McGrew, 2007. *Globalization/Anti-globalization*. Cambridge: Polity.

Held, D. 1980. *Introduction to Cultural Theory*. Berkeley: University of California Press.

Held. D. and J. Krieger, 1983. 'Accumulation, legitimation and the state', in D. Held (ed.), *States and Societies*. Oxford: Martin Robertson.

Helleiner, E. 1994. *States and the Re-emergence of Global Finance*. Ithaca, NY: Cornell University Press.

Henwood, D. 1997. *Wall Street*. London: Verso.

Hilferding, R. 1981 [1910]. *Finance Capital*. London: Routledge.

Hirsch, F. and J. H. Goldthorpe (eds), 1978. *The Political Economy of Inflation*. London: Martin Robertson.

Hirst, P. and G. Thompson, 1999. *Globalization in Question*. Cambridge: Polity.

Humphreys, M., J. Sachs and J. Stiglitz, 2007. *Escaping the Resource Curse*. New York: Columbia University Press.

Hutton, W. 2007. *The Writing on the Wall*. London: Little, Brown.

Ingham, G. 1974. *Strikes and Industrial Conflict*. London: Macmillan.

Ingham, G. 1984. *Capitalism Divided?* London: Macmillan.

Ingham, G. 1994. 'States and markets in the production of world money: sterling and the dollar', in S. Corbridge, N. Thrift and R. Martin (eds), *Money, Power and Space*. Oxford: Blackwell.

Ingham, G. 2002. 'Shock therapy in London', *New Left Review*, 14, Mar/Apr 2002, 152–8.

Ingham, G. 2003. 'Schumpeter and Weber on the institutions of capitalism', *Journal of Classical Sociology*, 3, 297–309.

Ingham, G. 2004. *The Nature of Money*. Cambridge: Polity.

Ingham, G. (ed.), 2005. *Concepts of Money*. Cheltenham: Edward Elgar.

Innes, A. M. 1914, 'The credit theory of money', in G. Ingham (ed.), 2005. *Concepts of Money*. Cheltenham: Edward Elgar.

International Financial Services, 2006. London.

James, H. 2001. *The End of Globalization: Lessons from the Great Depression*. Cambridge, MA: Harvard University Press.

James, H. 2006. *Family Capitalism*. Cambridge, MA: Harvard University Press.

Jameson, F. 1991. *Post-modernism and the Cultural Logic of Late Capitalism*. London: Verso.

Jessop, B. 1990. *State Theory*. Cambridge: Polity.

Jessop, B. 2001. *Regulation Theory and the Crisis of Capitalism*. Cheltenham: Edward Elgar.

Jessop, B. 2002. *The Future of the Capitalist State*. Cambridge: Polity.

Kalecki, M. 1943. 'Political aspects of full employment', *Political Quarterly*, 14, 322–31.

Kapstein, E. 1994. *Governing the Global Economy*. Cambridge, MA: Harvard University Press.

Keynes, J. M. 1924. *Tract on Monetary Reform*. London: Macmillan.

Keynes, J. M. 1930. *A Treatise on Money*. London: Macmillan.

Keynes, J. M. 1973 [1936]. *The General Theory of Employment, Interest and Money*. Cambridge: Cambridge University Press.

Keynes, J. M. 1980. *Collected Writings of John Maynard Keynes*, Vol. 25, ed. D. Moggeridge. Cambridge: Cambridge University Press.

Kindleberger, C. and R. Aliber, 2005. *Manias, Panics and Crashes*. Houndmills: Palgrave Macmillan.

King, D. 1987. *The New Right*. Basingstoke: Macmillan.

King, D. and S. Wood, 1999. 'The political economy of neoliberalism: Britain and the United States in the 1980s', in H. Kitschelt (ed.), *Continuity and Change in Contemporary Capitalism*. Cambridge: Cambridge University Press.

King, L. and I. Szelényi, 2005. 'The new capitalism of eastern Europe', in N. Smelser and R. Swedberg (eds), *The Handbook of Economic Sociology*, 2nd edn. Princeton: Princeton University Press.

Knorr Cetina, K. and A. Preda (eds), 2004. *The Sociology of Financial Markets*. Oxford: Oxford University Press.

Kolakowski, L. 1978. *Main Currents of Marxism*, Vols 1–3. Oxford: Oxford University Press.

Krippner, G. 2005. 'The financialization of the American economy', *Socio-Economic Review*, 3, 2, 173–208.

Lal, D. 2006. *Reviving the Invisible Hand: The Case for Classic Economic Liberalism*. Princeton: Princeton University Press.

Lane, C. 1989. *Management and Labour in Europe*. Aldershot: Edward Elgar.

Lane, C. 2003. 'Changes in corporate governance of German corporations: convergence to the Anglo-American model?', *Competition and Change*, 7, 2/3, 79–100.

Leach, W. 1993. *Land of Desire*. New York: Pantheon.

Lenin, V. I. 1963. *Selected Works, Vol.1*. London: Lawrence & Wishart.

Lindert, P. 2003. 'Voice and growth: was Churchill right?', *Journal of Economic History*, 63, 315–50.

Lipset, S. M. and G. Marks, 2001. *It Didn't Happen Here: Why Socialism Failed in the United States*. New York: Norton & Co.

MacKenzie D. 2006. *An Engine, Not a Camera: How Financial Models Shape Markets*. Cambridge, MA: MIT Press.

MacKenzie, D., M. Fabian and L. Sui (eds), 2007. *Do Economists Make Markets? On the Performativity of Economics*. Princeton: Princeton University Press.

Macpherson, C. 1973. *Democratic Theory*. Oxford: Oxford University Press.

Maddison, A. 1995. *Monitoring the World Economy. 1820–1992*. Paris: OECD.

Maier, C. 1978: 'The politics of inflation', in F. Hirsch and J. H. Goldthorpe (eds), *The Political Economy of Inflation*. London: Martin Robertson.

Mandeville, B. 1989 [1714]. *The Fable of the Bees, or Private Vice, Public Benefits*. Harmondsworth: Penguin.

Mann, M. 1970. 'The social cohesion of liberal democracy', *American Sociological Review*, 35, 423–39.

Mann, M. 1986. *The Sources of Social Power*. Cambridge: Cambridge University Press.

Mann, M. 2003. *Incoherent Empire*. London: Verso.

Marglin, S. 1974. 'What do bosses do?: the origins and functions of hierarchy in capitalist production', *Review of Radical Political Economy*, 6, 60–112.

Marglin, S. and J. Schor (eds), 1990. *The Golden Age of Capitalism*. Oxford: Oxford University Press.

Marshall, T. 1963 [1949]. 'Citizenship and social class', in T. Marshall, *Sociology at the Crossroads: And Other Essays*. London: Heinemann.

Marx, K. 1968 [1850]. 'The Manifesto of the Communist Party', Marx/Engels, *Selected Works*. London: Lawrence & Wishart.

Marx, K. 1976 [1867]. *Capital*, Vol. 1. Harmondsworth: Penguin.

Marx, K. and F. Engels, 1968. *Selected Works in One Volume*. London: Lawrence & Wishart.

Minsky, H. 1982. 'The financial instability hypothesis', in C. P. Kindleberger and J.-P. Lafarge (eds), *Financial Crises*. Cambridge: Cambridge University Press.

Mirowski, P. 1991. 'Post-modernism and the social theory of value', *Journal of Post-Keynesian Economics*, 13, 565–82.

Moore, Jr, B. 1966. *The Social Origins of Dictatorship and Democracy*. Harmondsworth: Penguin.

Morris, C. 2008. *The Trillion Dollar Meltdown*. New York: Public Affairs.

Murphy, T. 2000. 'Japan's economic crisis', *New Left Review*, Jan/ Feb, 25–51.

Nee, V. and R. Swedberg, 2005. *The Economic Sociology of Capitalism*. Princeton: Princeton University Press.

Noble, G. and J. Ravenhill (eds), 2000. *The Asian Financial Crisis*. Cambridge: Cambridge University Press.

Nolan, P. 2004. *China at the Crossroads*. Cambridge: Polity.

North, D. C. 1981. *Structure and Change in Economic History*. New York: Norton.

Olsen, M. 1982. *The Rise and Decline of Nations*. New Haven: Yale University Press.

Orléan, A. 2005. 'Crise de souveraineté et crise monétaire: hyperfinflation allemandes des anneés 1920', in B. Theret (ed.), *La Monnaie devoileé par les crises*. Paris: Odile Jacob.

Osberg, L. 2003. 'Long run trends in income inequality in the United States, UK, Sweden, Germany and Canada', *Eastern Economic Journal*, 29, 121–41.

Panic, M. 2007. 'Does Europe need neo-liberal reforms?', *Cambridge Journal of Economics*, 31, 145–69.

Phelps Brown, E. 1975. 'A non-monetarist view of the pay explosion', *Three Banks Review*, 105, 3–24.

Phillips, K. 1993. *Boiling Point*. New York: Random House.

Phillips, K. 2002. *Wealth and Democracy*. New York: Broadway Books.

Piore, M. and Sable, C. 1984. *The Second Industrial Divide*. New York: Basic Books.

Pixley, J. 2004. *Emotions in Finance*. Cambridge: Cambridge University Press.

Podolny, J. 1993. 'A status-based model of market competition', *American Journal of Sociology*, 98, 4, 829–872.

Polanyi, K. 1944. *The Great Transformation*. Boston: Beacon.

Polanyi, K. 1971 [1957]. 'The economy as an instituted process', in K. Polanyi, C. Arensberg and K. Pearson (eds), *Trade and Market in the Early Empires*. Chicago: Henry Regnery.

Pomeranz, K. 2000. *The Great Divergence: China, Europe and the Making of the Modern World*. Princeton: Princeton University Press.

Porter, T. 2005. *Globalization and Finance*. Cambridge: Polity.

Rajan, R. and L. Zingales, 2003. *Saving Capitalism from the Capitalists*. London: Random House.

Roe, M. 1994. *Strong Managers, Weak Owners: The Political Roots of American Corporate Finance*. Princeton: Princeton University Press.

Roe, M. 2003. *Political Determinants of Corporate Governance*. Oxford: Oxford University Press.

Rosenberg, J. 2000. *The Follies of Globalization Theory*. London: Verso.

Rosenberg, J. 2005. 'Globalization theory: a post-mortem', *International Politics*, 42, 2, 2–74.

Rousseau, P. and R. Sylla, 2006. 'Financial revolutions and economic growth', *Explorations in Economic History*, 43, 1–12.

Rueschmeyer, D., E. Huber Stephens and J. Stephens, 1992. *Capitalist Development and Democracy*. Cambridge: Polity.

Ruggie, J. 1993. 'Territoriality and beyond: problematizing modernity in international relations', *International Organization*, 41, 139–74.

Schmidt, V. 2002. *The Futures of European Capitalism*. Oxford: Oxford University Press.

Schumpeter, J. 1942. *Capitalism, Socialism and Democracy*. New York: Harper.

Schumpeter, J. 1961 [1911]. *The Theory of Economic Development*. Oxford: Oxford University Press.

Schumpeter, J. 1994 [1954]. *A History of Economic Analysis*. London: Routledge.

Scott, J. 1997. *Corporate Business and Capitalist Classes*. Oxford: Oxford University Press.

Searle, J. 1995. *The Construction of Social Reality*. Harmondsworth: Penguin.

Sennett, R. 1998. *The Corrosion of Character: The Personal Consequences of Work in the New Capitalism*. New York: Norton.

Sennett, R. 2006. *The Culture of the New Capitalism*. New Haven: Yale University Press.

Shiller, R. 2000. *Irrational Exuberance*. Princeton: Princeton University Press.

Shonfield, A. 1965. *Modern Capitalism*. Oxford: Oxford University Press.

Simmel, G. 1978 [1907]. *The Philosophy of Money*. London: Routledge.

Sinclair, T. 2005. *The New Masters of Capital: American Bond Rating Agencies and the Politics of Creditworthiness*. Cornell: Cornell University Press.

Slater, D. 1997. *Consumer Culture and Modernity*. Cambridge: Polity.

Smith, A. 1986 [1776]. *The Wealth of Nations.* Harmondsworth: Penguin Classics.

Smithin, J. 1996. *Macroeconomic Policy and the Future of Capitalism: The Revenge of the Rentier and the Threat to Prosperity.* Cheltenham: Edward Elgar.

Socio-economic Review, 2005, 3, 311–89.

Sombart, W. 1976 [1906]. *Why Is There no Socialism in the United States?* New York: Sharpe.

Soros, G. 2008. *The New Paradigm for Financial Markets: The Credit Crisis of 2008 and What it Means.* New York: Public Affairs.

Spruyt, H. 1994. *The Sovereign State and Its Competitors.* Princeton: Princeton University Press.

Stearns, L. and M. Mizruchi, 2005. 'Banking and financial markets', in N. Smelser and R. Swedberg (eds), *The Handbook of Economic Sociology,* 2nd edn. Princeton: Princeton University Press.

Stiglitz, J. E. and A. Weiss, 1981. 'Credit rationing in markets with imperfect information', *American Economic Review,* 71, 3, 333–421.

Story, J. 2000. 'The emerging world financial order and different forms of capitalism', in R. Stubbs and G. Underhill (eds), *Political Economy and the Changing Global Order,* 2nd edn. Oxford: Oxford University Press.

Strange, S. 1996. *Retreat of the State.* Cambridge: Cambridge University Press.

Streeck, W. and K. Thelen (eds), 2005. *Beyond Continuity: Institutional Change in Advanced Political Economies.* Oxford: Oxford University Press.

Streeck, W. and K. Yamamura, 2001. *The Origins of Non-liberal Capitalism,* Ithaca, NY: Cornell University Press.

Szelényi, I., K. Beckett and L. King, 1994. 'The socialist economic system', in N. Smelser and R. Swedberg (eds), *The Handbook of Economic Sociology.* Princeton: Princeton University Press.

Therborn, G. 1977. 'The rule of capital and the rise of democracy', *New Left Review,* 103, 3–42.

Thrift, N. 2005. *Knowing Capitalism.* London: Sage.

Tilly, C. 1990. *Coercion, Capital and European States, AD 900–1990.* Oxford: Blackwell.

Triglia, C. 2002. *Economic Sociology: State, Market and Society in Modern Capitalism.* London: Blackwell.

Tullock, G. 1987a. 'Public choice', *The New Palgrave Dictionary of Economics,* V, 1040–4.

Tullock, G. 1987b. 'Rent-seeking', *The New Palgrave Dictionary of Economics*, IV, 147–9.

Valdez, S. 2006. *Introduction to Global Financial Markets*, 4th edn. Houndmills: Palgrave Macmillan.

Van Rixtel, A. 2002. *Informality and Monetary Policy in Japan*. Cambridge: Cambridge University Press.

Varese, F. 2001. *The Russian Mafia*. Oxford: Oxford University Press.

Veblen, T. 1994 [1899]. *The Theory of the Leisure Class*. Harmondsworth: Penguin Classics.

Vitols, S. 2001. 'Varieties of corporate governance: comparing Germany and the UK', in P. Hall and D. Soskice (eds), *Varieties of Capitalism*. Oxford: Oxford University Press.

Vogel, S. 1996. *Freer Markets, More Rules*. Ithaca, NY: Cornell University Press.

Vogel, S. 2006. *Japan Remodelled: How Government and Industry Are Reforming Japanese Capitalism*. Ithaca, NY: Cornell University Press.

Vries, P. 2003. *Via Peking Back to Manchester: Britain, the Industrial Revolution, and China*. Leiden: Research School of Asian, African, and Amerindian Studies, Leiden University.

Wade, R. 2003 [1990] *Governing the Market*. 2nd edn. Princeton: Princeton University Press.

Wade, R. 2003. 'The invisible hand of the American empire', *Ethics and International Affairs*, 17, 2, 77–84.

Wade, R. and A. Kaletsky, 2007. 'Debate: is global finance out of control?', *Prospect*, December, 20–24.

Wade, R. and F. Veneroso, 1998. 'The Asian crisis', *New Left Review*, 228, 3–23.

Walter, A. 1993. *World Power and World Money*. Brighton: Harvester Wheatsheaf.

Warburton, P. 2000. *Debt and Delusion*. Harmondsworth: Penguin

Weber, M. 1978. *Economy and Society*. Berkeley: University of California Press.

Weber, M. 1981 [1927]. *General Economic History*. New Brunswick, NJ: Transaction Publishers.

Weber, M. 2001 [1904]. *The Protestant Ethic and the Spirit of Capitalism*. London: Routledge.

Weiss, L. (ed.), 2003. *States in the Global Economy*. Cambridge: Cambridge University Press.

White, H. 1981. 'Where do markets come from?', *American Journal of Sociology*, 87, 3, 517–47.

Whitely, R., S. Quack and G. Morgan (eds), 2000. *National Capitalisms, Global Competition, and National Performance*. Amsterdam: John Benjamins.

Williamson, O. 1975. *Markets and Hierarchies*. New York: The Free Press.

Williamson, O. 1985. *The Economic Institutions of Capitalism*. New York: The Free Press.

Wolf, M. 2005. *Why Globalization Works*. New Haven and London: Yale University Press.

Wolf, M. 2007. 'The new capitalism', *Financial Times*, 19 June.

Wolff, J. 2002. *Why Read Marx Today?* Oxford: Oxford University Press.

Woo-Cummings, M. (ed.), 2005. *The Developmental State*. Ithaca, NY: Cornell University Press.

Woodruff, D. 1999. *Money Unmade*. Ithaca, NY: Cornell University Press.

Woolcock, S. 1996. 'Competition among forms of corporate governance in Europe', in S. Berger and R. Dore (eds), *National Diversity and Global Capitalism*. Cornell: Cornell University Press.

Yergin, D. and J. Stanislaw, 1998. *The Commanding Heights*. New York: Simon & Shuster.

Zysman, J. 1983. *Governments, Markets and Growth*. Ithaca, NY: Cornell University Press.

Index

acquisitions *see* mergers and
  acquisitions
'adverse selection' and market
  failure, 98
advertising and
  consumption, 102, 103
aggregate demand, 48–50,
  103, 114, 132, 195–6
agriculture and factors of
  production, 8–9, 19
Akerlof, G., 237*n*
Althusser, Louis, 184
Amaranth, 167
analysts and stock market
  bubbles, 155
'anarchy of production', 105,
  106, 114
ancient world, 67, 240*n*;
  command economies, 92,
  236*n*; slavery, 16, 18, 19,
  119
Anglo-US liberal market
  capitalism, 204, 216,
  218–19, 221
'animal spirits', 45, 89
arbitrage, 150, 151
Argentina and failure of
  capitalism, 66

Arrighi, G., 3, 126
Asian capitalism *see* east Asian
  economies; Orient
assembly-line production
  methods, 135–6
'asset specificity', 122
asset-stripping, 159
assets *see* financial asset
  markets
'asymmetric information', 99
Augar, P., 156
Austrian economic theory,
  96–7, 223
authoritarian regimes, 43, 186,
  187, 201
authority and capitalist
  enterprise, 123
Automobile
  Association, 161–2

'backward sloping supply
  curve', 29
balanced budgets, 49, 77, 84
'bancor', 209
bank credit-money: adverse
  selection and market
  failure, 98; and capital
  markets, 148–9; and

capitalist enterprise, 129, 137, 138, 139–40, 142, 143, 144–5, 150; conflict and creation of money, 110–11; and consumption, 103–4, 115–16; debt and derivatives market, 164–9, 173; and development of capitalism, 29, 33, 51, 53, 54, 70–4; economic crisis and credit expansion, 89–90, 114–16, 151, 162, 165, 167, 168, 173; and financial instability, 40–3, 76, 115, 116, 151, 225–6; and Marx, 24; and money-multiplier, 75–6; private equity groups and hostile takeovers, 159–60; role as source of finance, 149–50; and Schumpeter, 24, 36, 38, 39–43, 51, 52, 53, 71, 111; and Smith, 228*n*; and Weber, 28–9, 35, *see also* financial markets
Bank of England, 32–3, 43, 72–3, 234*n*, 241*n*
banking system: and capitalist enterprise in Europe, 143, 144–5; and creation of money, 111; and derivatives market in US, 168–9; and development of capitalism in the West, 32–3, 39–43, 51, 53, 71–4; and finance for capitalism, 149–50, 220–1; and financial instability hypothesis, 40–3, 76, 115, 151, 225; investment banks and capitalist enterprise in US, 130, 137, 144; private credit and money multiplier, 75–6, *see also* bank credit-money; central banks; investment banks

Baring Brothers, 150, 167
barter exchange, 117; and money, 68
Bear Stearns, 169, 241*n*
Berle, A., 137–8
'big bangs', 152, 198
bills of exchange, 70–1
Black Wednesday, 234*n*
Blankenfield, Lloyd, 158
bonds, 149; government bonds, 77, 78, 79, 180
'boom and bust' cycles, 115–16, 132, 195–9, 225, *see also* credit 'crunch'/'squeeze'
Boots, 162
bourgeois political economy, 15, 17, 19, 21, 183
bourgeoisie and state, 32–3, 58, 72–4, 77, 126–7, 177
branded goods and monopolies, 101, 104
Braudel, Fernand, 3, 100, 157–8
Braverman, H., 135–6
Bretton Woods international monetary system, 50, 84–6, 164, 197, 209–10, 226
Britain, 43, 150, 241*n*; family capitalism in nineteenth century, 126, 127–9, 130; post-war Keynesian economy, 43–4, 196, 197, 209; trade unionism and class conflict, 23–4; universal franchise, 187, 194; and varieties of capitalism, 217; welfare state, 193, 194, *see also* Anglo-US liberal market capitalism; England; Treasury.
'bubbles', 115–16, 151–2, 154–5, 242*n*

Buffet, Warren, 167–8
Burawoy, M., 136
bureaucracy: of capitalist
    enterprise, 124–5, 129, 131;
    and market regulation, 118,
    198; Weber, 32, 34, 35,
    124–5, 236n
business cycles, 23, 115–16,
    132, 195–9, 225

calculation: and money as
    measure of value, 67, 68,
    91, *see also* rational capital
    accounting
California School, 227n
Cameron, David, 243n
Campbell, C., 102
capital: capitallabour
    relations, 107–10, 134–7,
    139, 142, 143, 145, 182,
    188, 213; and financial
    markets, 147–74; Marx's
    forces and relations of
    production, 19, 20, 21;
    politics and ownership,
    142–5; private
    ownership, 56–7, 58, 117,
    123–4; Smith's factors of
    production, 8–9, 19; and
    varieties of capitalism,
    220–1, *see also* bank credit-
    money; money-capital;
    physical capital; stock
    markets
capital accounting, 25–35, 40
capital markets, 147–74;
    definition, 148; and
    globalization, 206–13,
    245–6n; and Keynesian
    economics, 45–7, 49
capitalism: basic elements,
    52–62; classical theories,
    7–51; institutions, 63–203;
    varieties, 204, 214–22;
    vulnerabilities, 223–6

capitalist credit-money, 70–4
capitalist enterprise, 93, 117,
    119–46; deskilling and
    labour power, 108, 135–6;
    entrepreneurs and
    profit, 38–9, 53, 61; history
    of development, 126–33;
    and production, 53, 55–8;
    struggle for surplus, 133–45;
    theories of, 121–5, *see also*
    capitalist entrepreneurs;
    corporations; financial
    markets; mergers and
    acquisitions; takeovers
capitalist entrepreneurs:
    financial entrepreneurs,
    140–1; and profit, 38–9, 53,
    61
capitalist mode of production
    and Marx, 14–24
capitalist social relations and
    liberal democracy, 184–9,
    220
'capturing' the state, 179, 180,
    185, 186, 200–1
cartels, 101, 129, 130
'cash nexus', 65
central banks: and control of
    production of money, 67,
    74, 75, 77, 78–9; currency
    exchange controls, 210;
    interest rates and inflation
    targets, 88; as 'lenders of
    last resort', 42, 76, 115,
    150, 151, 168, 169, 178,
    242n; and liquidity, 150,
    199; and sovereign debt, 74,
    76–8
Chandler, A., 131, 239n
Charles II, king of
    England, 72, 126–7
'chartalist' theory of
    money, 70
Chartism, 128
Chase Manhattan, 155

China: demand and
inflation, 91; and
development of
capitalism, 34, 60, 186; and
'great divergence', 227*n*;
state capitalism, 56, 186,
201–2, 222
'churning', 153–4
'circular flow' model, 238*n*;
and Keynes, 43; Marx
on, 15–16; Schumpeter's
critique, 37–8, 39–40; and
Smith, 9–10, 15–16, 37–8
Citigroup, 157
citizenship: citizens as
stakeholders in
enterprise, 144, 219, 220;
statecitizen relationship,
31–5, 60, 194, 219
City of London, 129;
deregulation and 'big
bangs', 198, 240*n*;
eurodollar markets, 86
class conflict, 23–4, 188–9;
institutionalization, 187
classical liberal economics, 2,
7–14, 16, 43, 229–30*n*; and
private ownership, 161; and
role of money, 44–5; and
wage levels, 47–8
classical theories of
capitalism, 7–51; Smith,
7–14
'clearing' the market, 95, 236*n*
Coase, Ronald, 121
codetermination in
Germany, 143
coercion: costs, 127; and role
of state, 181–2
coins, 232*n*, 233*n*, *see also*
precious-metal currency
collateralized debt obligations
(CDOs), 165
collective bargaining, 108–9,
135, 139, 187, 188, 189

command economies: in
ancient world, 92, 236*n*; in
organized enterprises, 92–3,
see also planned economies
'commercial society' and Adam
Smith, 2, 8–13
commodities: enterprise as
commodity, 149, 158–62;
futures markets and
trading, 152, 163–4, 165;
labour *see* labour power;
Marx and exchange-
value, 17, 21; Marx's
'fetishism of
commodities', 61; as media
of exchange, 69; money as
commodity, 68; private
enterprise production, 53,
55–8
Commodity-Money-
Commodity (CMC)
exchange, 17, 18
communist economic
systems, 13, 185, 186;
primitive communism, 16,
18, *see also* post-communist
states
comparative advantage and
free trade, 227–8*n*
competitive deregulation, 144,
197, 198, 204, 210, 222,
240*n*
competitive markets, 94–100,
116–17, 204, 208;
contradictions, 113–16,
242*n*; and dynamic nature of
capitalism, 21, 34, 97, 106,
116; and economic
growth, 55, 94;
environmental effects, 224–
5; and equation with
capitalism, 93, 99–100, 116;
and equilibrium, 37, 82, 98–
9, 191; and Marx, 21; and
monopolistic

competitive markets (cont.)
  competition, 38, 94, 100–1,
  104–6, 117; perfect
  competition model, 94,
  95–6, 98–9, 111, 151; and
  price of goods, 13, 53–4;
  and profit-seeking
  behaviour, 61; and
  Schumpeter, 37, 38; and
  Smith, 7–14, 57, 95–6; and
  state intervention, 94,
  178–9, 185, 190–9, 216–17;
  and varieties of capitalism
  theory, 214–22; and wage
  levels, 47–8, 99, *see also* free
  market
'complementarity' and
  coordinated market
  economies, 220
conflicts of interest: capital–
  labour conflict, 107–10,
  134–7, 139, 143, 188; and
  market exchange, 93–4,
  106–16, 117; and rational
  capital accounting, 27, 120,
  236*n*; stock markets and
  investment bank
  oligopolies, 155, 157; and
  varieties of capitalism
  theory, 216, 217
conglomerates, 130; for
  mergers and acquisition, 159
'conspicuous consumption', 60,
  61
'constant capital' and 'variable
  capital', 21–2
consumer debt, 103–4
consumption, 100–6; and
  culture of capitalism, 60–1;
  and debt deflation, 90;
  development of
  consumerism, 101–2; and
  economic crisis, 114–15; and
  fixed exchange rates, 234*n*;
  and market exchange, 54,

93; mass consumption
  societies, 32; and Smith's
  factors of production, 9, *see
  also* mass consumption
contradictions: and crises, 94,
  112–16, 242*n*; and forces
  and relations of
  production, 16, 21–2
cooperative economy and
  'invisible hand', 44
coordinated market economies
  (CMEs), 215–16, 217; move
  to liberalization and
  convergence, 218–22
corporate governance, 134,
  137–9, 141–2; and scandals
  in US, 141, 169, 171–2
'corporate raiders', 149, 159,
  160
corporations: capitalist
  enterprise as legal
  entity, 133–4; and
  globalization, 205; growth
  in financial
  corporations, 147; joint-
  stock corporations, 124,
  126–7, 129; monopolistic
  competition and mass
  consumption, 99, 100–1,
  104–6; multi-
  divisional, multi/
  transnational corporations in
  US, 126, 130–3, 211, 221,
  222; organizational forms
  and US corporations, 132–3;
  and ownership of
  capital, 56, 142–5;
  transnational
  corporations, 122–3, 176,
  221, 222, *see also* capitalist
  enterprise; corporate
  governance; mergers and
  acquisitions; takeovers
corporatism and varieties of
  capitalism, 217

corruption and malpractice: Enron scandal, 170–2
costs: and capitalist enterprise, 125, 126, 135; cost-benefit analysis and 'public goods', 178–9, 193–4; protection costs, 127; social costs, 97, *see also* transaction costs
cotton textile industry in Britain, 127–8
counter-cyclical spending, 195–9
'creative destruction', 55, 200, 206; destructive phase of innovation, 38, 105–6, 129; and varieties of capital, 220–1
credit cards: and consumption, 103; as medium of transmission, 232n
credit 'crunch'/'squeeze', 42, 66, 76, 91, 114, 115, 169, 241–2n, *see also* recession
credit cycles, 114
credit-default-swaps (CDSs), 165, 173
credit-money: creation and historical development, 33, 36, 38, 39–43, 51, 53, 56, 69–70, 70–4; and dynamic nature of capitalism, 37, 38, 51, 66, 80, 91, 206, *see also* bank credit-money
credit-rating agencies, 79, 98, 111
credit-rationing, 98, 111
credit risk and derivatives market, 165–9
credit theory of money, 40
creditor and debtor class conflict, 111–12
crises *see* economic crises; financial crises

'crony capitalism', 124, 200–1, 216, 217
'cultural economy', 231n
culture and capitalism, 60–2, 101–2
currency: single currency and global trade, 203; stateless currency, 209, *see also* foreign exchange markets; money; precious-metal currency

debt, 29, 53; and consumption, 103–4; and economic crisis, 114, 116, 167, 168; and production of money, 69, 75–6, *see also* bank credit-money
debt contract and production of money, 39, 51, 66, 68
'debt deflation', 29, 42, 66, 76, 81–2, 88–91, 114, 115, 225; Japan, 88, 89–90; writing off debts, 90, 169
debtor and creditor class conflict, 111–12
'decommodification' of labour, 108
deficit finance, 49, 77, 103
deflation, 80–1, 81–2, 88–91; reverse Keynesianism, 50, *see also* debt deflation
demand shocks, 83
democracy *see* liberal democracy
deposits, 71, 75–6, 78, 111
depressions, 43, 84–5, 128–9
deregulation and competitive markets, 94, 113–14, 118, 144, 153, 197, 204; and 'big bangs', 152, 198; and global finance, 207, 245–6n; in US, 210, 222

derivatives markets, 148, 152, 163–9, 173, 208; Enron scandal, 170–2
deskilling of work, 108, 135–6
developmental states, 194
dialectical progression, 14–15, 21
'disembedded' economies, 57, 113
distribution: of income, 12–14, 50, 110, 212–13, 224; of production, 57, *see also* redistribution
dividends, 134, 149, 162, *see also* shareholders
division of labour: deskilling of work, 135–6; enterprise and organization of work, 123, 135; and globalization, 14, 230*n*; and 'putting out' system, 119, 121; Smith, 8, 9, 12, 14, 92
dollar standard, 207, 209, 210–11
dot.com bubble, 151, 154, 155, 171
double-entry bookkeeping, 25, 76
double movement, 84, 113, 114
downsizing workforce, 140
Dudley, William, 158
DuPont, 130
Durkheim, E., 113
Dutch East Indies Company, 127
Dutch joint-stock companies, 126, 127
dynamic nature of capitalism: and competitive markets, 21, 34, 97, 106, 116; and credit-money, 37, 38, 51, 66, 80, 91, 206; and financial asset markets, 55, 172; and varieties of

capitalism, 221, *see also* creative destruction
dynastic capitalism, 120, 124

east Asian economies, 204; financial crisis, 66, 211, 245*n*; and varieties of capitalism, 214, 216, 217, 245*n*, *see also* Japan
East India Company, 127
economic crises, 112–16, 149, 150, *see also* financial crises
economic growth, 55, 94, 106
economic liberalism and capitalism, 43, 84, 117, 183, 186, 190, 191, 199–201, 209
economies of scale, 130–1
Economist, The, 3, 157
economy and state, 177–81, 189–99, 200–2, 221
effective demand, 47–8, 114
efficiency and capitalist enterprise, 125
'efficient market hypothesis', 151, 152
Egypt, ancient, 57, 119, 236*n*
elective affinity, 60, 61
embedded economies, 57, 113
emissions trading, 98
employment *see* full employment; labour market
employment contracts, 108
employment protection, 143, 144–5, 192, 218
Enclosure Acts, 20, 128
'end of history', 223
energy industries, 27, 132, 165, 170–1, 194, 195, 200
Engels, Friedrich, 128
England: bourgeoisie and state, 32–3, 72–4, 77, 126–7; joint-stock companies, 126, 127; and varieties of capitalism, 216,

see also Bank of England;
    Britain
English East India
    Company, 127
Enron, 41, 170–2
enterprise *see* capitalist
    enterprise
entrepreneurs *see* capitalist
    entrepreneurs
environmental
    degradation, 224–5
equilibrium and markets, 13,
    37, 82, 98–9, 191
equity finance, 148, 150
'ethical dualism' in exchange
    relations, 32
eurodollar markets, 86
Europe: family capitalism, 120,
    138; and finance
    capital, 138, 143, 150, 220;
    politics and capitalist
    enterprise, 143, 144–5
European Commission, 118,
    245*n*
European ('Rhineland')
    capitalism, 204
European Union and deficit
    finance, 77
exchange: exchange relations in
    traditional societies, 32;
    money as media of
    exchange, 67, 68; non-
    market exchange relations in
    capitalist economy, 92–3,
    see also 'exchange value';
    market exchange
exchange rates, 50, 68, 85,
    164, 208, 209–10
'exchange value', 12–13,
    65–6, 69; Marx and
    exchange-value, 15, 16–17,
    21, 22
exploitation: capitalist
    enterprise, 128, 135;
    Marx, 15, 18, 19, 21–2,

35, 123–4, 135, 140, 183,
    192
exports, 7, 205, 233–4*n*
'externalities' *see* 'negative
    externalities'

factors of production:
    Marx, 15–16, 19; 'real'
    factors of production, 36,
    44; Smith, 8–9, 15, 19, 43;
    and value and
    distribution, 12–13
failure of capitalism:
    Argentina, 66; inter-war
    depression, 43, 84–5, 113
falling rate of profit, 21–2,
    114, 128–9
familial relations and
    economy, 57, 120, 124
family capitalism, 124, 126,
    127–9, 130, 188
family-owned enterprises, 120,
    124, 127–9, 130, 138, 143,
    160–1; and varieties of
    capitalism, 220–1
fascism and capitalism, 43,
    185–6, 187
'fetishism of commodities', 61
feudalism, 16, 18, 19
'fictitious capital', 36, 229*n*
finance capital, 52; and
    capitalist enterprise, 137–8,
    143, 144–5; Keynes and
    stock markets, 45–7; and
    varieties of
    capitalism, 220–1
financial asset markets, 67, 93,
    150–2, 174; complexity and
    range of instruments, 148;
    and globalization, 207, 208;
    and speculation, 16, 54, 55,
    115–16, 147, 150–2, 154–5,
    172, 173; and varieties of
    capitalism, 220, *see also*
    stock markets

financial corporations: growth in, 147

financial crises, 66, 149; management of, 225–6; and globalization, 211–12; and market exchange system, 94, 112–16, 224; Marx on, 15–16, 20, 21–2; and paper instruments, 28–9; role of central banks, 42, 76, 115, 150, 168; role of state, 58–9, 113–14, 178, 191, 195–9; and speculation, 24, 28, 41–2, 89–90, 114, 151–2, 154–5, 173, *see also* credit 'crunch'/'squeeze'; financial instability hypothesis

financial engineering, 148, 169, 208

financial entrepreneurs, 140–1, 145–6, 159–62; private equity groups, 144, 149, 159–60

financial globalization: politics and capitalist enterprise, 144–5

'financial instability hypothesis', 40–3, 76, 115, 116, 151, 225

financial intermediaries, 145–6, 152, 153–4; and insider trading, 153, 154, 155–6

financial markets, 147–74; and globalization, 206–13, 245–6*n*; primary markets, 148–50, 151, 172; regulation, 113–14, 118, 166, 171–2, 198–9; secondary markets, 150–2; and Weber, 28–9, *see also* capital markets; financial asset markets; money markets

Financial Services Authority (FSA)(UK), 154, 166

Financial Times, 3, 110

'financialization' of capitalism, 116, 147, 169, 174, 208, 213; and varieties of capitalism, 220–1, 222

firms: reasons for, 121–3, *see also* capitalist enterprise; corporations

fiscal constitution, 177

fixed exchange rates, 210, 234–5*n*

flexible labour markets, 108, 143, 145, 218, 220–1

'flexible specialization', 132

floating exchange rates and derivatives, 164, 208

forces and relations of production, 16, 18–22, 23; contradictions of, 16, 21–2

Ford, Henry, 102, 131, 136

'Fordist' stage of capitalism, 132

foreign exchange markets: and globalization, 207–12; Keynesian economics, 50, 85, 209–10; speculation, 116, 150, 164, 209–10, 211–12

forward contract trading, 163

fractional reserve, 75

France and varieties of capitalism, 217, 219

Frankfurt School, 183

free market: equation with capitalism, 93; and globalization, 207; and Keynes, 43, 84; and Marx, 15, 57, 113, 224; and Polanyi, 57, 113, 224–5; and Smith, 7–14; and socialism, 96–7; and varieties of capitalism, 204, 214–15; and Weber, 34, *see also* competitive markets; deregulation

free trade: and comparative advantage, 227–8*n*; and globalization, 14, 94, 96, 222; Keynesian economics and worldwide free trade, 50; and perfect competition model, 96; and state, 230*n*

French Regulation School/theory, 112, 214, 239*n*

Friedman, Milton, 14

Fukuyama, Francis, 93

Fulcher, J., 1, 3

full employment policy: post-war Keynesian economics, 43–4, 45, 49, 50, 83–4, 85–6, 196, 209–10; and labour power, 99, 109–10

fungible finance, 149, 172

futures markets and trading, 152, 163–4, 165

Galbraith, J.K., 138–9

General Agreement on Tariffs and Trade (GATT), 222

Germany: Bismarck and condition of labour force, 192; corporate governance and skilled labour force, 142; development of capitalist enterprise, 129; German philosophy and Marx, 14–15, 20–1; Hamburg commodity price crash (1799), 151; Third Reich's imperial project, 176; and varieties of capitalism theory, 215–17, 220, 221; worker representation, 142, 143

global markets, 202–3, 210–12, 222, 226

global recession, 91

globalization, 202–3, 204–13; and destabilization of capitalism, 114; effect on deflation and inflation, 91; financial globalization, 144–5; and free trade, 14, 94, 96, 222; and Smith's market capitalism, 14, 59–60, 226; state and 'logics of power', 176; and theory, 208–9; and varieties of capitalism, 221–2; and wage stagnation, 110

gold standard and money, 69, 73, 84–5, 111–12, 207, 209, 210

'golden age' of capitalism, 23, 44, 113, 196

Goldman Sachs, 157, 158

government bonds, 77, 78, 79, 180

Gowan, P., 240–1*n*

Gramsci, Antonio, 132, 184

Great Depression (1873–1896), 128–9

'great divergence', 227*n*

Greenspan, Alan, 151, 224

Grierson, P., 232*n*

Gucci, Mario, 120

Hall, P., 214–16

Hamburg commodity price crash (1799), 151

Hayek, Friedrich von, 14, 96–7

hedge finance, 41–2, 116, 152, 164–5, 167–8; remuneration of hedge-fund managers, 166, 173–4

hedgers in futures markets, 164, 165

Hegel, G.W.F., 14–15, 20–1

hegemony: economic hegemony
of US, 176–7, 221, 222; and
legitimacy of capitalism, 184
hierarchy and capitalist
enterprise, 122–3
high-status niche
markets, 104–5, 220
Hilferding, R., 52, 129, 138
historical progression and
Marx, 14–15, 16, 21, 37
history: development of
capitalism in the West, 31–
5, 33, 39–43, 51, 53, 70–4;
development of capitalist
enterprise, 126–33; Weber's
*General Economic
History*, 26–35
Hitler, Adolf, 176
Holland, 8, 35, 72, 126, 127,
151
hostile takeovers, 106, 116,
149, 159–60, 218–19
household debt, 103–4
human capital, 117, 179,
191–5
human relations
management, 136
'hybrid' capitalism, 204
hyperinflation, 83, 196

ideal type of capitalism:
Weber, 26–31, 244*n*
ideological state
apparatuses, 184
illiquid assets, 169, 173
imperfect information, 96–7,
121–2, 155
imperfections *see* contradictions
imperialism, 176–7
income distribution and
inequalities, 12–14, 50, 110,
212–13, 224
India, 27, 91, 127–8
individualism and
capitalism, 185, 186, 197

industrial relations, 107–10,
134–5, 136, 139, 182; in
Sweden, 188–9; worker
representation in
Germany, 142, 143
industrialisation, 31
inequality in market
exchange, 121–2; and
conflict, 107–12; and
dynamism of capitalism,
95–6; and
globalization, 212–13; and
labour power, 109–10; and
legitimacy of
capitalism, 183–4; and
Marx, 15, 20, *see also*
income distribution and
inequalities
inflation, 66, 74, 75, 80–8,
114, 225; and control of
interest rates, 78–9, 80, 88,
90–1, 226; and government
expenditure, 84, 179, 197,
218; Keynes and
management of aggregate
demand, 49, 50, 114, 196
inflation targets, 88
information: 'asymmetric
information', 99; imperfect
information, 96–7, 121–2,
155; perfect
information, 151, 152; and
power of US investment
bank oligopolies, 156–7
information and
communication
technology, 208–9
infrastructure and role of
state, 132, 194–5
Innes, A.M., 231*n*
innovation, 91; destructive
phase, 38, 105–6, 129
'insider trading', 153, 154,
155–6; Enron
scandal, 170–2

institutional control of money, 67, 74, 77, 111–12, 210

institutional investors, 141, 153, 166–7

institutionalization of class struggle, 187

institutions of capitalism, 63–203; and varieties of capitalism theory, 214–22

insurance markets and adverse selection, 97–8

inter-war depression, 43, 84–5, 113

interest rates: and control of production of money, 67, 78–9, 80, 111; domestic control, 226, 234–5n; and inflation, 78–9, 80, 88, 90–1; 'real' rate of interest, 80, 87; rises and financial instability, 41–2, 88–9, 89–90

intermediaries *see* financial intermediaries

International Monetary Fund, 210, 221, 222

international monetary system *see* Bretton Woods

internationalization, 205

investment banks, 148; and Anglo-US capitalism, 218–19; and capitalist enterprise in US, 130, 137, 144; and globalization, 211; and hedge fund debt, 168; stock markets and investment bank oligopoly, 152, 153, 154–8, 222

investment companies in London, 130

investment funds: institutional investors, 141, 153, 166–7, *see also* investment banks

'invisible hand', 111, 112, 226; and Keynes, 43, 44, 49; Smith, 9–10, 12, 13, 14, 15, 54–5, 100, 112, 183

Islamic countries and capitalism, 60

Italian city states, 35, 72, 126, 158

Japan: debt finance, 89–90, 150; deflation, 88, 89–90; development of capitalist enterprise, 129; management and organization of work, 132, 136; monopolies, 106, 192; and varieties of capitalism, 214, 216–17, 218, 219, 221, 245n

joint-stock capitalist enterprises, 124, 126–7, 129

JP Morgan, 130, 154

JP Morgan Chase, 157, 168, 241n

'just in time' production methods, 132

'just prices', 12

Kalecki, Michael, 50, 84

keiretsu in Japan, 90, 106, 192

Keynes, John Maynard, 1–2, 22, 42–50, 52, 77, 225, 226; Bretton Woods, 50, 84–6; and creation of money, 24, 78, 111; and deflation, 88–9; and 'golden age' of capitalism, 23, 44, 113, 196; and instability in stock market, 167–8; and macro-economic policy, 13–14, 114, 132, 198; and management of aggregate demand, 48–50, 103, 114, 132, 195–6; money of account, 68, 69; on relying

Keynes, John Maynard (cont.)
on the 'long run', 191; and
Smith's legacy, 13–14; and
speculation in financial
markets, 46–7, 49–50, 55,
116, 151–2, 209–10;
transition from Keynesianism
to neo-liberalism, 196–8, *see
also* full employment policy
Khodorkovsky, Mikhail, 27,
243*n*
Knapp's state theory of
money, 70

labour: capital–labour
relations, 107–10, 134–7,
139, 142, 143, 145, 182,
188, 213; commodification
see labour power;
employment protection, 143,
144–5, 192, 218; flexible
labour, 108, 143, 145, 218;
and globalization, 213; and
market exchange, 54; Marx
and capitalist mode of
production, 15, 17–18, 19,
20, 21–2, 124; and post-war
economy, 85–6; and private
equity companies, 161–2;
right to work, 194; Silesian
'backward sloping supply
curve', 29, 60–1; Smith's
factors of production, 9, 19;
state and welfare of, 191–4;
and value and
distribution, 20, 228–9*n*;
and varieties of
capitalism, 217, 220–1;
wage contract, 56–7, 107,
124; Weber and rational
capital accounting, 28, 109,
see also exploitation; wages
labour market, 93, 107; as
basic market of
capitalism, 54; capitalist

desire for flexibility, 108,
143, 145, 218;
deregulation, 197; Keynes
and effective demand, 47–8;
and market
imperfections, 99
labour movements, 87, 187,
see also industrial relations
'labour power': and
conflict, 107–10; Marx,
17–18, 21–2, 35, 56, 107,
123–4, 135
labourers: Smith's constituent
orders, 9, 19
Lal, D., 93
land: Smith's factors of
production, 9, 19
landlords: Smith's constituent
orders, 9, 19
large-scale construction
projects, 122–3
late development
capitalism, 214, 221
law and capitalist social
relations, 184–9
laying off workers, 28, 42,
143, 161
Leeson, Nick, 150, 167
legitimacy of capitalism, 182–4
Lenin, Vladimir Ilyich, 185,
187
leveraged buyouts
(LBOs), 140–1, 159
Levitt, Arthur, 157
Lewis, Ken, 141
liberal democracy: and
capitalist social
relations, 184–9, 220; and
'reflexivity', 223, 225; state
and economy, 179–81, 184,
197, 201, 221
liberal market economies
(LMEs), 215, 216;
convergence
towards, 218–22

liberalism and role of state, 59, 60, 179–80, 190–9, 221
liberalization: of coordinated market economies, 218–22, *see also* competitive markets; deregulation
Lindert, P., 243*n*
liquidity, 174, 206; dangers of pursuit of, 46, 171, 172–3; illiquid assets, 169, 173; Keynes's 'liquidity preference', 44–5; role of central banks, 150, 199; and varieties of capitalism, 220–1
loans, 29, 53, 75–6, 78, 103, 148–9, *see also* bank credit-money; debt
London Stock Exchange, 198
Long Term Credit Management, 165, 167, 168, 201
luxury goods, 101, 102, 103, 237*n*

Maastricht Treaty, 77
'machinofacture', 22, 128
macro-economic policy, 13–14, 114, 132, 178, 197–8
Mafia, 181
mail-order distribution, 132
managed capitalism, 214
management: and control of labour-process, 135–7; ex-military as early managers, 131; managers and struggle for ownership and control, 137–9, 140; as requirement of capitalist enterprise, 131; and varieties of capitalism, 220–1, *see also* bureaucracy; organization of work
managerial control of enterprises, 137–9

Mandeville, B., 10
manufacture and factors of production, 8–9, 19
marginal efficiency and state intervention, 178–9
'marginal utility' and prices, 229*n*
Marglin, Stephen, 239*n*
market capitalist system, 57, 211; and Smith, 8, 14; and state, 58–60; vulnerabilities, 224–6
market exchange, 92–118; as basic element of capitalism, 53–5; and emergence of capitalist enterprise, 123; and Marx, 15; and regulation, 94, 113–14, 117, 118, 198–9; role of state, 190; and Smith, 8, 9–10; in traditional societies, 117; role of state, 11–12, 58–9, 178, 190, *see also* financial crises
Marshall, Alfred, 236*n*
Marshall, T., 194
Marx, Karl, 1, 2, 14–24, 52, 54, 55, 105, 110, 186, 224; and capitalist control of state, 180; and capitalist enterprise, 123–4, 125, 128, 135, 192; and collapse of capitalism, 16, 19; contradictions, 112, 113, 114, 117; labour power, 17–18, 21–2, 35, 56, 107, 123–4, 135; and legitimacy of capitalism, 182, 183; and Schumpeter, 37; and Smith, 12, 14, 15–16, 17, 19, 57, 228–9*n*; and Weber, 30, 34, 35, *see also* socialism

mass consumption, 32, 100–6; and mass-communications industries, 131–2; and 'monopolistic competition', 100–1, 104–6, 117; and multi/transnational enterprise in US, 130, 131

mass production and consumption, 102; and multi/transnational enterprise in US, 130, 131–2

material forces of production, 18, 19, 20, 21–2, 23

Means, G., 137–8

means of payment: money as, 67

means of production, 18, 20, 35; and market exchange, 54, 93; private ownership, 56, 125; state ownership, 56

measure of value (money of account), 67, 68, 69, 70, 91

mechanization, 27, 128–9

media: mass-communications industries, 131–2

media of exchange: commodities as, 69; money as, 67, 68

media of transmission, 232n

'memorable alliance', 32–4, 58, 70, 127, 158, 177

mercantilism: neo-mercantilism, 242–3n; and Smith, 7–8, 10, 28, 175, 228n, 229–30n; and Weber, 32–3, 58, 176

merchants, 70–1; and joint-stock companies, 126; 'putting out' system, 119; and states, 177

'merchants of debt', 41, 51, 103, 172, 242n

mergers and acquisitions, 106, 143, 145–6, 158–62, 171, 218–19, *see also* takeovers

Merrill Lynch, 157

metallist theories of money, 229n

Mexico: state capitalism, 56

Mill, John Stuart, 186

Minsky, Hyman, 40–3, 76, 81, 115, 116, 151–2

Mises, Ludwig von, 96–7, 244n

mode of production: Marx and capitalist mode of production, 14–24

model villages, 128, 192

'monetarism', 74, 78, 87, 112

monetary disorders *see* deflation; inflation

monetary system: and bank-credit money, 53; Bretton Woods, 50, 84–6, 164, 197, 209–10; role of state, 199

money, 65–91; as abstract purchasing power, 68–9; and bank credit, 29, 53; and capitalism, 24, 36, 52; debt contract and production of money, 39, 51, 66, 68; functions and nature of, 67–70; and globalization, 206–7; 'liquidity preference' and profits, 44–5; metallist theories of money, 229n; origins of, 68; 'real' money, 40; Schumpeter on 'monetary' and 'real', 230n; Smith's relegation of, 10, 36; as 'veil', 44, 230n, *see also* liquidity; money-capital

money-capital, 91, 172–3, 228n; and Bretton Woods agreement, 85–6; global money-capital, 206–7, 213, 226; and Marx, 24, 36, 37;

money market and
production of, 54, 74–80,
110–12, 147, 148–9, *see also*
credit-money; money
markets
Money-Commodity-Money
(MCM) exchange, 17, 24,
54, 148
money-lending, 32, 71
money markets, 93; and
control of production of
money, 67, 75, 77, 78–9,
110–12; definition, 148; and
development of
capitalism, 33, 39–43, 54;
and Keynesian
economics, 50; and
production of credit-
money, 54, 74–80, 110–12,
147, 148–9
'money multiplier', 71, 75–6,
84, *see also* multiplier effect
money of account (measure of
value), 67, 68, 69, 70, 91
monopolies: and capitalist
enterprise, 129, 137; and
control of supply, 99; early
joint-stock companies, 127,
129; and economic
power, 99, 100–1, 104–6,
117, 137, 156–8; and
inflation, 84; labour
costs, 135, 192;
monopolistic competition
and mass consumption, 94,
100–1, 104–6, 117; and
post-war economy, 86, 195;
and production of
money, 70; Schumpeter and
capitalist entrepreneur, 38;
state intervention, 185
monopoly capitalism, 129
'moral hazard' and loans to
banks, 42, 115, 233*n*, 242*n*
Morgan Stanley, 155, 157

Morris, Charles, 241–2*n*
multi-divisional, multi/
transnational corporations in
US, 126, 130–3, 211, 221,
222, *see also* transnational
corporations
multinational
corporations, 205
multiplier effect, 49, 84, *see
also* money-multiplier
Myrdal, Gunnar, 84

nationalized industries, 194–5,
219
natural monopolies, 195
'natural price' of goods, 13
Nee, V., 1
needs and wants, 10, 25; and
consumption, 60, 61, 101,
103; and Marx, 15, 16, 19,
22; subsistence level, 29,
60–1, 92, 101
negative externalities, 97, 98;
environmental
degradation, 224–5; role of
state, 11–12, 178, 179,
191–5
neo-classical economics, 245*n*
neo-liberal economics, 196–7;
and competitive markets, 94,
204; and environmental
degradation, 225; and role
of state, 178–9, 179–80,
190; Smith's legacy, 14; and
speculation on foreign
exchange markets, 212; and
varieties of capitalism
theory, 214–15, 218–22;
and wage levels, 47
neo-mercantilism, 242–3*n*
Neutral Money concept, 44,
230*n*
New Economy, 23, 113,
154
'new spirit of capitalism', 62

niche markets and monopolistic
  competition, 104–5, 220
nominal money-wages, 47
'non-excludable' goods, 97
'non-rival goods', 97
Northern Rock, 150, 168,
  169, 190, 241*n*, 242*n*

occupational skills and labour
  power, 107–8, 142
oil companies in US, 130–1
oligopolies, 99, 105, 117, 129,
  130, 131; and hedge fund
  debt, 168; in Russia, 182,
  243*n*; stock markets and
  investment banks, 152, 153,
  154–8, 222, *see also*
  monopolies
opportunism and human
  nature, 122
options trading, 163
organization of work, 119–20,
  121, 127; capital–labour
  conflict, 135–7, 139, 143,
  188
Orient, 25, 26, 30, 70, 124
Ottoman empire, 233*n*
overproduction, 24; and
  economic crisis, 114–15,
  128–9, 225; use-value and
  exchange-value, 17, 21–2
ownership: and control of
  capitalist enterprise, 137–45;
  of forces of production, 19,
  20, 35, 125; private
  ownership of capital, 56–7,
  58, 117, 123–4, *see also*
  mergers and acquisitions

'path dependency' and
  institutional variety,
  216–17
'patient capital', 215, 220
patrimonial state, 201
Paulson, Hank, 158

Pecora, Ferdinand, 154
Pemex, 56
perfect competition model, 94,
  95–6, 98–9, 111, 151, *see
  also* competitive markets
'perfect liberty' and market, 9,
  11, 12, 57, 60, 183, 185
'performativity', 94, 231*n*
philosophy: German
  philosophy, 14–15, 20–1
physical capital, 19, 36, 40,
  54, 56; and rational capital
  accounting, 26; speculation
  in financial asset
  markets, 115–16
Pickens, T Boone, 159, 166
Piore, Michael J., 132
planned economies: fall of, 14,
  93; loss of dynamism, 180,
  236*n*, *see also* command
  economies
Polanyi, K., 57, 113, 224–5,
  228*n*
political capitalism, 27–8,
  201
political elites and state, 200–1
political liberalism and
  capitalism, 186
political parties, 187
politics: crisis of state and
  inflation, 83; and ownership
  of capital, 142–5; and role
  of state, 59, 179–80, 190–9;
  and Smith's 'commercial
  society', 10–11; and varieties
  of capitalism, 217, *see also*
  state
Ponzi finance, 41–2
post-communist states, 13–14,
  94, 186, 204, 223
power relations: capitalist
  enterprise and organization
  of work, 123, 125; conflicts
  and contradictions of
  capitalism, 106–16, 117;

corporate governance, 134;
economic power and
monopolies, 99, 100–1,
104–6, 117, 137, 156–8;
institutional control of
money, 67, 74, 111–12,
210; and market
exchange, 55, 93–4; and
Marx, 15, 19, 20, 56, 125;
ownership and control of
capitalist enterprise, 137–45,
158–62; and post-war
economy, 85–6; and
prices, 34; state and two
logics of power, 175–81,
199–200; and Weber, 28,
34, *see also* monopolies
pre-capitalist society *see*
ancient world; traditional
societies
precious-metal currency: credit-
money replaces, 70–1, 73,
111; as medium of
exchange, 68, 69; scarcity
value, 40, 75; unproductive
hoarding, 10, *see also* coins
'predators', 16, 157–8
prices: and competitive
markets, 13, 53–4; and
conflict, 27, 34; financial
assets, 54, 67, 150–2;
futures markets, 152, 163–4,
165; and market failure,
97–8; and money as measure
of value, 68; monopolies
and price fixing, 100–1, 104;
share prices, 46, *see also*
deflation; inflation
primary financial
markets, 148–50, 151, 172
primitive communism, 16, 18
printers' unions and labour
power, 108
private credit and money
multiplier, 75–6

private debt and public
money, 73, 74, 75
private enterprise *see* capitalist
enterprise
private equity groups, 144,
149, 159–60, 173, 218–19
private ownership of
capital, 56–7, 58, 115–16,
117, 123–4; Bretton Woods
and foreign exchange
controls, 85; management
of, 225–6; and ownership of
capital enterprise, 137–45,
158–62; private economic
power and state, 175–81,
190, 199–200, 221
private property: Marx and
collapse of capitalism, 16,
19
private sector: commercial
money, 71, 75; and
government
expenditure, 190, 218; and
monetary authorities in
Japan, 89; and Smith, 11
privatization, 94, 193, 197,
202, 219
producer markets, 93, *see also*
monopolies
producers' alliance, 139, 142,
221
production: markets, 54, 93;
private enterprise
production, 53, 55–8, 122
production chain, 122, 127,
129, 130, 132
productive capital and post-
war economy, 85–6
productivity and profit:
capitalist enterprise, 128;
and Marx, 21–2, 114
profit: and circular flow
model, 37, 238*n*; falling rate
of profit, 21–2, 114, 128–9;
Keynes and 'liquidity

profit (cont.)
    preference', 44–5; and
    labour power, 18, 19, 20,
    21–2; Schumpeter on
    capitalist entrepreneur,
    38–9, 53; and
    shareholders, 61, 124,
    133–4; and struggle for
    ownership of capital
    enterprise, 139–45; and
    traditional societies, 29–30,
    see also rational capital
    accounting; surplus
profit-seeking behaviour, 25,
    29–30, 61, 65, 128; and
    Protestantism, 30, 61,
    101–2
proletariat, 20, 123–4, 128
promissory notes, 71
property prices in Japan, 89
property relations and
    capital, 57–8, 186, 187
property rights, 11, 55, 108,
    144–5, 178, 182
protection costs, 127
protectionism and
    mercantilism, 229*n*
Protestantism, 30, 61, 101–2
public banking, 33, 35, 72–3
'public choice' theory, 179
'public goods', 58; and market
    failure, 97, 98; and role of
    state, 190, 191–5, 219; and
    Smith, 11, 14, 97, 178; state
    and cost-benefit
    analysis, 178–9, 193–4, *see
    also* welfare
Pujo Commmittee (US
    Senate), 137
purchasing power *see* abstract
    purchasing power
Putin, Vladimir, 27, 33–4,
    182, 243*n*
'putting out' system, 119, 121,
    128, 130

Rajan, R., 93
rational capital
    accounting, 24–35, 40, 53,
    61, 82, 120, 124–5, 191,
    236*n*
rational-legal legitimacy, 184
rationing credit, 98, 111
Reaganomics, 87
'real' factors of production, 36,
    44
'real' money, 40
'real' money-wages, 47
'real' rate of interest, 80
recession: and deflation, 82,
    91; financial instability
    hypothesis, 42, 233*n*; global
    recession, 91; and
    Marx, 21, 22; and
    stimulation of
    consumption, 61; and
    welfare of workers, 191–2,
    see also credit
    'crunch'/'squeeze'
reciprocity, 8, 92, 113
redistribution, 8, 57, 92, 110,
    113, 131, 160
'reflexivity', 223, 225
regulation: hedge funds and
    financial regulation, 166,
    167–8; of markets, 113–14,
    117, 118, 171, 185, 198–9,
    see also corporate
    governance; deregulation
regulation school/theory, 112,
    214, 239*n*
relational contracting, 132
relations of production *see*
    forces and relations of
    production
religion and profit, 30
remuneration: and corporate
    governance, 141; financial
    sector, 166, 173–4, 213, 224
rent as social category, 19, 20
'rent-seeking', 200, 217

rentiers: 'revenge of the
rentier', 139–42, 225–6
representative democracy, 185,
186–7, 197
reskilling work, 136
'revenge of the rentier', 139–
42, 225–6
Rhineland capitalism, 204
Ricardo, David, 227–8*n*,
229–30*n*
right to work, 194
risk: and Keynesian
economics, 45; risk
management and
speculation, 163–9
'risk averse' banks, 42, 115
Rockerfeller conglomerate, 130
Roe, M., 240*n*
'rolling back' the state, 197,
198
Romanticism and
consumption, 102
Rubin, Robert, 158, 245–6*n*
rule of law, 11
rulers and fortunes of
states, 7–8, 58, 177
ruling class: and 'capture' of
the state, 180; ownership of
forces of production, 19, 20,
35, 56; pre-capitalist
societies, 92, 101, 126
Russia: and capitalism, 27, 33–
4, 65, 202, 243*n*; monetary
disorders, 81; organized
violence, 182

Sabel, Charles F., 132
Salt, Sir Titus, 128
Sarbanes-Oxley Act (US), 156,
171–2
Sarkozy, Nicolas, 219
Saudi Arabia: state
capitalism, 56
Saudi Aramco, 56
Savings and Loan, 168

Scandinavian social
democracy, 180–1, 188–9,
218
scarcity: control of production
of money, 75, 79, 111–12;
and market failure, 97, 98;
and Smith's 'invisible
hand', 9, 13; suppliers and
small-numbers
bargaining, 122; supply of
labour power, 107–8; and
Weber, 27
Schumpeter, Joseph, 1–2, 3,
35; and creation of
money, 24, 36, 38, 39–43,
51, 52, 53, 71, 111; creative
destruction, 55; credit
crunches/squeezes, 115;
monopolies, 106
'scientific management', 135–6
secondary financial
markets, 150–2, 153–8
Securities and Exchange
Commission (SEC)(US), 154,
166
'securitization', 149–50; and
sub-prime mortgages in
US, 149, 168–9, 173, 241*n*
seignorage, 233*n*
self-destructive capacity of free
markets, 113, 117
self-government of pre-
capitalist markets, 238–9*n*
self-interest, 117, 122; Marx
on capitalist production,
15–16; and Smith, 9, 10–11,
44; and Weber, 25
share prices, 46, 140–1
shareholders: ownership and
control of capitalist
enterprise, 137–45; and
profits, 61, 124, 133–4
shares as capital, 148–9, 162
'shock therapy' in post-
communist state, 94

Silesian peasants, 29, 60–1
Simmel, G., 68
Slater-Walker, 159
slavery in ancient world, 16, 18, 19, 119
'small-numbers bargaining', 122
Smith, Adam, 2, 7–14, 35, 52, 116; division of labour, 8, 9, 12, 14, 92; and Marx, 12, 14, 15–16, 17, 19, 57, 228–9n; and mercantilism, 7–8, 10, 28, 175, 228n, 229–30n; and money as capital, 36, 39–40; 'perfect liberty' and market, 9, 11, 12, 57, 60, 95, 183, 185; and Schumpeter, 37; state provision of 'public goods', 11, 14, 97, 178, *see also* 'invisible hand'
social democratic politics: and capitalist enterprise, 143, 179, 187, 188–9; Scandinavian model, 180–1, 188–9; and welfare provision, 193–4
social peace, 181–4, 217, 221
social relations of production, 18, 19, 20, 22, 23, 57–8; and 'cash nexus', 65; and legitimacy of capitalism, 182–3, 220, *see also* capitalist social relations
socialism: effect on economy, 180; and environment, 224–5; Marx and economic system, 16, 19, 22, 35; planned economies, 14, 93, 180, 236n; socialist calculation debate, 96–7; and state capitalism, 56, *see also* post-

communist states; social democratic politics
sociological view of capitalism, 1–2, 214–15; conflicts and contradictions, 106–16, 117; enterprise, 123–5; and reflexivity, 223, 225
Soros, George, 166, 242n
Soskice, D., 214–16
'sound money', 49, 77, 79, 81, 84, 87, 226
South Sea Bubble, 66, 151, 154
south-east Asia *see* east Asian economies
sovereign consumer, 229n
sovereign debt, 74, 75, 76–8, 79–80, 177
speculation: derivatives markets, 148, 173, 208; financial asset markets, 16, 54, 55, 115–16, 147, 150–2, 154–5, 172, 173; and financial crises, 24, 28, 41–2, 89–90, 114, 151–2, 154–5, 173; financial markets and risk management, 163–9; foreign exchange markets, 116, 150, 164, 209–10, 211–12; and Keynes, 46–7, 49–50, 55, 116, 151–2, 209–10
speculators in futures markets, 164, 165
'spirit of capitalism', 61; 'new spirit of capitalism', 62
Spitzer, Eliot, 154–5, 156
'stagflation', 91, 196
stagnation, 82, 112, 114, 128–9; Japan, 89–90, 106; and monopolies, 106; and socialism, 180; of wages, 110
Standard Oil Trust, 130, 131

state, 175–203; authoritarian economic programmes, 43; and capitalism, 56, 179–81, 182–4, 194–5; and capitalist credit-money, 72–4; and capitalist enterprise, 132, 179, 180, 221; and citizenship, 31–5, 60, 194, 219; competitive markets and intervention, 94, 178–9, 185, 190–9, 216–17; and the economy, 177–81, 189–99, 200–2, 221; globalization and role of, 14, 31; and globalization theory, 209; government expenditure and economy, 80, 84, 179, 190, 197, 198, 218; and inflation and deflation, 81, 83, 196; Keynes and management of aggregate demand, 48–50, 132, 195–6; and legitimacy of capitalism, 182–4; macro-economic policy, 13–14, 114, 132, 178, 197–8; and market capitalist system, 58–60; ownership of means of production, 56; regulation of markets, 113–14, 117, 118, 185, 198–9; 'rolling back' the state, 197, 198; and Smith's 'commercial society', 8, 10–12; sovereign debt, 74, 75, 76–8, 79–80, 177; and two logics of power, 175–81, 199–200; Weber and political capitalism, 27–8, *see also* politics

state capitalism, 56, 194–5, 201–2, 214, 217, 222
state currency, 72–3
state ownership of enterprise, 194–5, 219
'state theory' of money, 70

status competition and consumption, 102–3, 104–5
Stewart, Martha, 156
stock markets, 148, 150, 153–8; and Anglo-US capitalism, 218–19; 'big bangs', 152, 198; and investment bank oligopoly, 152, 153, 154–8, 222; Keynes on, 45–7; and ownership of capitalist enterprise, 139–42, 142–3, 144, 149, 158–62, *see also* insider trading
stock options, 140
stocks: capital as, 36, 40, 148–9, *see also* joint-stock capitalist enterprises; stock market
strikes, 136, 139, 187, 188
sub-contracting, 122
sub-prime mortgages in US, 149, 168–9, 173, 224, 241*n*
supply and demand: and equilibrium, 37, 82, 98–9, 191; fluctuations and economic crisis, 114; and inflation, 82–3; Keynes and management of aggregate demand, 48–50, 103, 114, 132, 195–6; labour power and conflict, 107–10; and marginal utility, 229*n*; and market failure, 97–9; and monetary system, 53, 68; money markets and production of credit-money, 74–5, 78–9, 110–12; monopolies control of supply, 99, 100–1, 104–6; Smith's 'invisible hand', 9–10, 13, 100
supply shocks, 82

surplus: and capitalist
enterprise, 133–45; and
monopolistic
competition, 101;
redistribution, 57, 110, 131,
160, *see also* profit
'surplus value', 18, 19, 20,
21–2, 37, 124
surveillance of workers and
technology, 136
Swedberg, R., 1
Sweden, 188–9, 218

takeovers: hostile
takeovers, 106, 116, 149,
159–60, 218–19; leveraged
buyouts, 140–1, 159, *see
also* mergers and acquisitions
taxation, 77, 243n
Taylor,
F. W./Taylorism, 135–6
technological invention, 37,
91, 159; and deskilling of
work, 135–6
territorial power of state,
175–6, 177, 199–200
textile production, 119, 123,
127–8
Thatcherism, 87, 108, 143,
197, 217
trade unions, 87, 187;
Britain, 23–4, 108;
Sweden, 188–9, *see also*
collective bargaining
traditional societies: and
consumption, 60–1; ethical
dualism in exchange
relations, 32; and market
exchange, 117; and
production, 57; and
profit, 29–30; subsistence
needs and wants, 29, 60–1,
92, 101
'transactions costs', 121–3,
125, 128

transferable debt, 39
transitional capitalism, 204
transnational
corporations, 122–3, 176,
205, 221, 222
transnational flows, 206–7
Treasury (UK), 43, 150, 241n
Triffin dilemma, 244n
Triglia, C., 1
'trilemma', 234n
Tulip Mania in Holland, 151

uncertainty: and Keynesian
economics, 45, 46–7, 49;
and speculative capital
markets, 152, 164–9
under-consumption and
crisis, 114–15, 225
unemployment: and classical
economics, 47; and market
imperfections, 99; and role
of state, 58–9, *see also* full
employment
United States: and Bretton
Woods agreement, 210;
corporate governance, 141,
171–2; economic
hegemony, 176–7, 221, 222;
economic power and
monopolies, 99, 100–1,
104–6, 137; Enron
scandal, 41, 170–2; and
global free markets, 222;
globalization and foreign
exchange markets, 210–11;
Goldman Sachs personnel in
government posts, 158;
multi-divisional, multi/
transnational
corporations, 126, 130–3,
211, 221, 222; politics and
capitalist enterprise, 144,
189; private health
insurance, 193; return of
gold standard, 111–12;

securitization of sub-prime
mortgages, 149, 168–9, 173,
241*n*; stock markets and
investment bank
oligopoly, 152, 153, 154–8,
222; and varieties of
capitalism theory, 215, 217,
see also Anglo-US liberal
market capitalism
unrestricted foreign exchange
markets, 234–5*n*
'use-values', 15, 16–17, 22
usury prohibition, 32

value: and distribution, 12–13;
Marx's labour theory of
value, 17–18; money
and, 67, *see also* exchange
value; measure of value;
use-values
variable capital and constant
capital, 21–2
'varieties of capitalism', 204,
214–22; convergence
theory, 218–22
Veblen, T., 102
vertical integration of the
firm, 121, 122, 123, 129
violence and role of
state, 181–2
'visible hand' in Keynesian
economics, 48–9
Vogel, S., 118

wage contract, 56–7, 107, 124
wages: and capitalist
enterprise, 132–3, 134–5,
139, 142, 143, 191–2;
consequences of full
employment, 50, 83–4, 86;
flexibility and
rigidities, 108–9; and
globalization, 213; and
market imperfections, 99;
Marx's variable capital, 21;

orthodox economics and
wage levels, 43, 47–8, 99;
and Smith's factors of
production, 9, 19;
stagnation, 110, *see also*
labour power
Wall Street Crash (1929), 42,
66, 88–9, 154
Walras, Leon, 236*n*
wants *see* needs and wants
war: and development of
capitalism, 32–3; and
inflation and deflation, 83,
225; and welfare of human
capital, 192–3
Washington consensus, 221
wealth inequalities, 212–13,
224
Weber, Max, 2, 24–35, 55,
109, 110, 117;
bureaucracy, 32, 34, 35,
124–5, 236*n*; and
empires, 176; *General
Economic History*, 26–35;
ideal type of capitalism,
26–31, 244*n*; and market
exchange, 118; and
mercantilism, 32–3, 58, 176;
and patrimonial state, 201;
and profit-seeking
behaviour, 25, 29–30, 60–1,
101–2; *Protestant Ethic*, 1,
30, 61, 101–2; rational
capital accounting, 24–35,
40, 53, 61, 82, 120, 124–5,
191, 236*n*; and state in
capitalist society, 180, 184,
200, 202
welfare: government
expenditure and
inflation, 80, 84, 179, 196,
218; and Keynesian
economics, 44, 49, 196;
redistributive transfers, 92;
and role of state, 117,

welfare (cont.)
178–9, 191–4, 196, 197;
of workers, 128, 191–4,
see also 'public goods'
welfare states, 193
wergeld (worthpayment)
systems, 232*n*
West: development of
capitalism in, 31–5, 33,
39–43, 51, 53, 70–4
William of Orange (William
III), 72–3
Williamson, Oliver, 121–2
Wolf, Martin, 93, 224

work *see* labour; organization
of work
worker representation, 142,
143
workers' political parties,
187
World Bank, 210, 221, 222
World Trade Organization
(WTO), 222

Yeltsin, Boris, 243*n*

zaibatsu, 192
Zingales, L., 93